AMERICAN RESTORATION EXTENDED EDITION

REBUILDING THE FOUNDATIONS OF
DEMOCRACY NOW WITH READER'S GUIDES

AMERICAN RENEWAL SERIES
BOOK 2

JIM VINCENT

JIM VINCENT US

American Renewal: Extended Edition

© 2025 Jim Vincent

All rights reserved.

No part of this publication may be reproduced, stored in a retrieval system, or transmitted in any form or by any means—electronic, mechanical, photocopy, recording, or otherwise—without the prior written permission of the publisher, except for brief quotations used in reviews, articles, or scholarly analysis.

This is a work of nonfiction. Every effort has been made to ensure accuracy. Any errors are the responsibility of the author. Opinions expressed are the author's own and do not represent any organization or institution. This book is for informational and educational purposes only and does not constitute legal advice. The author is not a lawyer and makes no guarantees regarding legal outcomes. Readers should consult qualified legal counsel or trusted advocacy organizations before taking action based on this material.

Cover design by Jim Vincent.

Published by Vincent Press

Printed and distributed by IngramSpark

Printed in 2025 • VP Edition 1.0.is

ISBN 978-1-7641693-3-2 (paperback)

For more information, visit: https://jimvincent.us

EPIGRAPH

"No nation remains a democracy by accident. The people must defend its laws, rebuild its frame, and renew its soul."
— JP Vincent

Democracy is not self-sustaining. It must be guarded by law, shaped by design, and animated by the will of an informed public. This book begins with that premise—and proceeds with the conviction that what was broken for power can be rebuilt for principle. These reforms are not partisan ambitions. They are democratic necessities. Each one answers a failure that made corruption possible. Together, they form a plan—not to tilt the system toward one party, but to return it to the people.

CONTENTS

Foreword	vii
Preface to the Extended Edition	ix
Preface	xi
Introduction	xiii

1. American Restoration: The Stakes — 1
   Part I. Elections That Count Every Voice — 3
2. Campaign Finance Reform — 9
3. Voting Rights Protection — 19
4. Electoral College Reform — 25
5. Redistricting Reform — 33
6. Election Certification and Peaceful Transition — 41
7. Elections That Work - Five Reforms, One Democracy — 49
   Part II - The Limits to Presidential Power — 53
8. Power Without Boundary — 59
9. Law Without Consequence — 67
10. Office Without Honor — 77
11. Constraint Without Exception — 85
    Part III. A Judiciary That Upholds Law, Not Loyalty — 91
12. Judicial Assignment Reform and Case Integrity — 99
13. Judicial Ethics Reform and Federal Accountability — 107
14. Court Transparency and Shadow Docket Oversight — 115
15. Supreme Court Term Limits and Generational Balance — 125
16. Lower Court Expansion and Access to Justice — 131
17. Transparency Reform and Public Access to Information — 141
18. The Rule of Law Is What We Build It To Be — 149
    Part IV. Rebuilding an Informed Public — 155
19. Disinformation and Platform Transparency — 165
20. Fairness in Broadcast Media — 175
21. Civic Education and Democratic Literacy — 185
22. The Six That Hold — 193

23. If We Are to Last	201
Appendix A - Eighteen Items in the Reformation Agenda	207
Appendix B - The Legal Web of Presidential Constraint	213
Appendix C: The Summary of Presidential Constraint	229
Appendix D: The Unwritten Guardrails	235
Appendix E: Notes on Judicial Corruption and Influence	243
Appendix F: Manipulation of Supreme Court Procedure to Advance Ideology	251
Appendix G: Restoration Spine	255
Appendix H: Epigraphs of the Restoration	261
Appendix I: Selected Sources and Citations	269
Reader's Guides	273
Afterword	387
Colophon	389
Also by Jim Vincent	391
About the Author	393

FOREWORD

This is the extended edition of *American Restoration*, the second volume in a trilogy that began with *American Renewal*. That first book was written in the shadow of collapse. This one was written in the light of possibility. And this version—expanded, annotated, and reframed—is offered to those ready to do the work.

The original *American Restoration* laid out a structural response to democratic decay. Twenty-seven chapters. Seven appendices. Each one traced a failure of law, design, or institutional will—and offered a remedy. This was not commentary. It was construction. Not a lament for what had been lost, but a blueprint for what must be rebuilt if democracy is to mean anything at all.

This edition adds nearly 120 pages of Reader's Guides. They do not repeat what has been said. They help us use it. Each guide distills the stakes, clarifies the structure, outlines the collapse, and proposes specific remedies. They include action lists, strategic rationale, and discussion prompts—designed not just for understanding, but for mobilizing. For educators. For organizers. For everyone who believes democracy is a system we must rebuild together.

If *American Renewal* was about endurance, *American Restoration* is about reconstruction. It begins with six constitutional promises—justice, peace, defense, prosperity, liberty, and unity—and insists that they must now be made real. Not with rhetoric. With law. With structure. With the moral clarity of citizens who know we are running out of time.

The final volume, *American Redemption*, will take up the next task: delivering outcomes that match those promises. But that work depends on this one. Before we build a better future, we must fix what no longer works. This is the blueprint.

Let the restoration begin. Again—and this time, together.

PREFACE TO THE EXTENDED EDITION

This Extended Edition adds something new: a Reader's Guide for every chapter. These guides are not summaries. They are tools. Each one breaks down the stakes, structure, collapse, and remedy of the chapter. It includes strategic rationale, concrete actions, and ten open-ended questions for discussion or reflection. These guides are designed for use—in classrooms, reading groups, workshops, campaign strategy sessions, and wherever people gather to confront what comes next.

Why now? Because the danger is no longer hypothetical. Trump's second term is dismantling the guardrails we failed to secure. What was once a warning is now a reckoning. These guides transform the book from blueprint to instrument—from argument to action. They exist to help others carry this work forward, wherever they are, with whatever they have.

This is not a second edition. The chapters remain as they were. But the invitation has changed. This version is meant to be shared. Taught. Used aloud. Used together. The book in your hands is not longer for its own sake—it is longer because the danger has grown, and so must our clarity, our courage, and our reach.

So take it up. Use it. Host a reading group. Start a conversation. Plan a campaign. Give it to someone who doesn't yet see the urgency —or someone who does but doesn't yet have the words. Give a copy to your representatives, both state and national. There is a lot of work to do, and the time to do it is short. Mere reading is not the action. Sharing is. It is how we muster the force we need for what comes next. Begin here. Begin with the chapters. Move to the guides —and then act. Not alone. Not like a drop in the ocean, but like a river breaking through the dam.

PREFACE

───◆───

This book begins with collapse—not as metaphor, but as a structural diagnosis. The first volume, *American Renewal*, laid out the scale of constitutional failure and mapped the five-phase plan for democratic recovery: Defense, Resistance, Restoration, Redemption, Reinstitution. What you hold now is the second step. This is where the plan becomes construction. It is where we begin to rebuild the republic not by memory, but by design.

American Restoration is not a return to normalcy. It is the work of rebuilding from what has failed, been corrupted, or hollowed out. These chapters name the reforms required to make democracy functional again: fair elections, ethical courts, accountable power, and a government that earns public trust through structure, not sentiment. This book is not theoretical. It is architectural. Each chapter is a beam, a wall, a bearing joint. Together, they form a republic capable of lasting.

The reforms offered here are not final. They will evolve. They may be revised. That is how democracies grow. What matters is that the structure be sound, the purpose be clear, and the public be engaged not only in resisting collapse, but in building what comes next. These proposals are not presented as gospel. They are meant to provoke debate, sharpen strategy, and invite contribution from those already doing the work.

There will be no single moment when this project is declared finished. No Philadelphia convention. No final parchment. The work ahead will be scattered, decentralized, and often invisible. It will unfold in courtrooms and classrooms, in statehouses and organizing calls, in ballots cast and laws enforced. That is how republics are made real—through the steady labor of citizens who decide that democracy must not just survive, but work.

We begin here. Not because the plan is perfect, but because the need is urgent. Democracy will not restore itself. It will take shared labor, moral clarity, and the refusal to abandon what must be repaired. This book is not the handoff. It is the shoulder pressed to the work. Let's begin—fully, collectively, and without illusion—until the foundation holds.

INTRODUCTION

———— ✦ ————

Restoration is not the beginning of something new. It is the act of returning what was broken to a state where it can serve its original purpose. This book is not a sequel—it is a continuation. The crisis that required *American Renewal* has not passed. The damage has not been undone. The promise of democracy has not been fulfilled. What has changed is what we now know: that holding the line is not enough. Resistance buys time. Restoration builds futures. This volume is not about protest. It is about design. It is the blueprint for reclaiming a government that still bears the name of a republic, but no longer answers to its people.

We have lived too long in a democracy by illusion—where elections are held but rigged through maps, where judges wear robes but rule like partisans, where the people still vote, but the outcomes are foregone. The republic continues only in ritual. But ritual without fairness is not democracy. It is performance. And performance cannot protect a people from tyranny.

This is the turning point—when resistance becomes design, and protest becomes plan.

This is not a revolution. It is repair. The American system was never designed for minority rule, but it has been twisted to deliver exactly that. The Electoral College lets a president govern without winning the people. The Senate grants veto power to geography. The Supreme Court, captured by ideology, blocks reform even when passed by overwhelming consensus. And the rules of elections—who can vote, how votes are counted, which votes matter—are written by those who benefit from fewer votes. These are not accidents. They are outcomes by design.

American Restoration is built to reverse them. It consists of eighteen reforms across four domains: political design, electoral integrity, judicial power, and civic legitimacy. Each chapter is a blueprint—not for partisan gain, but for democratic repair. And each is shaped not by ideology, but by the question that must now govern all constitutional design: what does democracy require?

This book does not stop at diagnosis. It offers direction. Every reform is grounded in law, history, and institutional architecture. Seven strategic appendices offer the constitutional basis, implementation path, or ethical imperative for the changes proposed. Together, they form the structural scaffolding of a republic restored.

Collected at the back of this volume are Reader's Guides—one for each chapter. They are meant not just to reflect, but to activate. Use them to teach, organize, challenge, revise, and lead. Use them where you are, with whoever is ready.

But reform does not begin in theory alone. Implementation depends on two victories: a pro-democracy majority in Congress in 2026, and the presidency in 2028. Those battles are assumed, not analyzed here. This volume begins where restoration becomes real—when power has been reclaimed, and repair must begin: to mend what was broken, replace what was dismantled, and restore what was sold, ignored, or corrupted in the long decay that led to 2029.

The order matters. Some reforms shield the rest. That strategic sequence is reflected in the chapters that follow—and it will determine whether restoration holds, or is undone.

These reforms are not final. Some may be flawed, revised, or surpassed. That is not failure. That is democracy.

This volume offers a beginning.

Let the work begin.

1

AMERICAN RESTORATION: THE STAKES

WHAT BROKE, WHO BROKE IT, AND HOW WE RESTORE THE REPUBLIC

"You do not become a tyranny overnight. You become a tyranny by design, by neglect, and by delay."
— JP Vincent

Democracy in the United States has failed to deliver on its most basic promises: fair elections, equal justice, and responsive governance. The collapse was not sudden. It came by design—through distortion of representation, corrosion of truth, capture of the courts, and the slow retreat of public power from public hands. What remains is not a functioning republic, but a brittle simulation of one—where outcomes are preordained, laws favor the powerful, and the people's voice grows fainter with each election. We have not lost the Constitution by coup. We have abandoned it by cowardice, delay, and design.

What once held this country together—shared facts, mutual legitimacy, and institutional boundaries—has been deliberately unraveled. Elections are manipulated through maps and money.

Power is concentrated in the hands of those immune to oversight. And the rule of law is now contingent not on justice, but on jurisdiction. The promises of the Preamble—justice, tranquility, welfare, liberty—are not just unmet. They are mocked by a system that rewards those who break it, and punishes those who dare to fix it. This is not the tyranny the Framers feared. It is the failure they did not finish protecting us from.

This book does not merely name what has gone wrong. It lays out the architecture for repair. *American Restoration* is not a slogan. It is a structural response to a structural crisis. It proposes twenty reforms—not to turn back time, but to finish what democracy never fully built. Some reforms will restore what was lost. Others will realize what was promised. Still others will construct what was never conceived. But together, they form a single objective: to build a democracy that serves the governed—and is strong enough to survive.

This restoration is not a single fix. It is a systemic rescue—across four domains: elections and representation, the presidency and executive power, the courts and rule of law, and the truth-based public square. Each domain contains fractures that can no longer be ignored. Each reform responds to a deliberate sabotage or historic omission. And each chapter that follows makes the case not just for what must change—but why it must change now.

The United States does not need new ideals. It needs a government that honors them. It needs elections that reflect the public, laws that bind the powerful, courts that answer to truth, and a culture that does not treat disinformation as freedom. The Restoration is not an agenda of the left. It is the rescue plan of the republic. And the only way forward is through it.

PART I. ELECTIONS THAT COUNT EVERY VOICE

WHEN VOTING IS PERFORMANCE, DEMOCRACY IS A LIE

―――― ✦ ――――

"The ballot is stronger than the bullet."
— Abraham Lincoln

We begin with elections—not because they are symbolic, but because they are structural. Before we can restore democracy, we must fix the five systems that determine who can run, who can vote, and whether that vote counts. In a democracy, the vote is more than a mechanism. It is the source of consent, the means by which the governed shape the laws that govern them. But when the system of elections is distorted, delayed, or purchased, that promise collapses. A vote that cannot be cast, counted, or trusted is not democratic participation. It is performance. And no nation can long survive on performance alone.

The United States has reached that threshold. Elections still occur—but they no longer reflect the people as they are, or the will they express. Maps are rigged. Districts are drawn to nullify voters before they speak. Candidates are selected by donors long before ballots are cast. And those ballots, once sacred, are now subject to purges, disqualifications, delays, and doubt. What remains is a democracy in appearance, not in function. And the longer we tolerate the illusion, the harder it becomes to recover the real thing.

That is why this section begins with a comprehensive agenda for electoral repair. Each chapter that follows addresses a different point of failure: how elections are financed, who is allowed to vote, how those votes are weighted, how districts are drawn, and how results are certified. Each of these reforms is essential on its own. But together, they form the foundation for everything else *American Restoration* proposes. No policy, however just, and no law, however needed, can endure if the process that delivers power is itself broken.

Campaign finance is where the distortion begins. In a healthy democracy, elections are contests of ideas. In the United States, they have become contests of capital. Candidates are not chosen by voters—they are pre-selected by donors. Just 0.5% of Americans now provide the majority of campaign funds. A handful of billionaires bankroll election cycles. Super PACs shape races through untraceable ads and coordinated spending. Corporate interests flood the process through shell companies and dark money networks. The result is a system where the public still votes—but for candidates elevated by money, shielded from scrutiny, and backed by investors who expect a return. This is not representation. It is market capture.

And it does not end with the election. Once in office, those who have been funded are not free. They are dependent on the very networks that financed their rise—and that will determine whether they can stay. The result is not just influence. It is servitude. Every hearing, every bill, every silence is shaped by the need to retain donor favor. When a drug company spends $300 million lobbying Congress to block generic competition and protect profits, it is not participating in democracy. It is purchasing policy. Officials cannot serve the public if they are owned by their patrons. Until that structure is broken—until elected office is no longer a debt owed to wealth—democracy will remain hostage to those who never stand for election.

Voting access is the second fault line. The right to vote is the foundation of every other right in a democracy. But in the United States, that right has never been guaranteed—only contested. From poll taxes to literacy tests, from grandfather clauses to voter purges, the history of American democracy is also the history of American exclusion. And that exclusion continues. Today, voter suppression is not declared—it is engineered. Precincts are closed. Ballots are rejected. Registration rolls are purged. Rules are rewritten not to protect elections, but to control who participates in them.

The targets are always the same: Black voters, poor voters, young voters, new citizens. Communities that are growing, changing, and challenging entrenched power. And the tactics have grown more sophisticated. Voter ID laws, signature mismatches, provisional ballot games, and disinformation campaigns all serve one purpose: to raise the cost of participation until enough people give up. Real reform means guaranteeing the vote—automatically, universally, and securely. Until access is equal, power will not be. And a vote that cannot be cast cannot count.

The Electoral College was not designed to undermine democracy—but that is now its effect. What once solved a logistical challenge has become a tool for minority rule. In the late 1700s, the United States was a nation of vast distances, poor roads, and limited communication. Most voters had never seen a presidential candidate, heard a speech, or read a platform. The Electoral College allowed states to appoint informed intermediaries. It also reflected the compromises of the time—between large and small states, slave states and free. For a time, it served. But what served in the age of handwritten ballots and horseback travel no longer serves in the age of instant information.

Today, the system distorts representation and diminishes trust. A candidate can lose the popular vote and still win the presidency. Voters in battleground states are courted relentlessly. Voters elsewhere are ignored. Most Americans know their ballot will not change the outcome. And most candidates know which states matter—and which do not. The result is not democratic legitimacy. It is strategic disenfranchisement. Real reform must move us toward a system where every vote counts equally and every citizen has a reason to participate. The principle must come first: a democracy cannot endure if the people choose one candidate and the system installs another.

Gerrymandering is the fourth breach. In a representative government, voters are meant to choose their leaders. But under partisan gerrymandering, it is leaders who choose their voters. District lines are drawn not to reflect communities, but to entrench power—dividing neighborhoods, diluting blocs, and isolating opposition. Sophisticated software now allows politicians to predict voting patterns down to the household, and to redraw boundaries with surgical precision. The result is elections decided before they begin, where the outcome is not debated but engineered.

Gerrymandering is not just manipulation. It is disenfranchisement by design. In some states, a party can win a minority of votes and still claim a supermajority of seats. Competitive districts vanish. Extremes flourish. And the link between public will and public policy dissolves. Real reform means creating independent redistricting commissions, bound by transparency, community coherence, and proportional fairness. Representation must begin with a map that reflects the people—not one that divides them to preserve power.

Certification is the final gate. An election is not over when the last ballot is cast. It is over when the result is certified. That final step—once a formality—has become a fault line. In recent years, partisan officials have begun to challenge, delay, or outright refuse certification of legitimate results. Laws have been rewritten to allow legislatures to override local vote counts. Extremist campaigns have harassed election workers, threatened secretaries of state, and positioned loyalists to seize control of certification.

This is not election integrity. It is election sabotage. No democracy can survive if losing is treated as illegitimate. The peaceful transfer of power depends on shared rules, honest actors, and a process that cannot be hijacked by partisan will. Real reform means protecting nonpartisan certification procedures, enforcing criminal penalties for interference, and insulating election officials from political retaliation. Without those safeguards, even the most secure vote can be nullified after the fact—and democracy collapses not in chaos, but in silence.

None of these reforms can wait. A republic does not fail all at once. It fails step by step—when elections are bought, when votes are suppressed, when outcomes are distorted, when maps are rigged, and when results are denied. Each distortion reinforces the next. And together, they form a system that no longer reflects the people it claims to represent. We still call it democracy. But we know what it has become.

These are not technical adjustments. They are structural repairs. Campaign finance, voting rights, electoral fairness, redistricting, and certification are not policy debates. They are the rules of the game. And right now, the game is rigged. Every other reform in this agenda depends on these five. Until power can be won fairly, it cannot be exercised legitimately. Until elections are real, government is not accountable. And until the people can choose their leaders freely, they do not govern at all.

This is not a crisis that outrage alone can solve. We must answer design with design—intentional, strategic, and structural. That means passing laws, not slogans. Building coalitions, not echo chambers. Restoring legitimacy one safeguard at a time. The enemies of democracy have been working for decades. We will not undo that work in one election. But we can begin. And we must.

The promise of this country was never that wealth would govern. It was that the people would. These five reforms are not a return to what was. They are a step toward what was promised—and never delivered. That work begins here. Democracy is not restored by hope—it is restored by law. And that law must begin with the vote.

2

CAMPAIGN FINANCE REFORM
ENDING THE AUCTION, RESTORING THE VOTE

"A representative cannot serve both the people and their patrons."
— JP Vincent

Before any policy can be debated, any law proposed, or any grievance redressed, a decision must be made about who holds power. In a democracy, that decision is made by vote. But what determines whose voice is heard before the vote is cast? The answer is money. Money shapes the field, frames the debate, decides who runs, who gets seen, and who gets silenced. It does not merely influence elections—it defines them. And while the vote transfers power, money determines the choices. That is why campaign finance reform is not an accessory to democracy. It is its precondition.

That is why campaign finance reform is first. Because if elections are bought, democracy is only rented. And the people cannot govern if their voice is drowned by wealth. Today, candidates do not win by persuasion. They win by fundraising. Power is brokered, not earned.

Donors expect returns. And the public, left on the margins, watches a system speak in a language they cannot afford to learn. This is not democracy. It is auction.

It wasn't always this way. In the earliest years of the republic, campaigning was seen as almost shameful—evidence of ambition rather than virtue. Candidates did not seek votes directly. They remained distant, while electors chose leaders presumed to be disinterested, independent, and known to the public. As the country opened the vote to more citizens, that model eroded—but not overnight. For much of the nineteenth century, elections remained modest in scale and cost. Campaigns were local. Communication was personal. Persuasion came by letter, speech, or handbill—not by saturation. But as railroads shrank distance, printing presses expanded literacy, and federal power began reaching into infrastructure, commerce, and law, the stakes grew. The government could now shape markets, award contracts, and enforce—or ignore—monopolies. To win office was no longer merely to serve. It was to gain access to a lever with the power to transform economies, rewrite regulations, and someday, decide everything from land use to healthcare to marriage to what we see, say, buy, and eat.

By the late 1800s, the United States had entered what would be called the Gilded Age—a time of immense industrial growth, staggering inequality, and thinly veiled corruption. The gap between money and power had vanished. Industrial magnates didn't just influence elections. They purchased them. Party bosses became access brokers, trading financial support for control over policy, appointments, and law. The result wasn't governance. It was a bidding war. Reformers tried to intervene. The Tillman Act of 1907 banned direct corporate contributions—but enforcement was symbolic. The money remained. And then came Watergate. That scandal revealed not only lawbreaking, but how money had become both shield and sword: hiding crimes, purchasing silence, and turning public office into a private weapon. In response, Congress passed real reform—contribution limits, public financing for presidential candidates, and the creation of the Federal Election Commission. For a moment, the tide turned.

But that moment did not last. The courts intervened. In *Buckley v. Valeo* (1976), the Supreme Court equated spending money with speaking freely. From that single distortion flowed decades of dysfunction. In *Citizens United v. FEC* (2010), the Court removed nearly all limits on independent political spending—giving corporations, unions, and ultra-wealthy individuals license to flood elections with untraceable cash. Super PACs emerged. Dark money networks flourished. Donors no longer needed parties or platforms. They could fund not just ads, but entire movements—and do it in secret. In a system where power is anonymous, accountability disappears. One person, one vote may still apply. But one voice? Not when a single billionaire can speak louder than ten million citizens and never show their face.

This is not merely corruption. It is distortion, institutionalized at scale. Elected officials no longer raise money just to win—they raise money to remain. The moment the victory speech ends, the calls begin. Members of Congress now spend 20, 30, even 40 percent of their time dialing for dollars—not governing, not listening, not legislating. And the donors they call are not average citizens. They are the wealthy, the well-organized, the ideologically extreme. The result is policy that reflects the priorities of patrons, not the people. And because that truth cannot be seen too clearly, another distortion follows: secrecy. The rise of dark money is not an accident. It is protection—concealing the allegiance of the elected so the public can go on believing they are still the ones being served.

And what is all this money spent on? Not on policy research. Not on public-minded staff. Not on town halls or community casework. It is spent on advertising—almost all of it. The largest expense in any major campaign is the ad buy: television, digital, social, mail. Not to explain ideas. Not to argue positions. But to flood the airwaves, overwhelm the opposition, and leave no silence unfilled. In presidential campaigns, ad spending now exceeds half a billion dollars. In close Senate races, tens of millions are spent by outside groups on messages the candidate may never even read—let alone write. The purpose is not persuasion. It is domination. It substitutes repetition for trust, and disorients the voter until voting becomes reflex—disconnected from thought, stripped of meaning, and emptied of choice.

And the content of these ads? Rarely proposals. Rarely solutions. Instead, they deliver a war of narratives where the opponent is never just wrong—but dangerous, corrupt, criminal, even traitorous. Each cycle, the accusations escalate, the production sharpens, and the connection to fact weakens. Negative advertising is no longer a tactic. It is the grammar of campaigning itself. And beneath the volume, a darker pattern has emerged: not just character attacks, but conspiracy; not just innuendo, but explicit dehumanization. We are no longer debating policy. We are being primed—for loyalty, for outrage, and for division.

The result is exhaustion. Bombarded with lies, contradictions, fear, and contempt, the voter does not become engaged. They become numb. They tune out. They assume the worst. And in that assumption, the distortion completes itself. The public ceases to believe that truth is knowable, that candidates can be trusted, or that elections are vehicles of change. This is not apathy. It is not ignorance. It is defense—against a system that teaches sincerity is weakness and information is a weapon. And as more voters disengage, fewer need to be persuaded. The system becomes cheaper to manipulate. And those who engineered the distrust now thrive on the silence it created.

At this point, the cycle sustains itself. Candidates must raise enormous sums to compete in an environment dominated by ad warfare. Donors, having invested, expect results. Messaging narrows. Allegiances harden. And the public—supposedly the beneficiary of this democratic energy—becomes the target of a marketing machine where truth is incidental and victory is everything. The more the system rewards saturation, the more money it demands. And the more money it demands, the less space remains for deliberation, dissent, or doubt. Elections become echo chambers. Policy becomes product. And public trust becomes collateral damage.

Meanwhile, the media—dependent on advertising revenue—has become complicit. Campaign lies are aired as coverage. Rally clips run without context. Conspiracies are repeated without correction in the name of balance. Even in public debates, lies go unchecked, rules are ignored, and questions go unanswered—while moderators, networks, and platforms avoid correction for fear of losing access, ratings, or political favor. Every falsehood, no matter how grotesque, is given oxygen. This is not journalism. It is participation. And the system does not punish it, funding it instead.

Unchecked financing is not merely a domestic distortion. It opens the door to foreign influence, funneled through shell entities, nonprofits, or digital platforms—turning campaign finance not only into a tool of inequality, but a vector of interference.

But it does not have to be this way. Other democracies face the same temptations—money, influence, partisanship. But they have drawn different lines. France bans political advertising on television and radio. The United Kingdom enforces strict limits on campaign duration and spending. Germany provides public funding and mandates donation transparency. Australia is moving toward real-time donor disclosure and truth-in-political-advertising laws. None of these systems is perfect. But none permit what we do. Nowhere else is there such a sustained fusion of unlimited money, unregulated advertising, and unchecked falsehood. These nations disagree fiercely about policy. But they agree on something more foundational: that elections must be fair, factual, and answer to the public they serve.

Reform must begin with what should never have been compromised: transparency. If money is speech, as the courts now insist, then it must speak with a name attached. Every donation, every expenditure—whether direct to a candidate or routed through a nonprofit or Super PAC—must be disclosed publicly, promptly, and accessibly. Real-time transparency is no longer a luxury. It is a precondition for accountability. If a lawmaker cannot be questioned about who is financing their career, they cannot be trusted to represent the public. They represent their donors. The First Amendment protects speech—but not secrecy. A whisper may be speech. But when whispered through a billion-dollar amplifier and aimed at the outcome of elections and legislation, it becomes something else entirely: an evasion of democracy disguised as a right.

But disclosure alone is not enough. Knowing who funds the noise does not reduce its volume. Campaigns are no longer contests of vision. They are competitions in capital. Today, the loudest voice is not the most persuasive. It is the best funded. Political advertising has become a race to saturate, overwhelm, and dominate—not to inform, but to outspend. In this environment, truth loses not by argument, but by repetition. And the most effective repetitions are now amplified by algorithm—optimized for outrage, precision-targeted by data, and immune to rebuttal in the time it takes for damage to be done.

When huge donations meet total anonymity, and fiscal dependency meets unchecked ambition, the result is not just elections that can be bought. It is candidates—pre-selected, pre-approved, and privately owned. And those candidates often campaign in gerrymandered districts, where the general election is a formality and all messaging is aimed at a narrow, controlled slice of the electorate. Thus, the financing and the maps reinforce each other—concentrating power, hardening partisanship, and lowering the cost of capture.

Political advertising in the United States is exempt from the truth-in-advertising laws that govern nearly every other product. A candidate may lie about their opponent's record, their own experience, even basic facts—and face no legal consequence. A Super PAC may fabricate a crisis, promote a conspiracy, or invent accusations out of whole cloth. As long as the message is technically independent, it can run unchallenged on national media. We cannot demand that candidates fulfill every promise. But we can demand that political ads tell the truth—about who they are, what has happened, who did it, and the current state of the world. To allow unchecked lies in campaign messaging is not free speech. It is weaponized disinformation. And if a soap company cannot lie about what it removes from stains—under Federal Trade Commission rules—a campaign should not be allowed to lie about what its candidate has done. Democracy is not strengthened by falsehood. It is devoured by it.

Reform will not come easily. The beneficiaries of the current system—candidates, consultants, donors, and even some journalists—will resist. They will claim that every restriction is censorship. That every limit is unconstitutional. That any attempt to restore balance is a partisan power grab. But democracy was never meant to be defined by the consent of the powerful. It is defined by the consent of the governed—and consent without clarity, without voice, without trust, is no consent at all. The question is not whether reform will be hard. It is whether democracy is worth what it takes to restore it.

Reform is not a dream from a distant land. It is already happening. In New York, small donations are matched with public funds to amplify ordinary voices. In Seattle, every registered voter receives four $25 "democracy vouchers" to give to candidates of their choice. Maine and Arizona have sustained public financing systems for state races. None are perfect. All face legal and political attack. But they exist. They work. And they point to a future in which running for office is not a luxury good, and campaigning is not a code word for fundraising. These measures do not eliminate the influence of money. But they dilute it, compete with it, and in some cases, displace it. That alone makes them worth protecting—and replicating. But they remain local, limited, and rare. If reform is to restore democracy, it must be national in scope—and free of exceptions for the wealthy, the connected, or the already empowered.

After decades of legal manipulation and institutional abuse, no single campaign finance reform will be enough. Public financing without advertising limits simply subsidizes participation in the same contaminated system. Disclosure without consequences is transparency in name only. Donation caps help, but not if independent expenditures are allowed to drown out campaigns entirely. The real challenge is not choosing among fixes—it is confronting the architecture of distortion itself. A system built on dependency cannot be redeemed through minor repairs. It must be replaced with one that centers voters, not donors. A system where the loudest voice is not the richest. Where truth, not repetition, prevails. And where public trust is not a casualty of power—but its condition.

There are those who already try to live this ethic. Some candidates refuse corporate PAC money. Others rely entirely on small-dollar donors. A few prioritize public town halls over high-dollar fundraisers. These exceptions matter. They are acts of resistance. They prove it can be done. But a democracy cannot depend on personal heroism. It must be sustained by structure. A healthy republic should not rely on the strength of a few to resist the pull of corruption. It must build rules that prevent corruption from taking root in the first place. If it takes courage to remain clean, the system itself is dirty. The solution is not to hope for better candidates in a system where character rarely determines outcome. It is to demand a better system—one that rewards character and public service instead of private obedience.

Let us be clear: this is not about silencing dissent. It is about restoring authentic disagreement—the kind democracy depends on.

Conflict is not the enemy. In a functioning republic, citizens must argue over values, policies, and priorities. But today's system doesn't promote debate. It replaces it with spectacle. With noise. With saturation campaigns designed to distort, not clarify. Billion-dollar arsenals of deception don't fuel disagreement. They erase it—beneath a flood of attack ads, conspiracy, and caricature. Real debate begins when truth has space to breathe—and when those speaking it aren't forced to shout through walls of cash.

There was a time—however flawed—when public service was a duty, not a career. When candidates were chosen for judgment, conscience, and trust. When elected officials served their districts, then returned home to resume life as teachers, farmers, scientists, or shopkeepers. That vision has eroded. Today, if you are not already wealthy—or cannot secure a wealthy benefactor—you cannot run. And if you do win, you spend half your time trying to stay. The pressures are relentless. Even those who enter with principle are pushed to conform, to fundraise, to obey. No one should have to silence their conscience to keep a seat. Representation should not be for sale. And democracy cannot survive in a system that punishes truth, rewards distortion, and drives honest voices out. This will not correct itself. It must be fought—relentlessly, structurally, and in every place where influence now overrules consent.

We do not offer a simple solution. We offer a principle: representation must be earned—not bought. Democracy begins when the people are heard, and it ends when they are drowned out. Every lever—public financing, donation caps, real-time transparency, truth in advertising, limits on saturation—is a tool to restore that core promise. None is sufficient alone. But together, they reclaim what has been stolen: the right of citizens to shape their future without selling their voice. If we want a government worthy of public trust—one where honest, talented, and committed people can serve—we must build a system that cannot be bought. That work begins here. And it cannot wait.

3

VOTING RIGHTS PROTECTION
FROM PERMISSION TO POWER: SECURING THE RIGHT TO VOTE IN A BROKEN SYSTEM

---✦---

"A system that filters participation through race, class, or ZIP code is not broken. It is rigged."
— JP Vincent

Many Americans believe the right to vote is guaranteed. It is not. The Constitution does not grant it. It does not define it. It does not protect it. Instead, it avoids the question entirely. The Framers were afraid of democracy, and they built a system that delegated control of voting to the states. From that silence, exclusion has grown. From property thresholds to poll taxes, literacy tests to registration traps, the ballot has never been freely given. It has always been contested. Today, that contest is more blatant but no less strategic. Ballot access is narrowed. Registration is restricted. Entire categories of citizens are deliberately made invisible—not by accident, but by design. For by exclusion, power is guaranteed—not earned, not fairly contested, not won.

The absence of a constitutional guarantee was not a mistake. It was a deliberate decision born of fear, history, and circumstance. The Framers had just fought a war to break free from monarchy. They were terrified of building another. The Bill of Rights reads like a direct rebuke of the world they left behind: no king, no quartered soldiers, no prison without trial, no forced religion, no censorship of dissent. But their caution ran deeper. Across Europe, the poor were rioting, revolting, starving. In France, the people had not just deposed their king—they had beheaded him. Democracy looked dangerous. Popular rule looked like anarchy.

At the same time, the new republic faced vast distances, poor infrastructure, and a scattered, largely uneducated population. A national vote seemed unworkable. So the Framers placed their trust elsewhere—in property, order, and elite judgment. They built a system mediated by legislatures, electors, and Senate chambers—not the public. The Constitution does not require citizens to vote, does not mandate equal access, and does not promise that the most votes must win. Democracy was not its foundation. It was a risk, delegated to the states.

What we now call voting rights entered the Constitution only through struggle—and only as prohibitions, not guarantees. The 15th Amendment barred racial exclusion. The 19th barred sex-based denial. The 24th outlawed poll taxes. The 26th ensured no one over eighteen could be turned away because of age. But none of these affirm the vote as an inherent right. Each says only who cannot be excluded—not that anyone must be included. Each depends on Congress to enforce them. And enforcement has grown weaker with time.

Again and again, the courts have eroded voting protections not with one blow, but with sustained attrition. In *Shelby County v. Holder*, the Supreme Court invalidated the preclearance formula of the Voting Rights Act. In *Brnovich v. DNC*, it raised the burden of proof for racial discrimination. In *Bush v. Gore*, it voided recount procedures without setting precedent. The Court speaks the language of democracy while enabling those who undermine it. Voting is declared fundamental in principle, but optional in practice.

As suffrage expanded—to Black men, women, immigrants, and the young—a new strategy emerged: contain the impact. Jim Crow laws, language requirements, residency rules—all were designed not to bar voters openly, but to discourage participation. If new voters could change outcomes, make it harder for them. The motive was no longer fear of disorder, but fear of losing power.

That battle moved to the states. With discretion over voting and partisan incentives, legislatures refined suppression into strategy. Polling places closed without notice. Voter rolls purged by algorithm. Ballots disqualified over signatures. IDs demanded that few possess. Every barrier—however small—adds friction, especially for communities long excluded. This is not election security. It is systemic prevention.

The data reveals the intent. In Texas, population growth has surged—but voter participation remains low. In Georgia, after record turnout in 2020, the state restricted early voting, absentee access, and mobile voting centers. As the electorate expands, access contracts. Each gain in population is met with exclusion. The pattern is deliberate.

Republican-led legislatures have introduced thousands of voting laws in recent years—not to protect votes, but to shape the electorate. Their agenda is unpopular. Their base is shrinking. They do not adapt their message—they adapt the rules. Close precincts. Purge rolls. Require obscure ID. The method changes. The motive does not. If you cannot win the majority, change who counts as one.

Their defense is always the same: election integrity. But fraud is vanishingly rare. What exists is almost always Republican. Trump claimed the 2020 election was stolen—yet no credible fraud was found. What remains is manufactured uncertainty: partisan officials, rule confusion, delays, intimidation. Armed observers. Fake robocalls. ICE threats. These are not glitches. They are tactics. And when voters disengage, the distortion completes itself.

Meanwhile, those claiming fraud have undermined integrity themselves. Trump dismantled the Cybersecurity and Infrastructure Security Agency after it affirmed 2020's legitimacy. States refused help. Machines were denounced, then reused. We trust digital systems to run banks, hospitals, and defense. But secure online voting is dismissed as impossible. It isn't. It's just inconvenient for those who profit from exclusion.

The United States is not the world's strongest democracy. It is among the most exclusionary. In Australia and Greece, voting is mandatory. Canada and Germany ensure universal registration. Estonia votes online. France and Mexico offer secure digital options abroad. These systems are not perfect—but they are designed to include. Ours is increasingly designed to exclude. That's not a flaw. It's intent.

With policies this unpopular, Republicans cannot win by persuasion. So they win by restriction. They narrow the electorate. They claim sanctity for the process of denial. Power, once defined by race, is now protected by wealth, cynicism, and fear. Not by offering more to the people—but by allowing fewer to choose.

Every expansion of voting rights has met resistance. Today, it arrives cloaked in legality and framed as protection. Gerrymanders are blessed by the courts. Disenfranchisement is sold as fairness. The fear that once shaped the Founders now justifies denying the democracy they never finished. We do not lack will. We lack the power to enact what the public already supports. That is not governance. It is capture.

But what has been denied can still be won. The technology exists. The models exist. Other nations use them. So must we. Early voting. Mail voting. Online voting. In-person voting. Each protected by design, audited by law, and expanded by default. Democracy does not resist inclusion. It is defined by it.

In an exclusionary system, registration is a hurdle. In a just democracy, it is automatic. The first time a citizen interacts with the government—filing taxes, applying for Social Security, entering customs—they should be enrolled. One identity. One record. One line on the rolls. The state counts us for taxes and the census. It must count us to vote. No just democracy waits for permission to include its people.

And with registration must come access. The method must not limit the right. A just democracy meets people where they are: at home or work, online or on paper, in illness or motion. Election Day should remain for those who want tradition. But early, online, and mail options must become equal, secure, and universal. Voters must never lose their voice to distance, fatigue, or routine.

This will not be welcomed by those who rule through restriction. Their strategy is clear. Their advantage depends on turnout gaps, access blocks, and friction disguised as fairness. But law can serve justice as well as power. What once excluded can be rewritten to include. What once protected privilege can secure participation. And what once denied can now be declared: a right to vote, national, structural, and real.

That right must be federal. One standard. One guarantee. One law that overrides the thousand cuts of partisan sabotage. Automatic registration. Universal access. Paper trails and secure machines. Transparent certification. Enforced by a fully funded, modern infrastructure. And insulated from partisan override. Votes must determine outcomes—not power.

The clock is short. By 2030, new state legislatures will draw new maps. That window cannot be missed. Federal voting rights legislation must pass in 2029—and implementation must begin immediately. If the states sue, let them. If the Court intervenes, expand it. The same Court that permits insurrectionists on ballots can uphold the vote. Our task is not to restore the Founders' vision. It is to complete what they began. They built a system that could become democratic. We must make it so.

A vote uncounted is a voice unheard. The right to vote must no longer be filtered by ancestry, income, or address. A system that filters access is not broken. It is rigged. And it must be replaced—openly, lawfully, structurally, and without apology. Democracy is not self-enforcing. It is self-made. We may not be the ones who finish it. But we are the only ones who can start it.

4

ELECTORAL COLLEGE REFORM
WHY THE ELECTORAL COLLEGE MUST BE REPLACED—OR RENDERED FAIR

---✦---

"A democracy worthy of its people must let every voice count equally."
— Stacey Abrams

The Framers of the Constitution were not fools. They had just overthrown monarchy and knew firsthand the dangers of concentrated power—but also of unrestrained mobs. Across the Atlantic, the French Revolution was becoming a bloodbath. England's masses were so impoverished that petty criminals were shipped in chains to Australia. No functioning democracy existed to emulate. America was not yet a nation of equals or of information—it was an experiment, fragile and untested. In that context, the idea of a direct popular vote for president felt not only risky, but reckless. Their solution was not democratic in the modern sense, but it was defensible: choose wise electors who could be trusted to act in the republic's interest.

The Electoral College was not an expression of principle but a concession to circumstance. In a country with no common media, no national infrastructure, and no means to travel faster than a horse, a direct election was logistically absurd. Communication was limited to town criers, pamphlets, and month-old news carried westward by word of mouth. The country was too vast, the people too scattered. So the Constitution passed the problem to the states. Each would select electors—men presumed to be informed and rational—who would deliberate and choose the president. It was, in essence, a workaround, not a vision.

Two and a half centuries later, the conditions that justified the Electoral College no longer exist. Today, one can travel across the country in the time it once took to reach the next town. News arrives in seconds, not weeks. Citizens are educated, connected, and informed in ways unimaginable to the Framers. But the system remains—unchanged, ossified, and dangerous. Like leaded paint or DDT, what once passed for progress now poisons the institutions it was meant to protect. The Electoral College was born of necessity. But necessity has passed, and all that remains is distortion—and danger to a fair democracy.

In 48 states, the Electoral College uses a winner-take-all system: whichever candidate wins the most votes statewide—by one vote or one million—receives all the electoral votes. In states where one party dominates, every other vote is effectively discarded. A Republican in California or a Democrat in South Carolina may vote in large numbers, but unless they flip the statewide outcome, their ballots have no bearing on the result. This distorts not only representation, but campaign strategy. Presidential candidates focus almost entirely on the few states that could swing either way, bypassing the rest. Elections present as national contests, but in practice they are narrow campaigns fought on selective ground. Most Americans are not courted, not persuaded, not heard. Their participation is noted—but rarely matters. And their consent, the foundation of democracy, is treated as incidental.

This distortion is not just unfair. It is dangerous. In two of the last six elections, the Electoral College delivered the presidency to candidates who lost the national popular vote. The results were not simply narrow—they reversed the expressed will of the people. Far from a statistical quirk, this is the predictable outcome of a system designed to misrepresent. And because it enables minority rule, it encourages extremism. There is no incentive to reach a national consensus. There is every incentive to inflame, divide, and capture the right geography. The College doesn't moderate. It magnifies.

As detailed in Chapter Two, campaign finance flows toward power—and power flows to swing states. There is no need to persuade the country when eight or ten states will decide the outcome. Billions are spent targeting these battlegrounds while the rest of the country fades into electoral silence. A voter in Florida or Wisconsin is not just more likely to see a candidate in person—they are more likely to matter. In the eyes of campaign strategists, everyone else is background noise. The modern presidency is not won by building a majority. It is won by gaming a map.

When power is concentrated in a handful of battlegrounds, policy follows. Presidents allocate attention, promises, and resources to the places that decide elections—not the ones that need them most. Disaster relief, infrastructure funding, and even federal appointments often reflect political calculus more than public need. A community in Pennsylvania might receive three campaign visits and billions in funding while one in Mississippi sees nothing—not because of merit, but because one is electorally decisive and the other is not. This is not representative democracy. It is a transactional map where lives matter only if votes do.

There is no moral principle embedded in the Electoral College. It was not handed down as sacred doctrine. It was a workaround—a temporary patch for a new country too fragmented to run a national election. The Constitution gave states the authority to choose electors because the federal government couldn't. It left implementation vague because uniformity was impossible. What emerged was less a system than a shrug: let each state solve it. That flexibility served a practical purpose in 1787. But today it serves only those who exploit chaos to override consent.

The United States is the only major democracy where a candidate can win the highest office while losing the national vote. In most parliamentary systems—like the United Kingdom, Australia, New Zealand, and Canada—the head of government is selected by the majority party or coalition in the national legislature. In presidential systems such as France, South Korea, and Brazil, the president is elected directly by the people through national popular vote. Even in monarchies like Sweden, Denmark, or the Netherlands, the monarch is ceremonial; real power lies with elected leaders chosen by democratic means. The concept is neither radical nor rare. The United States stands virtually alone in maintaining a system that rewards minority rule. National leadership by national vote is not utopian theory. It is the global norm.

The obvious fix—abolishing the Electoral College—is practically impossible. Constitutional amendments require two-thirds of both chambers of Congress and ratification by three-fourths of the states. That threshold was designed for permanence, not urgency. And those who benefit from the College have no incentive to dismantle it. It is a unicorn with a newspaper—mythical and already outdated. But there are other legal paths. The National Popular Vote Interstate Compact allows states to pledge their electors to the national popular vote winner, taking effect once the 270 threshold is reached. And two states—Maine and Nebraska—already allocate their electors proportionally based on the vote in each congressional district, with statewide winners receiving the remaining two. It's an imperfect model, but it proves the College can be modified without waiting for a miracle.

The National Popular Vote Interstate Compact (NPVIC) is simple in principle, elegant in execution. Each participating state passes a law: it will award all its electoral votes to the candidate who wins the national popular vote. But the law takes effect only when states totaling at least 270 electoral votes have joined—enough to decide the presidency. No amendment. No federal approval. As of today, 16 states and the District of Columbia have signed on, totaling 196 votes. We are close. But close is not enough. The next stolen election will not wait for permission to act.

Proportional allocation of electors—used now only in Maine and Nebraska—offers another route to reform. Instead of awarding all electors to the statewide winner, states could assign them by congressional district, with two additional votes going to the statewide popular vote winner. But district-level allocation inherits another distortion: gerrymandering. Without redistricting reform, proportional systems merely replicate partisan bias in miniature. An alternative is true statewide proportionality, assigning electors in direct proportion to each candidate's share of the state vote. This reduces winner-take-all effects without requiring national coordination. These two solutions—NPVIC, already ratified by 16 states, and proportional allocation, already proven in two—are the only legal and operational reforms available within the Restoration timeframe. Others may be imagined, even proposed. But these two can be enacted.

Even if the Compact reaches 270 or all 50 states adopt proportional allocation of electors, fair elections cannot survive ambiguity. In the past, electors were free to ignore the will of voters—casting ballots for losing candidates, alternate parties, or personal favorites. Today, most states bind their electors, but not all. The risk is not theoretical. In 2016, seven electors broke ranks. In a close election, even a handful could shatter legitimacy. National law must make clear: electors are agents, not deciders. Whether assigned by statewide winner, national popular vote, or proportional allocation, their duty is fixed. They have no discretion, no autonomy, no veto.

The Electoral College may remain on paper. But in practice, it must become a reflection of the popular will.

Any national effort to bind electors or change how they are allocated will be challenged in court. Opponents will argue it infringes on state sovereignty, violates constitutional tradition, or undermines federalism. If Trump has taught us anything, it is that power unchecked will test every limit—and often prevail. A Democratic trifecta in 2029 must anticipate this. Legislation must be airtight. Contingencies must be ready. And if the Supreme Court, packed with ideologues, seeks to invalidate lawful reform, then expansion must be on the table—not as revenge, but as repair. If Thomas and Alito can invent presidential immunity, a rebalanced court can restore constitutional reality and defend election fairness.

The existing system does not, as some believe, protect small states. It does not serve the union. It serves the minority that has mastered its distortions. Campaign operatives, redistricting strategists, and candidates who cannot win a national majority all benefit from the College's perversions. Republicans have relied on it to remain competitive while narrowing their appeal to the wealthy, the white, and the rural. The system rewards division, regional manipulation, and the politics of exclusion—not national unity. It is a firewall for minority rule—by design, by habit, and increasingly by intent.

By contrast, a national popular vote or proportional allocation changes everything. It forces parties to persuade, not suppress. It breaks the cycle of swing-state favoritism and turns every voter into a stakeholder. Candidates would need to campaign everywhere—not just in Pennsylvania, Georgia, or Arizona, but in Idaho, Oregon, and South Dakota. Safe states would become relevant. Minorities in every region would regain a voice, and the presidency would return to its rightful owner: the people. A real democracy should not fear its voters. It should depend on them.

But the Electoral College is not the only distortion. It is one piece in a broader system engineered over decades to entrench minority power through fragmentation: gerrymandered districts, unlimited money, voter suppression, and judicial manipulation. Reforming one without the others is like patching a leak while the roof collapses. The system is interconnected. Power flows through all its channels. If we do not secure them all—elections, financing, redistricting, and representation—then even good reforms will rot from within. The goal is not a better illusion. It is a working democracy.

A true democracy holds elections where every vote counts equally. Where campaigns seek support from voters in every state—not just a handful. Where a Democrat in Alabama and a Republican in Oregon know their voices matter. Where presidents are elected by persuasion, not precision targeting. This is not an idealistic dream. It is the norm in most functioning democracies. It produces more representative leaders, more inclusive debates, and less incentive to divide. A government elected by all the people, and accountable to all the people. The Electoral College is not a necessary safeguard. It is an obsolete solution to a problem that no longer exists—now an engineered vulnerability. And the remedy is not revolution. It is a set of clear, lawful reforms that make the people's voice equal, empowered, and decisive. That is what democracy looks like.

If Democrats win a trifecta in 2029, they must act swiftly. National legislation can encourage proportional elector allocation. Federal incentives can reward states that join the Compact or enact binding elector laws. Congress can attach democratic conditions to federal election funding—just as it does for education or infrastructure. And it can clarify that the right to vote includes the right to equal weight in choosing the presidency. We cannot rely on voluntary state action alone. Power must be used to restore representation. Not someday. Not later. Immediately.

January 6, 2021, was not only a riot. It was a coordinated attempt to subvert the peaceful transfer of power—a stress test of the system, and a preview of what may come. Members of Congress objected to certified state results. Armed protesters breached the Capitol to delay or prevent the final count. The goal was not protest. It was disruption—and possibly reversal. If the Electoral College delivers the presidency to a losing candidate in a future election, the crisis will be worse. Not because of what the losers might do—but because of what the victors will claim. We have seen it before. In 2024, Trump narrowly won the popular vote but secured a wide Electoral College margin—and declared a "mandate." That fiction became the justification for unprecedented overreach, systemic abuses, and the illegal consolidation of power. A distorted win can be weaponized as legitimacy. A corrupted system can be used to entrench minority rule. The danger is not just a stolen election. It is the slow, legal theft of the future. Democracy cannot survive in the shadow of permanent doubt.

We have outgrown the Electoral College. We must now outlive it. To delay reform is to tolerate fraud in slow motion. Every cycle it distorts tightens the grip of minority rule. Every delay emboldens those who no longer seek majority support. But we are not bound to the past. The Constitution was not written to serve tyranny in fragments. The people are sovereign. Their will is not a threat—it is the republic's foundation. We can reform this system lawfully, nationally, and completely. The question is not whether it can be done. The question is whether we will.

5

REDISTRICTING REFORM

WHY AMERICA'S ELECTORAL MAPS NO LONGER REFLECT THE WILL OF THE PEOPLE— AND HOW WE FIX THEM BEFORE 2030.

---◆---

"The lines that divide us do more than shape elections—they shape who matters."
— JP Vincent

Redistricting is not just broken. It has been weaponized. The drawing of legislative maps—a once-routine act of civic maintenance—has become a calculated assault on democracy. With each decade, the distortion grows. Districts are twisted into shapes that silence dissent and cement control. One election victory becomes a ten-year lock on power. The public cannot vote their way out of it because the system has already decided which votes matter. This is not politics. It is cartographic warfare. And in too many states, it has succeeded. The map is no longer a mirror of the people. It is a cage built to contain them or ignore them.

Representation begins with geography. Lines on a map define who votes where. But when those lines are drawn to favor one party

—and, too often, whose vote will count—the result is not just partisan advantage. It is institutional rot. Gerrymandering incubates extremism. It rewards loyalty to party over duty to constituents. And it breeds candidates of breathtaking cynicism: Marjorie Taylor Greene, Lauren Boebert, Matt Gaetz—elected not because they represent the public, but because the public was partitioned to ensure their victory. In a fair district, character matters. In a safe one, it does not. The people didn't choose them. The map did.

The Framers understood that representation required balance, even if they failed to achieve it. Article I, Section 2 mandates apportionment by population. The Fourteenth Amendment later affirmed equal protection as a constitutional requirement. Redistricting was meant to adjust for population shifts—to preserve fairness, not to engineer outcomes. It was never meant to empower the majority party in a state legislature to rewrite the rules of representation in its own favor. But over time, that is precisely what happened. The system we inherited was fragile, built for the honesty and technology of the 1780s. It required good faith. It assumed restraint. When that restraint disappeared and good faith became optional, the architecture of representation was turned against itself.

The irony is inescapable. The practice is named for Elbridge Gerry, Governor of Massachusetts (1810-1812), who signed a grotesquely shaped Massachusetts district into law in 1812—but fiercely opposed the practice itself. He understood its danger: that politicians could redraw maps to preserve their own power, not to reflect the will of the people. Today, that fear has become fact. And the tools have evolved far beyond what the Framers and even Gerry could have imagined. The modern gerrymander is not hand-drawn. It is built by algorithms, fed by voter data, optimized to minimize opposition, and engineered to give the desired outcomes for a decade or more. This is no longer mere unfairness. It is engineered disenfranchisement—silent, systematic, and built to last.

In its earliest form, redistricting was often clumsy and uneven—

but it still bore some allegiance to fairness, logic, and geography. Districts followed counties, rivers, or cities. They reflected, however imperfectly, a map of people and place. But over the next few censuses, that changed. From clumsy redistricting to racial partitioning to partisan gerrymandering took only a few decades. As the enormous power of redistricting became apparent, the goal evolved. First, to dilute Black political power. Now, to erase competition in elections entirely. What began as uneven representation became engineered suppression. Racial gerrymanders aimed to keep people from voting—or to keep them from counting. Partisan gerrymanders aim to stay in power even when unpopular. Both are unfair. Both are undemocratic. But only racial gerrymandering is illegal.

Partisan gerrymandering has never been outlawed by Congress or constrained by a constitutional standard. The courts have long struggled to define what fairness means in political mapmaking. Some rulings chipped away at racial injustice or malapportionment, but the core question remained: how much partisanship is too much? The answer came in 2019. In *Rucho v. Common Cause*, the Supreme Court declared that partisan gerrymandering was a "political question" beyond the reach of federal courts. Chief Justice Roberts, joined by Justices Alito and Thomas, acknowledged the injustice—and rejected the remedy. The Court did not merely permit distortion. It legitimized it. The justices understood exactly what they were doing. And no law was there to stop them.

Taking full advantage of this legal vacuum, state legislatures have pushed gerrymandering into open defiance. In North Carolina, after courts struck down racially and politically biased maps, the legislature drew new ones—just as rigged. In Ohio, lawmakers ignored a state constitutional amendment and defied multiple rulings from their own supreme court. In Alabama and Arkansas, federal judges increasingly sided with legislators, not voters. These are not isolated abuses. They are coordinated signals: that power will protect itself, that law can be bypassed, and that consent no longer matters. Control is now the guiding principle.

The effect is both immediate and long-term. Capture a legislature once—just once at the right time—and a party can draw maps that lock in control for a decade. During that time, it can entrench its power by rewriting election laws, sidelining independent commissions, replacing officials with loyalists, and even rigging the rules for the next census. With each cycle, the distortions grow. What begins as advantage becomes permanence. What was once a campaign becomes a fortified empire. And because the maps guarantee safe seats, even unpopular, unqualified, or unethical lawmakers face no real competition. Elections still happen, but the outcomes are known in advance. The people may vote—but it is the party lines that have already decided.

This is not just political distortion. It is structural collapse. Unfair maps reduce the number of competitive districts, concentrating campaign money in the few that remain. In a truly representative system, those funds would be spread across hundreds of races. But with gerrymandering, billions are funneled toward a few thousand swing voters in a few dozen decisive contests. The result is a perfect storm. Safe districts protect incumbents from the people. Concentrated districts empower donors over voters. Propaganda intensifies. Accountability disappears. The lines on the map do not just shape politics. They shape whose voices are heard—and whose are drowned in money.

It quickly becomes a perfect cycle: capture the map, secure safe seats, target the rest, win more seats, redraw the map, repeat. It does not require national support—only control of a single statehouse at the right moment. One distorted cycle becomes two. Two become three, then four, then more. Within just a few redistricting cycles, the system no longer rewards responsiveness or consent—only loyalty, timing, and ruthless precision. And with safe seats comes moral decay. In districts where outcomes are preordained, character no longer matters. The only test is loyalty to party. Extremists flourish not despite gerrymandering but because of it. They cannot be removed by election, only by scandal—and sometimes not even then. The result is a House of Representatives littered with conspiracy theorists, demagogues, opportunists, and even criminals. People who could never survive a competitive race. They would never even be nominated. And still the cycle continues. Every gerrymandered map begets more corruption, more silence, more distortion of the vision of a fair democracy. The republic decays not from war or invasion, but from the slow, silent erosion of choice—drawn one line at a time.

The results are visible across the country. In Wisconsin, Republicans hold near-supermajorities in both legislative chambers despite consistently losing the statewide vote. In Ohio, gerrymandered maps have produced a legislature immune to democratic shifts. In North Carolina, a near-even electorate is ruled by maps drawn to favor one party by design. These are not anomalies. They are blueprints. Once a party controls redistricting, it can secure disproportionate power indefinitely. In some states, these distorted majorities have become supermajorities—able to override vetoes, expel opponents, and even rewrite constitutional rules without public consent. This is minority rule. And while it is utterly undemocratic, it is stable, legal, and insulated from court restrictions.

This is not merely a political failure. It is a moral breach. Democracy depends not only on the right to vote, but on the ability of that vote to shape outcomes. Gerrymandering violates that promise. It silences millions not by taking away their vote, but by making that vote irrelevant. It gives the illusion of participation while nullifying its effect. And it creates two classes of citizens—those whose votes matter, and those whose votes are managed. In doing so, it destroys the central covenant of a self-governing republic: that each person counts equally. Without that, we are not governed by consent. We are ruled.

Other democracies have faced these same challenges—and fixed them. In Australia, federal electoral boundaries are drawn by independent commissions using uniform rules, reviewed for population equity and community continuity. Canada and the United Kingdom use similar approaches. Their maps are not perfect, but they are legitimate. The result is not just fairer outcomes, but greater public trust. When people believe the system is rigged, they withdraw. But when they believe the lines are drawn fairly—when the contest is honest—they participate, even when they lose. Other countries have not ended partisanship. But they have ended this particular abuse. So can we.

Fair maps do not require a single method. They require a single standard. If one party wins 52 percent of the statewide vote, it should win roughly 52 percent of the seats. That is the outcome. Whether by commission, algorithm, judicial oversight, or voter initiative, the method matters less than the result. No party should win two-thirds of the seats with half the vote. No district map should silence a competitive region. And no state should be allowed to draw maps that give one party every safe seat while denying the other any. Fairness does not mean every race is close. It means every vote is counted equally.

That kind of fairness cannot be left to the states alone. The Supreme Court's retreat in Rucho made one thing clear: only Congress can impose a national standard. Without it, the United States becomes a patchwork of manipulation and reform—fair in some places, fraudulent in others. A real solution requires federal action. The Fair Maps Act must be passed as national law: banning partisan gerrymandering, requiring population parity, mandating transparency, and establishing legal thresholds for representational symmetry. This is not interference. It is constitutional repair. The right to representation is not regional. It is national. And it must be protected as such.

That federal reform must begin in 2029 and be fully in place before new maps are drawn in 2030. If Democrats win the presidency and both chambers of Congress, they must act immediately to set national standards for how districts are drawn. But even that will not be enough. Because the process is controlled at the state level, we must also reclaim the power to shape it. The goal is clear: flip at least seven key legislatures by 2030. Arizona, Georgia, Pennsylvania, North Carolina, Wisconsin, Michigan, and New Hampshire are all within reach. Each has elected Democrats statewide in recent years. But under distorted maps, those votes have not translated into legislative control. That must change.

Why these states? Because they are both vulnerable and winnable. Arizona and Georgia have shifting demographics and tight statewide margins. Pennsylvania, Wisconsin, and Michigan have a history of political balance, but distorted maps that tilt right. North Carolina is a perennial swing state governed by locked-in Republican lines. And New Hampshire, small but strategically vital, swings on local organization. None of these states are beyond reach. But none will flip by accident. It will take national coordination, local strategy, and relentless organizing to take back the power to draw the lines fairly. If we miss the window, we may not get another for a decade.

2030 is not just another census year. It is the next inflection point —the moment when new maps will shape representation until 2042. Every legislature that controls that process will define political reality for a generation. And every unfair map drawn in 2030 will harden the ground against reform in 2040. The damage compounds. Unfair maps do not merely distort the present. They rig the future. And each distortion ratifies the last, justifying more extreme manipulation. This is not a cycle. It is an upward ratchet—tightening with every turn, until democracy can no longer breathe.

We are not powerless. But we are on borrowed time. Every unfair map solidifies the next. Every rigged district helps shield the machinery that draws the next decade's lines. Delay is not neutral. It is surrender. If we want to rebuild a republic in which every voice matters and every vote counts, we must act before the next redistricting cycle begins. This is not a procedural issue. It is a structural emergency. And it will not fix itself. To outlive the gerrymander, we must out-organize it, outvote it, and outlast it. There is no other path. There is no other plan.

Because the shape of our districts shapes the shape of our democracy. And the shape of our democracy determines whether we live in a nation of rulers or a nation of citizens. Gerrymandering is not just unfair. It is un-American. It violates the promise of representation. It erases accountability. And it severs the link between the people and their government. But it can be undone. Maps can be redrawn. Power can be restored to the people—if we fight for it. We are not bound to the lines drawn by the last party in power. We can draw new ones—lines of fairness, of truth, of equal voice. And with them, a new future.

6

ELECTION CERTIFICATION AND PEACEFUL TRANSITION

TRUMP EXPOSED WHAT THE CONSTITUTION NEVER SECURED: THAT THE MOST VITAL STEPS IN A DEMOCRATIC ELECTION ARE STILL OPTIONAL.

―――― ✦ ――――

"The law must finish what the people begin."
— JP Vincent

Certification is democracy's final gate. It is the moment when counted votes become lawful power. Until then, every ballot remains provisional, every margin vulnerable to challenge, every outcome subject to sabotage. For two centuries, Americans treated this final step as routine—an administrative act so reliable it became invisible. But like so much of the system built by the Framers, certification depended on restraint. It relied not on law but on the willingness of those vying for power to accept the voters' decision. That illusion shattered in 2020, and what followed made clear: certification and peaceful transition are not traditions to honor. They are weaknesses to exploit—unless we make them law.

The Constitution says nothing about certification. It empowers states to choose electors "in such Manner as the Legislature thereof may direct," but never defines how to validate results or secure them against sabotage. The 12th Amendment outlines how Congress counts votes, but not how they are protected along the way. That machinery developed piecemeal—state by state, decade by decade—built on the assumption that those who lost would accept the outcome. It was never designed to withstand a president willing to destroy it. In 2020, that is what we faced. And what preserved the republic was not law. It was three men: a state official who refused to falsify the count, a vice president who refused to reject the result, and a Capitol officer who led the mob away from the fleeing Congress. Trump's failure to overturn the election was not proof that the system worked. It was proof that it had already failed—and survived only because, for one day, the right people stood in the gap.

That fragility is no accident. The United States was built on deference to state power, elite discretion, individual integrity, and procedural informality. The Electoral Count Act of 1887, passed in response to the disputed Hayes-Tilden election, offered a timeline and structure for resolving competing slates. But it left critical terms undefined. What counted as a "safe harbor"—the deadline after which Congress was supposed to accept a state's results as conclusive? Who determined which slate was legitimate? Could Congress override state certifications? The act functioned for more than a century not because it was sound, but because no president had dared to weaponize its ambiguity. Trump did. And what it revealed was not merely crisis—it was architectural failure. The most dangerous president in American history did not break the law. He used it.

Trump's plan was not improvisational. It was a coordinated attempt to exploit every weakness in the system. He pressured state officials to "find votes." He dispatched Rudy Giuliani to Arizona, Pennsylvania, and elsewhere to coach legislators on how to overturn certified results. He encouraged seven states to produce false elector slates and sent forged certificates to the National Archives. His allies harassed and defamed local poll workers in Atlanta. His campaign filed more than sixty lawsuits—most baseless, all rejected. He summoned local officials to the White House, urged them to delay or discard certification, and pressured the Vice President to ignore certified results and reject the electoral count. When that failed, he orchestrated objections in Congress to swing-state certifications—objecting not to fraud, but to outcome. And when Congress resisted, he summoned the crowd. Even as the Capitol was under siege, he delayed telling the mob to leave—because the chaos served his purpose: to halt the lawful transfer of power. This was not a tantrum. It was a blueprint—and one others may adopt.

Trump's refusal to transition power cut both ways—once in denial of victory, and again in disdain for responsibility. In 2020, he refused to initiate the formal transition process, denying his incoming administration access to critical resources, national security briefings, and interagency coordination. He declined to sign the paperwork that would have triggered the handover—an act that, while not legally required, had become essential in modern governance. The result was delay during a deadly pandemic, fractured communications with allies, and obstruction across every level of planning. Then in 2024, the pattern repeated. Trump, now returning to power, again refused to engage fully with the outgoing administration. Allies were left guessing. Required financial reports under the Presidential Transition Act were delayed. Turnover conversations with key departments simply never happened. Though both transitions occurred without riots, neither upheld the legal or civic responsibilities the moment demanded. That this behaviour remains legal is not a defense. It is proof that the law has not caught up with the danger.

What these two failures—certification and transition—share is a common flaw: each was built on the assumption of good faith. Neither was fortified by enforceable law. Until 2022, the Electoral Count Act still allowed a single member of each chamber to object to certified results, regardless of merit. Until 2021, nothing prohibited state parties from submitting false slates of electors; the only law they risked breaking was the forgery of a government document. And to this day, no statute requires a sitting president to facilitate transition—or penalises one who obstructs it. These are not minor oversights. They are standing invitations to sabotage, awaiting the next lawless actor willing to exploit them. Trump tried and failed. The next may try and succeed.

Some progress has been made. The Electoral Count Reform Act of 2022 clarified key parts of the certification process: governors must certify electors by a firm deadline; Congress can only object with the support of one-fifth of each chamber; the role of the Vice President is purely ceremonial. But the law leaves major holes untouched. There are still no national penalties for submitting false electors. No guaranteed federal protection for state and local election officials. And the Presidential Transition Act—passed in 1963 and only modestly updated since—contains no requirement that outgoing administrations cooperate in good faith with their successors, or that incoming administrations engage with those they replace. The foundation remains exposed—and the next storm may not pass us by.

The fix is not complex. Certification and transition must be bound by law, not left to custom—and certainly not reliant on integrity. States must be required to criminalise false electors and certify lawful results on time. Federal protection must be extended to election officials facing harassment or coercion. Outgoing administrations must be required by statute to begin the transition process within a fixed period after certification, with civil and criminal consequences for delay. These reforms are not about punishing Trump. They are about closing the open doors he walked through. A system that can be undone by a single man—with no penalty—is not a system at all. It is an invitation.

Authoritarians follow a pattern: if they cannot rig the vote, they delay the count. If they cannot delay the count, they discredit the certification. And if all else fails, they block the transfer of power itself. It has happened in Turkey, Hungary, Venezuela, and Russia. It nearly happened here. And the tools remain on the table—sharpened now by precedent. The next attempt may come from a different candidate, a different party, or a more disciplined version of the same. We cannot wait to see which. The path back to democratic normalcy is not paved by memory. It is secured by law.

What makes certification and transition so dangerous when left unsecured is not just their position at the end of the democratic process—it is their visibility. These are the moments when power is most openly contested, and when bad actors, foreign and domestic, are most motivated to interfere. Unlike voter suppression, which hides in procedure, or gerrymandering, which operates upstream, certification and transfer are public, global, binary, and final. That is what makes them vulnerable—and what makes reform urgent. The system must not present its weakest defence at its most critical juncture.

Trump's refusal to certify or facilitate transition revealed something deeper than defiance. It exposed a worldview in which losing power is not part of the democratic process—it is betrayal. In that worldview, power is personal, not institutional. Laws are obstacles, not obligations. The peaceful transfer of power, once a defining trait of the American republic, becomes optional. That belief did not fade when Trump left office. It returned with him—and it has taken root in a growing movement within the Republican Party that treats any loss as fraud and any transition as surrender.

But in a functioning republic, transitions are not acts of grace. They are acts of duty. From Adams to Jefferson, from Hoover to Roosevelt, from Bush to Obama, transfers of power have ranged from tense to warm—but they have always occurred. Until now. Trump broke that continuity. He proved the system has no fail-safe. If the loser refuses to cooperate, there is no mechanism to compel them. That is not just a procedural flaw. It is a national security threat. Nuclear protocols, health infrastructure, and international diplomacy all depend on the speed and completeness of transition. Delay is not symbolic. It is deadly.

To leave this vulnerability in place is to invite future sabotage. Every delayed transition erodes public trust. Every baseless challenge to certification pushes the next actor further. We are not standing still. We are sliding. And the only thing that can halt that descent is a hard wall of law: clear standards, enforceable deadlines, real consequences. This is not partisan. It is structural. If Democrats or Republicans cannot rely on certified results and guaranteed transfer of power, then neither can the people they represent. Democracy becomes brinkmanship—and every loser becomes a threat.

It is not enough to hope that future leaders will behave better. Hope is not a policy. Character is not a defense. The only guarantee of democratic continuity is law—law that does not rely on cooperation, but compels it. Just as we protect ballots with chain of custody and voting machines with tamper-proof seals, we must protect certification and transition with legal mechanisms that do not bend to will or whim. In 2020, democracy held. In 2024, it limped. In 2028, it must not be left to chance. This chapter of reform is not about reliving crisis. It is about refusing to risk it again.

The reforms we propose are not radical. They are constitutional affirmations. To certify an election is to recognize the will of the people. To transfer power is to obey it—publicly, and without condition. These are not acts of surrender. They are acts of allegiance—to the law, not the leader. We do not need new ideals to secure these processes. We need statutes that reflect the ones we already claim to hold. No person should face threats for certifying a lawful vote. No president should obstruct a transition and remain untouched. No election should remain vulnerable to sabotage by silence.

The reforms are simple—and entirely within reach. Congress can require all states to criminalize false elector slates and certify results by a federal deadline. It can mandate protection for election officials under threat. It can impose civil and criminal penalties for obstructing transition. And it can create a permanent, nonpartisan authority to ensure that power changes hands peacefully, even when presidents refuse. None of this demands a constitutional amendment. It demands only the will to act.

Other democracies have long since recognized what America still resists: that democracy cannot rely on self-restraint alone. They transfer certified results within hours, impose penalties for false claims of victory, and establish caretaker governments to limit obstruction. These are not signs of instability. They are signs of maturity. We have learned—too late and at great cost—that the right to vote does not end with the ballot. It ends with lawful certification and peaceful transfer. If any step can be delayed, denied, or ignored, the process fails. The "stolen election" lie feeds on ambiguity. The only cure is clarity—and clarity can only be secured by law. The law must finish what the people begin. And no future candidate —however lawless—must ever again be allowed to decide whether democracy continues.

7

ELECTIONS THAT WORK - FIVE REFORMS, ONE DEMOCRACY

WHY FAIR ELECTIONS REQUIRE ALL FIVE— AND FAIL IF MISSING ANY ONE

---✦---

"The price of freedom is eternal vigilance."
— Thomas Jefferson.

The Constitution never told us how to run an election. It could not. There was no precedent to follow, no functioning model of nationwide democratic consent. Monarchy had been rejected, but nothing had replaced it. And the founders were not naïve: they had witnessed the instability of France, the cruelty of Britain, the failures of confederation. They feared the mob as much as the king. So they did not design a national democracy. They designed a federation—and left the vote to the states.

In Britain, the poor were criminals. In France, they were revolutionaries. In America, they were both—farmers and freedmen, outcasts and indentured labor, convicts and conscripts. There was no shared public, only property. The vote, therefore, was restricted to the propertied. The Framers assumed that local elites would act with restraint, that state legislatures would handle the mechanics of elections, and that power would pass peacefully among gentlemen. That assumption died slowly, then all at once.

From the start, America's electoral system was a federation of fragments—each reform layered atop the last, but never forged into a whole. Over time, reforms emerged not from design, but from failure. Campaign finance laws arose only after industrial capital bought the Gilded Age. Redistricting reform came only after racial gerrymanders violated the Voting Rights Act. Certification remained a formality—until it became a battlefield. None of these solutions were conceived together. Each was built to patch a hole in the boat. But patchwork is not a plan. And now, the boat is sinking.

For decades, Americans were told these problems were separate. Gerrymandering was a districting issue. Voting rights were a race issue. Campaign finance was a corruption issue. Certification was a procedural issue. The Electoral College was a math problem. But they were wrong. These are not isolated flaws. They are five parts of one broken system—and unless they are reformed together, none will hold.

We do not need a new theory. We need a working democracy: one where every citizen can vote, every vote is counted, the candidate with the most votes wins, and power changes hands—publicly, without delay, blood, or resistance. That is not five goals. It is one. What we call five reforms are five histories—divided only by time and terminology. What they form now is one imperative.

Redistricting reform ensures representation is not rigged before the vote is cast. Without it, a minority of voters can win a majority of seats—and a majority of Americans can be locked out of power for a decade. It was once used to silence Black voters. It is now used to silence all dissent. No democracy can survive a map designed to prevent change.

Voting rights are the doorway to participation. Without federal guarantees of equal access, the ballot becomes a privilege, not a right. Voter ID laws, registration purges, and racial filtering are not neutral—they are strategic weapons. When access is blocked, democracy becomes theater. Participation shrinks. Extremism grows. And no reform can reach those who are denied the chance to choose it.

Campaign finance laws determine whether the public decides elections—or whether billionaires do. Dark money, super PACs, and untraceable shell donations have turned representation into auction. No reform—of voting rights, redistricting, or certification—can succeed if the winners are chosen before the first vote is cast. The power of one person, one vote, means nothing if one dollar, one donor, can silence ten thousand citizens.

The Electoral College was a compromise born of mistrust—of the public, of direct democracy, of anything that might bind the presidency too closely to the will of the people. It has failed in every way imaginable: electing second-place candidates, enabling minority rule, and turning a few swing states into permanent battlegrounds while ignoring the rest. It rewards manipulation. It punishes participation. And no electoral reform is complete if the presidency remains structurally untethered from the people.

Certification was long ignored because it was long assumed. For over two centuries, America treated the peaceful transfer of power as a tradition—until one man refused it. In 2020, and again in 2024, the weakness of that assumption was exposed. Without strong certification law, a losing president can still win. A governor, a secretary of state, or a gerrymandered legislature can block or falsify the final step. And when that step fails, every other reform fails with it.

Each of these reforms, taken alone, solves a vital problem. But taken together, they do something more. They lock the system. They make it possible not just to vote, but to govern based on that vote. They ensure that elections are not performative, not provisional, but final. This is not a to-do list. It is a design. And unless it is completed in full, it will be undone in full.

Gerrymandering without campaign finance reform becomes minority rule funded by billionaires. Voting rights without certification becomes turnout without transfer. Electoral reform without equal access becomes mathematical fairness on a rigged field. And finance reform without the rest simply reroutes the money to new choke points. The system seeks its weakest link. Break one, and the whole collapses.

This is not theory. We have lived it. We have seen how power cheats. And if any loophole remains, someone will find it—and exploit it. That is not a prophecy. It is a pattern. In American history, no gap in the democratic system has ever gone unused. And now that those gaps have been mapped, they are being widened into roads.

To restore faith in elections, we must make cheating impossible—not just illegal. That means closing every known breach: rigged maps, blocked access, bought outcomes, inverted results, and false certification. No single reform can do that. But all five, together, can. What began as five separate fights must now become one solution.

This is not about perfection. It is about protection. We do not need to love the system. We need to make it real, lawful, and safe. Only then can we restore what has been lost—not just legitimacy, but trust. Not just fairness, but peace. Not just the right to vote, but the right to be heard—and counted.

We rebuild by doing all five—not as idealists, but as realists. Because we know where the fractures are. We know who profits from them. And we know that unless we seal them all, democracy will fail again—by design, not by accident.

PART II - THE LIMITS TO PRESIDENTIAL POWER
HOW THE PRESIDENCY BECAME IMMUNE TO LAW, OVERSIGHT, AND SHAME

"The Constitution was never meant to survive a man without shame."
— JP Vincent

No single office in the American system is meant to rule alone. The presidency was created to carry out the law, not to invent it. Its powers are drawn narrowly, its duties specific, and its limits presumed. Executive orders are designed to direct agencies in the faithful execution of laws passed by Congress. Emergency powers are meant to respond to urgent threats—temporarily, and only with oversight. The pardon power is intended to temper justice, not obstruct it. And the Justice Department is meant to uphold the law, not shield the executive from it. Under Trump, each of these tools is turned inward—against the Constitution, against accountability, and against the republic itself.

He issues orders to bypass legislation, declares emergencies to implement an agenda by fiat, rewards loyalty with clemency, and directs prosecutions toward critics. These are not occasional breaches. They are the governing method. They are precedent. They are proof that constraint in the modern presidency no longer functions—not in consequence, not in law, and not in practice.

This chapter does not ask how the guardrails failed. That comes next. It names the failure for what it is: collapse. Not a single breakdown of oversight or accountability, but the simultaneous erosion of three interlocking foundations—constitutional constraint, legal enforcement, and democratic tradition—each once thought strong enough to hold on its own. Together they formed the triangle of presidential restraint. But when defied all at once by a man who respects none of them, the structure does not bend. It gives way.

Constitutional design is supposed to prevent this. The separation of powers, the oath of office, the "take care" clause, the impeachment clause, and judicial review—each exists to contain executive overreach. The President swears to "preserve, protect, and defend the Constitution." He is commanded to "take care that the laws be faithfully executed." But every one of these restraints relies on compliance. The Constitution does not enforce itself. It assumes cooperation, mutual respect, and institutional courage.

But it was never built to withstand a man like Trump. He does not comply. He defies subpoenas, violates laws by fiat, claims immunity, and campaigns in open defiance. He is allowed to seek office even after inciting an insurrection. He treats the Constitution not as constraint but as stagecraft—an inconvenience, an obstacle, something to challenge or ignore. And while some courts have tried to hold him accountable, Congress and his political allies defend him. The Constitution offers no remedy for bad faith. And in the absence of shame, it has proven powerless.

Where the Constitution created structure, Congress has passed laws to make that structure robust, current, and enforceable. The Inspector General Act, the Freedom of Information Act, the Whistleblower Protection Act, the Impoundment Control Act, the Presidential Records Act—each was designed to operationalize restraint, enforce transparency, and protect the public interest. Trump violates them all. He fires inspectors general, suppresses reports, conceals records, withholds funds, and retaliates against whistleblowers. The Office of Management and Budget, once an administrative executor of congressional will, is now a command post—defunding universities, research, and programs like Head Start when they displease him. Court orders are delayed or defied. Congressional appropriations are ignored. Legal obligations are treated as options, making compliance a game of "Catch Me If You Can" that the nation is losing.

The Constitution defined a system built on balance: three branches, co-equal and adversarial, each meant to restrain the others. But that balance no longer exists. Congress no longer checks the executive. It shields him. The courts no longer reliably constrain him. They invent immunity, delay review, or decline to intervene. Oversight is defunded. Subpoenas are ignored. Laws are broken, and the legislative branch rewards the defiance. What was once a triangle of resistance is now a hierarchy of compliance. The presidency stands above both law and legislature. And the republic, stripped of balance, begins to tip.

The judiciary is the only constraint still standing. But it is overwhelmed. More than two lawsuits per day are filed against Trump and his administration—by individuals, universities, nonprofit watchdogs, legal societies, and states. The courts are working. Judges continue to issue rulings, injunctions, and findings of fact. But they cannot keep pace. Of the 249 cases filed, only nine have reached resolution. The rest are buried in appeals, procedural delay, defense stallings, or ignored outright by an executive who violates faster than the system can respond. Infractions accumulate. Court calendars fill. Orders are defied. Statutes remain on the books. Evidence mounts. But the scale is now the shield. The presidency does not defeat justice. It drowns it.

The third foundation of restraint is tradition—never written into law, but once respected as binding. For generations, presidents released tax returns, disclosed their health, submitted to press briefings, honored the State of the Union, published speeches and interviews, and separated private gain from public duty. These were not partisan gestures. They were rituals of democratic legitimacy. Trump mocks them all. He turns official events into campaign rallies. Speeches go unpublished. Interviews are unrecorded. Public statements are later denied with "I never said that" and "I don't know anything about that." He hosts foreign governments at properties from which he profits. He erases call logs, cancels visitor records, and withholds even basic information after a reported assassination attempt. While claiming "the most transparent presidency in history," he treats the office as private property—and the public as trespassers.

These traditions were not written into law because they were built on something older: a shared understanding of honor, duty, and public service. But when a president possesses none of these—no shame, no duty, no loyalty to the people—he simply discards what once bound the office. And he is unopposed: Republicans are compliant and complicit; Democrats lack both the power and the leadership to stop him.

This is not a hypothetical. He is president again. He is issuing orders, targeting enemies, defunding opposition, and using the Department of Justice as a political weapon. He has pardoned past co-conspirators and is promising pardons for future ones. He is installing loyalists in oversight roles and asserting total immunity for crimes—past, present, and still to come. The Supreme Court, in return, invents doctrines of de facto kingship—granting him protection the Constitution never intended, no president ever claimed, and no law ever allowed. It is now the defender of the Constitution in name only. Again and again, when asked to uphold their oath, Justices Thomas and Alito protect the president instead. And the rest either agree, remain silent, or are outvoted.

Other democracies do not allow this. South Korea impeached and imprisoned a sitting president. France convicted Chirac. Israel sentenced Olmert. Brazil, Italy, Taiwan—each has held its leaders accountable through trial, sentencing, and disqualification. But in the United States, a man convicted of 34 felonies, sued over 200 times, who incited insurrection, suppressed oversight, and ignored court orders, now governs again—without penalty, without consequence, with the open support of his party—and the protection of a hand-picked Court. The difference is not legal complexity. It is that in other democracies, oversight works—constitutional, legal, and cultural. In the United States, none of it does.

Each of the next four chapters examines one of the failed foundations of constraint. Chapter 10, Power Without Boundary, traces how constitutional checks relied too heavily on virtue—and failed when virtue vanished. Chapter 11, Law Without Consequence, shows how Trump exposed the fragility of legal enforcement when institutions chose delay and deluge over defense. Chapter 12, Office Without Honor, reveals how democratic tradition, once powerful, now means nothing when ignored. And Chapter 13, Constraint Without Exception, offers not a proposal, but a design: the reforms that must be enacted to ensure that no future president—no matter how shameless or lawless—can do what Trump is doing now.

This book does not seek to weaken the presidency. It seeks to restore the republic. The office was never meant to be immune. But without structural reform, it has become sovereign in everything but name. The power to declare emergencies, issue decrees, fire investigators, defund agencies, pardon co-conspirators, and claim legal immunity—this is not balanced governance. It is one-man rule. And it will not stop on its own.

The Constitution assumed character. It assumed integrity. It assumed that those entrusted with power would defend the structure that gave it. But it guaranteed none of those things. When a man without shame met a party without conscience, every unwritten rule collapsed. What was built as a system of checks became a stage for impunity. The safeguards did not break. They were bypassed. And unless we act, the next president who walks through these same breaches will be more deliberate, more prepared, and more permanent.

The chapters that follow do not ask whether constraint is necessary. They answer how it must be restored—fully, forcefully, and without exception. The republic cannot survive another presidency without boundaries. And it will not survive at all if we choose to leave those boundaries broken.

We must remove the crown and dismantle the throne.

8

POWER WITHOUT BOUNDARY
A SYSTEM BUILT ON HONOR COLLAPSES AT THE HAND OF A MAN WHO HAS NONE

---✦---

"A constitution is not the end of a struggle. It is the record of it—and the path to keep fighting."
— JP Vincent

The Constitution was written to prevent the return of a king. The nation had just fought a brutal war to free itself from a sovereign who governed by decree, commanded armies without consent, dismissed legislatures at will, and claimed to rule by divine right. In response, the Framers drafted a document that placed power in chains. The President would not reign for life but serve a fixed term. He would not command unchecked, but be subject to Congress and law. He would not declare war, suspend courts, or tax unilaterally. And if he abused the public trust, he could be impeached and removed. The Bill of Rights, added immediately after ratification, was not an afterthought. It was a corrective—a list of the very abuses the colonists had endured and would no longer allow: censorship, unlawful imprisonment, forced quartering, seizures without cause, trials without justice, rule without consent.

That design was precise and intentional. The presidency was given force, but not freedom. Each power—commander-in-chief, pardon, veto, appointment, enforcement—was hedged by conditions. Congress would raise armies and declare wars. The courts would interpret law. The people, through elections, would grant temporary authority—not permanent rule. The President would take an oath to "preserve, protect and defend the Constitution of the United States." And he would be constrained not only by written limits, but by the vigilance of other branches, the press, and the public. For nearly 250 years, that architecture held. Presidents tested its boundaries, but none dissolved them. Ambition checked ambition. Law restrained power. The presidency remained an office—not a throne.

But one flaw was never repaired: the system assumed that men of dishonor would never be elevated to its highest post. It presumed that those who sought to violate the Constitution would never succeed in swearing to uphold it. That presumption lay dormant for two and a half centuries. Then came a man who understood the limits of law not as barriers, but as invitations to break them—and a party willing to follow him, not in spite of his lawlessness, but because of it. Trump did not create the flaw. He revealed it: the fatal overreliance on the honor of those who hold power. And what he revealed was how fragile the promise truly was—and how quickly it could be broken, not by revolution, but by the election of a man with no honor and no integrity.

The Constitution grants the President substantial power, but never absolute power. He is tasked with executing the laws, not making them. He may command the military, but only Congress may declare war. He may negotiate treaties, but only with Senate approval. He may nominate judges, but only with advice and consent. He may veto legislation, but Congress can override him.

These are not symbolic gestures. They are structural limits, embedded in the very design of Article II and counterbalanced by Articles I and III. The presidency was created as one branch among three—not a sovereign authority, but a conditional trust.

Even the qualifications for office were designed to constrain. The President must be a natural-born citizen, at least thirty-five years old, and resident in the United States for fourteen years. He is elected indirectly, not by popular vote but through electors chosen by the states—a mechanism meant to temper demagoguery. His term is fixed, not open-ended. He must swear an oath to preserve, protect, and defend the Constitution—not the flag, the land, or himself, but the governing document that binds him. These requirements reflect a belief that the office should be held by someone shaped by the country, loyal to its laws, and willing to serve rather than rule.

To guard against corruption, the Constitution also imposes prohibitions. No President may accept gifts, titles, or emoluments from foreign states without the consent of Congress. No President may hold office after engaging in insurrection or rebellion. No President may suspend habeas corpus, quarter troops in homes, or seize property without due process—rights reinforced by the Bill of Rights. The power to pardon exists, but cannot shield a President from impeachment. The right to lead is framed by the duty to be led —by law, by public accountability, and by constitutional boundaries that apply not only in word, but in practice.

The most powerful constraints on the presidency do not rest solely in government. They reside in the public. The First Amendment forbids the President from punishing speech, suppressing dissent, or retaliating against critics. The people may protest, publish, assemble, and petition without fear. They may vote him out —openly and lawfully. The Fourth and Fifth Amendments limit his power to seize, detain, or punish without due process. The judiciary may strike down unlawful acts. The legislature may investigate and remove. These provisions were not theoretical. They were born of tyranny—designed to ensure that no future executive could silence opposition, rule by decree, or treat public power as private right.

For most of American history, the Constitution did not merely exist. It functioned. When presidents overreached, the system responded. Andrew Jackson was censured by the Senate for defying a Supreme Court ruling. Abraham Lincoln, though wielding emergency power during war, still sought congressional authorization to raise troops and suspend habeas corpus. Richard Nixon resigned rather than face certain impeachment after the courts, Congress, and the press exposed a sweeping criminal conspiracy. Bill Clinton was impeached by the House for perjury and obstruction of justice. Each case affirmed the principle that no President stood above the law—and that accountability, however delayed, would come. Even unpopular or controversial presidents were checked by the democratic mechanisms the Constitution guarantees. Lyndon Johnson, deeply criticized for escalating the Vietnam War, faced mass protest that reshaped public opinion and forced his withdrawal from the 1968 race. Jimmy Carter, confronted with the Iran hostage crisis and economic upheaval, lost re-election amid widespread public dissatisfaction. George W. Bush's claims about weapons of mass destruction led to congressional investigations and public distrust that cost his party politically. These were not coups or conspiracies. They were consequences—imposed not by violence, but by law, elections, and public scrutiny.

Judicial constraint has also played a defining role. The courts have repeatedly struck down executive overreach—from Truman's seizure of steel mills during the Korean War to Obama's deferred action policies blocked by injunction. In each case, the constitutional balance of power was reaffirmed: presidents may act decisively, but not unilaterally. The Supreme Court, though not immune to politics, once stood as a guardrail. Lower courts, often less visible, regularly checked the presidency through injunctions, rulings, and statutory interpretation. These were not mere gestures. They were acts of enforcement—proof the law still ruled, and that constitutional design centuries old still was able to limit presidential power.

And through it all, the First Amendment remained the most constant safeguard. Protesters marched against war, against racial injustice, against corruption. Journalists uncovered scandals, exposed abuse, and published truths the powerful sought to hide. Citizens voted—sometimes in affirmation, often in rejection—and their choices altered history. The people, armed with rights and protected by law, have always been the final restraint. That was the genius of the system: power would exist, but never without limit—and never without consequence.

Until Trump.

Trump did not bend the Constitution. He broke it. Within hours of taking the oath of office in his second term, he issued an executive order attempting to nullify birthright citizenship—directly violating the Fourteenth Amendment. The oath itself, which binds the President to "preserve, protect, and defend the Constitution," was shattered in real time. He does not see the Constitution as a covenant. He sees it as an obstacle—something to bypass, reinterpret, or discard. The President is charged with ensuring the faithful execution of the laws. Trump ensures that laws are obeyed by everyone but himself.

He has violated the Emoluments Clause by accepting gifts and payments from foreign states—most recently from Qatar, whose regime has ties to terrorist financing. Instead of disclosing the gift or seeking congressional consent, he claimed it as personal property. He auctions off dinner invitations and White House access through a cryptocurrency token bearing his name—a direct monetization of access forbidden under the Emoluments Clause. He continues to profit from domestic and foreign entities doing business with his properties, while the Justice Department—under his direct influence—refuses to investigate. The Constitution forbids the use of public office for private gain. Trump treats office as inheritance.

He has trampled the First Amendment by threatening journalists and the media, directing agencies to investigate media outlets, and calling for the criminal prosecution of protestors. He has used federal law enforcement to attack peaceful demonstrators and dispatched the National Guard to intimidate political opponents. He has violated the Fourth Amendment's protections against unlawful search and seizure by targeting migrants, protestors, and private citizens with mass surveillance and warrantless raids. He has defied the Fifth Amendment's promise of due process by calling for executions without trial, denying bail by fiat, and pressuring courts to rule in his favor. He has degraded the Eighth Amendment by deporting undocumented immigrants not to their country of origin, but to a maximum-security prison in El Salvador—known for torture—without hearing, review, or the hope of return. These are not isolated abuses. They are part of a governing philosophy that treats constitutional rights as obstacles to power.

He has been granted, and daily uses, immunity from prosecution for any crime committed while in office—an assertion the Court, now shaped by his appointees and protected by Justices who refuse to recuse, is poised to legitimize. He has declared that Section 3 of the Fourteenth Amendment, which disqualifies insurrectionists from office, does not apply to him. He has encouraged states to disregard court rulings, pressed agencies to defy congressional subpoenas, and used the pardon power not to temper justice but to reward silence and secure loyalty. Every constitutional limit that once bound the presidency has now been tested—and many have been torn away entirely.

The Constitution cannot defend itself. It was never built to survive a President who rejects its limits or a Court that rewrites its meaning. It assumes good faith and honorable behavior where none remains. It relies on institutions already captured—and on a public willing to act before it is too late. Amendment—the only permanent remedy—requires a political unity that has long since vanished. What remains is not a system of balanced restraint, but one of loopholes wide enough for tyranny. The danger is not just that Trump broke the Constitution. It is that he proved how easily it could be broken—and how few are willing to stop him.

Donald Trump took the oath with the same mouth that spews lies without end, without rebuttal, without shame. And, as expected, he broke it. Within minutes. He will not preserve, protect, and defend the Constitution, so we must. Against all enemies, foreign and domestic. Against his party. Against his Court. Against him.

To keep democracy, we must take that oath—and keep it.

9

LAW WITHOUT CONSEQUENCE

THE PRESIDENCY IS BREAKING THE LAW. THE SYSTEM BUILT TO STOP HIM IS BREAKING TOO.

"The sea did what it liked, and what it liked was destruction."
— Charles Dickens, *A Tale of Two Cities*

The President of the United States is not immune. Not from accountability, not from oversight, not from the law. That is the constitutional promise. Article I gives Congress the power to legislate, appropriate, and oversee. Article III gives the courts power to interpret and check. Article II binds the President to execute those laws faithfully. Constraint is not a suggestion. It is the architecture of power in a republic. But that structure depends on enforcement. It depends on Congress doing its job, on the Courts doing theirs, on the public knowing what is being done in its name, and on institutions refusing to obey unlawful orders. If any of those fail, law becomes performance. And that is where we now stand.

The Constitution was never intended to operate alone. It provides the foundation, but not the scaffolding. It sketches the branches of government, but leaves the details—the limits, the safeguards, the procedures—to legislation. Congress was given the sole power to make law for a reason: because every abuse of power in the executive would eventually require a legal remedy. And for most of American history, Congress delivered. It passed laws to restrain the President's budgetary power, constrain emergency declarations, protect federal employees, preserve environmental safeguards, and ensure transparency. The law grew in response to abuse. That was the system working.

It worked not because the presidency was trustworthy, but because it was bound. Richard Nixon was brought down by inspectors general and the Freedom of Information Act. Ronald Reagan's excesses in Central America were exposed through whistleblower protections and the GAO. George W. Bush's detention practices were reined in by the courts through habeas corpus. Barack Obama faced limits on appointments, disclosures, and war powers. The laws passed in the aftermath of Vietnam, Watergate, and Iraq were imperfect—but they worked. They reminded the presidency that power was not self-justifying, and that law would outlast the occupant.

That is no longer true. The law has not changed, but the presidency has. And this Congress—the one elected in 2024—is no longer acting as a co-equal branch. It is enabling lawbreaking in real time. When President Trump signed a budget in February 2025 that included an illegal provision barring federal judges from issuing injunctions against him, Congress did not object. When he canceled billions in research funding in direct violation of appropriated law, Congress did not resist. When he reinstated Schedule F to purge career civil servants, rewrote NEPA by executive fiat, and used loyalty screenings to reshape federal departments, Congress did not investigate. It voted yes. Unanimously.

Nor has the judiciary fulfilled its role. The Constitution envisioned three co-equal branches, each a check on the others. Lower courts still attempt to hold the line—some at great personal risk—

but without institutional backing, their rulings stall, reverse, or disappear. Meanwhile, the Supreme Court has abandoned that responsibility. It has refused to hear urgent constitutional challenges. It has intervened in matters where it had no standing to rule. And two justices in particular—Clarence Thomas and Samuel Alito—have signaled through their votes that there is no act too corrupt, too violent, or too expressly prohibited that they will not defend. Again and again, they have dissented alone to shield Trump from consequence. And now, with the Court enshrining "presidential immunity" as a legal doctrine conjured from nothing, the branch once tasked with interpreting the law as a check on executive power has instead begun dismantling it. This is not judicial review. It is judicial complicity.

With two branches abdicating their duty to check executive power—and this Congress in particular refusing even to investigate violations, let alone write new constraints—the only resistance that remains is the legal architecture built by earlier legislatures. These laws were written when the presidency was still assumed to require limits. They span nearly every domain of executive action: investigations, transparency, military deployments, civil service protections, land use, research grants, emergency declarations, and digital security. None were passed in abstraction. Each was forged in response to a specific abuse—Watergate, Vietnam, Iran-Contra, 9/11, Iraq. Together, they form a kind of institutional immune system: not just a list of rules, but a structure built to detect, resist, and correct presidential overreach. The full list appears in Appendix B. It is not a catalog. It is a record of what the United States once valued—and what it now needs to defend. The legal web was never self-executing. Its safeguards worked only when upheld.

Trump has not dismantled this web. He has simply chosen to step through it. In his second term alone, he has violated the Impoundment Control Act by canceling congressionally authorized grants to universities and research labs. He has sidestepped the

Federal Vacancies Reform Act by installing acting officials without Senate approval. He has nullified the National Environmental Policy Act through sweeping "emergency" waivers. He has denied FOIA requests indefinitely, refused to preserve presidential records, and directed agencies to bypass GAO oversight. Each of these actions breaks a law. None has produced consequences. And with "presidential immunity" now conjured into doctrine, consequence is no longer expected. It is prohibited.

The Department of Government Efficiency, created by executive order and placed under the de facto control of Elon Musk, unelected and unconfirmed, became a legal black box—accessing personnel, benefits, medical, and financial data across federal systems without oversight or transparency. It operated outside standard federal reporting structures, refused to disclose protocols, and answered to no inspector general. Its practices likely violated the Privacy Act, HIPAA, the Federal Information Security Management Act (FISMA), and other statutes. Though Musk has since distanced himself —his interest seemingly limited to the data itself—the infrastructure remains. DOGE still functions, now under new leadership, but with the same systems in place and the same absence of accountability. No court has intervened. No congressional committee has curtailed its scope.

The defiance is not limited to Musk's agency. The Veterans Administration has transferred mental health and disability records to be cross-referenced for "suitability" assessments. The Department of the Interior has issued oil and gas leases in protected zones without new environmental review. The Office of Management and Budget has halted disbursements to institutions deemed ideologically unfriendly. These are not bureaucratic missteps. They are unlawful acts—deliberate, visible, and answered with silence.

No prior president has operated with such open contempt for legal constraint—not even Nixon. And no Congress in modern history has shown such comprehensive indifference and abdication of duty. The web of law has not failed because it was weak. It has failed because those charged with defending it have not. Inspectors general have been fired or silenced. Oversight agencies sit defunded or leaderless. The courts still have jurisdiction, but are swamped—buried beneath a flood of lawbreaking that outpaces their capacity to respond. The statutes still exist, but the enforcement has gone dark. This is not the spectacle of unraveling. It is a slow-motion constitutional exam. One we are taking in full view. And one that, if failed, will never be retaken.

This is the essence of law without consequence: not the absence of rules, but the evaporation of enforcement. Donald Trump does not need to repeal the statutes that bind him. He only needs to ignore them until they are hollow. In his first term, he tested the boundaries. In his second, he has erased them. He defies subpoenas, withholds documents, refuses court orders, and announces policy by proclamation. Each time he violates a legal norm, he watches for resistance. And finding none, he advances further.

This is what unchecked executive power looks like. Trump has defunded Harvard and dismantled medical research grants. He has renamed the Gulf of Mexico in a symbolic decree—a stunt without legal standing, but with authoritarian bravado. He has attacked law firms, targeted journalists, and excluded critical media from official access. He has canceled collective bargaining rights, fired career civil servants with legal protections, and terminated those on fixed terms. He has deported lawful residents, detained citizens, and auctioned off access to the White House through his own cryptocurrency. He has invoked invasion emergencies and economic crises to justify tariffs, land sales, and oil leases. He has eliminated pennies, declared English the sole official language, and claimed peacetime war powers to override statutory limits. He has canceled constitutionally guaranteed birthright citizenship. And all of it—every action—has been wrapped in executive orders, signed at record pace, often with the ink still wet from previous violations.

He has been sued more than any president in history. Protested more widely. Challenged more often. But challenges do not matter if the law cannot be enforced. A system designed to constrain ambition is now overrun by it. These are not isolated abuses. They are the scaffolding of something new.

This is not government. It is occupation—by a political force that recognizes no law but its own expansion. The structure still stands, but its function has changed. The Constitution is still cited, but only to justify what it was written to prevent. The agencies remain, but serve only the executive. The courts exist, but are bent toward delay or deference. Congress convenes, but does not constrain. And the presidency, once an office bound by oath and oversight, now governs through impulse, vengeance, and spectacle—guided by an agenda drafted for him by the Heritage Foundation. The legal web is still there, but it hangs like abandoned scaffolding: visible, in tatters, and utterly bypassed.

Consider the Schedule F executive order. It reclassifies career civil servants as at-will employees, stripping them of legal protection and replacing expertise with loyalty. The Civil Service Reform Act forbids this. So does the Pendleton Act. But Trump issued the order anyway—and federal agencies obeyed. Hundreds were reassigned, fired, or forced out. Loyalty screenings, once unthinkable in a professional civil service, are now normalized. The law was clear. The violation was public. No response came.

Or consider his "Big Beautiful Budget Bill." Not only does it propose to redirect funds in violation of the Impoundment Control Act, it includes a provision forbidding courts from issuing injunctions against presidential action. This is unconstitutional on its face. Yet no member of the majority party in the House objected. The Department of Justice defended it. The President praised it. The bill passed the House. It has not passed the Senate. It is not yet law. But the message is clear: the Constitution does not enforce itself. It must be enforced—or it becomes a decoration.

Even the judicial branch—once seen as the final bastion of constraint—has begun to fracture. Trump's legal team routinely defies court protocols: refusing to produce requested documents and witnesses, presenting arguments unmoored from established legal theory or precedent, missing deadlines, and then ignoring orders by claiming they interpreted them as optional. In one notable instance, a Trump lawyer, when questioned, admitted he had no idea and nothing to say—a performance that led to his replacement by day's end. Judges, understandably, are growing increasingly frustrated and infuriated by these tactics.

While Chief Justice Roberts has publicly admonished Trump for his attacks on the judiciary—actions that earned him threats of impeachment—and Justice Barrett has voted against Trump's legal positions, inciting ire from the MAGA faction in Congress, such instances of resistance are exceptions rather than the rule. The Supreme Court, now dominated by justices aligned with a vision of expansive executive power, has delayed rulings, narrowed precedent, and signaled deference. The DOJ, under Trump's influence, spends considerable resources defending his illegal actions instead of prosecuting federal crimes, effectively transforming from a prosecutorial agency into the president's personal defense team. The message is unmistakable: not every crime will be punished. Not every abuse will be stopped. Some will be protected.

Meanwhile, the Department of Government Efficiency continues to consolidate power without legal charter, congressional authorization, or public oversight. DOGE still accesses medical records, employment histories, tax filings, and internal agency communications. It answers to no inspector general, issues no public reports, and follows no codified rules. Its creation was never debated. Its structure was never ratified. Its actions are shielded from FOIA and exempt from accountability. It functions as a parallel government—unregulated, unreviewed, and increasingly untouchable.

The press, too, is under threat. Journalists investigating Trump's second-term actions have faced surveillance, source subpoenas, targeted IRS audits, and denial of access. The Privacy Protection Act forbids the seizure of journalistic materials. DOJ guidelines prohibit targeting reporters except under extraordinary circumstances. These laws remain in force. But they are not enforced. Worse, laws meant to protect the country are now turned against those who report on it. Immigration codes are used to threaten foreign correspondents with visa revocation. Defamation laws, once meant to deter public malice, are weaponized against news outlets that show opponents in a favorable light. The message is clear: publish what the President approves—or risk your platform, your access, or your freedom.

This is how a republic ends its fidelity to law: not with a repeal, but with a shrug. The legal web that once restrained the presidency was not mythical. It was real. Documented. Enforceable. It had rules, procedures, and consequences. But now it lies torn—cut by the very hands it was designed to bind. And still, no one moves to repair it. The public watches. The press reports. The Congress yields. The President acts. And acts. And acts. Until illegality becomes ordinary. Until outrage becomes frustration and then resignation.

If legal constraint fails—and it is failing—then only two institutions remain with the power to resist: the free judiciary and the free press. They are imperfect. They are under siege. But they are the last forms of lawful accountability still operating in real time. They must be protected—not as symbols, but as tools. The press must be funded, defended, and kept free. The judiciary must be shielded from sabotage, not hollowed out by loyalty and fear. If these fall, only one force remains: the people. Not resigned. Not fatigued. Outraged—and unyielding.

The legal web is not gone. It can still be repaired. But only if we remember what allowed it to break: not just corruption at the top, but exhaustion at the bottom. The President has not rewritten the law. He has revealed that the law, without force behind it, will not restrain him. This is not just a legal test. It is a civic one. If institutions will not act, citizens must. If courts fall silent, the people must speak. The law is not a wall. It is a warning—unless enforced by those it was written to protect.

10

OFFICE WITHOUT HONOR

THE COLLAPSE OF PRESIDENTIAL RESTRAINT AND THE RISE OF SHAMELESSNESS

———✦———

"The presidency is not merely an administrative office. That is the least of it. It is preeminently a place of moral leadership."
— Franklin D. Roosevelt

The presidency was not built on trust. It was built on fear—of monarchy, of tyranny, of unrestrained ambition. The Constitution offered structure: powers separated, offices limited, terms defined. But structure alone could not guarantee restraint. That guarantee came later, and not through law. It came through behavior. Through habit. Through shame. Over time, a web of expectation formed around the office—not codified, not enforceable, but real. Its strength lay in its invisibility. As long as it was honored, it needed no defense. That illusion is gone now. Trump didn't merely violate tradition. He revealed it as optional—and showed the cost of a system built on honor in an age without it.

The first restraint was humility. Washington declined a crown. Adams surrendered power. Jefferson walked to his inauguration.

The early republic, wary of kings, judged a president not only by what he did but by what he refused. No parades. No palaces. No permanence. The rituals were small, but their message was colossal: this office is not yours—it is borrowed. That principle, though never law, carried forward. Presidents did not campaign in person. They mourned national losses above party. They used words carefully, stayed out of courts, and waited to be invited to speak. Even in scandal, the role demanded gravity. That sense of measure has now vanished.

By the 20th century, humility gave way to transparency. Wilson's failure to share his health crisis led to a quiet panic: who was governing? FDR, in turn, spoke directly to the nation. Eisenhower published his medical charts. Kennedy disclosed almost nothing—and the result was silence during crisis. So his successors overcorrected. Johnson, Nixon, Carter, even Reagan made disclosure a civic expectation. Tax returns. Medical records. Visitor logs. They governed as if the public had a right to know, because trust depended on visibility. By the 1990s, the expectation was nearly automatic—until Trump. He offered secrecy, then spectacle. Mystery, then misinformation. Never transparency. And never shame.

After transparency came engagement. As presidential power expanded through war, media, and bureaucracy, so too did the expectations of accountability. Press briefings became daily ritual. Testimony before Congress became routine. The White House opened its gates—at least on paper. Presidents debated their critics, answered questions, explained decisions. These were not legal requirements. They were performances of legitimacy. Reagan held prime-time addresses. Clinton submitted to hours of deposition. Obama published visitor logs, agency rules, and his own criticisms. They understood that power must be seen explaining itself—or it would be seen as illegitimate. Trump reversed this entirely. Explanation was replaced by spin. Accountability by aggression.

Then came the era of honor. Post-Watergate, honor was not just ornament—it was the final guardrail. Presidents now faced the expectation that they would rise above. No attacking judges. No personal profit. No pardons for allies. No interference in law enforcement. No glorifying the self above the state. These weren't traditions born of aristocracy. They were earned in disgrace. After Nixon, presidents honored these norms to avoid triggering collapse again. They submitted to ethics offices, published disclosures, kept the military apolitical, and accepted defeat with grace. In other words, they restrained themselves—because the law, alone, could not. Trump refused that restraint from the start.

He did not quietly abandon tradition. He bulldozed it—and celebrated the wreckage. He turned the presidency into a branding platform, a tool of retribution, a source of profit, and a theater of grievance. He refused to concede. He kept his businesses and insisted the government use them. He appointed unqualified loyalists, retaliated against whistleblowers, and attacked courts, journalists, governors, and generals. He boasted of violating norms: "I alone can fix it." It wasn't just traditions that collapsed under Trump. It was the idea that there was any tradition at all. That collapse did not end with his first term. It expanded in his second, with vengeance as policy and loyalty as law.

This chapter does not catalog one breach of decorum. It documents fifty. And still, that is not the whole. Each was a thread in the moral fabric that once clothed the office in civic dignity. Alone, each breach might be survivable. Together, they expose a vacuum. A presidency without humility governs for self. A presidency without transparency governs in darkness. A presidency without engagement rules by fiat. And a presidency without honor becomes, not a leader of a republic, but a sovereign over subjects. That is the office Trump has created: not bound by past expectation, not shaped by shared norms, but sculpted to fit the ambitions of one man. And one party.

It began with the smallest choices: no tax returns. No medical records. No visitor logs. Each was a test: would the system object? It didn't. So he went further. Press briefings disappeared. Cabinet officials refused to testify. Executive orders were signed without explanation. Again, silence. Then came the open violations. He encouraged a coup. Pardoned co-conspirators. Campaigned from federal property. Profited from public office. And still, the system did not respond. By the end of his first term, Trump no longer had to break norms—he had already erased them. There was no longer a line to cross. Only a throne to keep.

In his second term, the office continues to mutate. Loyalists staff agencies. Daily schedules are withheld. Retaliation is routine. The Department of Justice functions as an instrument of protection and punishment. The Office of Government Ethics is sidelined. Oversight requests are ignored. The military is politicized. And state ceremonies are used to elevate personality over country. These are not accidents of erosion. They are acts of design. Trump did not inherit a dishonorable presidency. He brought dishonor to it— because it served his purpose better that way. He did not invent the collapse. But he made its final form unmistakable. And he did it not because he could, but because no one stopped him.

The damage is not only institutional. It is cultural. A generation is growing up with no memory of the office as honorable. With no example of self-restraint. With no model of loss accepted, criticism endured, or power relinquished with grace. And the danger is not only that they will admire Trump. The true danger is that they will learn from him. That power justifies itself. That truth bends to the strong. That honor is naïve. That shame is weakness. And that restraint is optional—unless forced. That is the legacy now etched into the office itself. It will not erase easily. Nor should it.

Every prior chapter of this book has shown a different breach— constitutional, legal, structural. But this chapter is different. It is not about powers taken or laws broken. It is about the vanishing of internal restraint. The erosion of the idea that the presidency is a duty, not a possession. That it must be preserved, not consumed. That it represents the nation, not the man. These were never laws because we thought they did not need to be. Now we know better. Trump shattered the illusion of honor. And what came next was not correction—it was imitation.

For a decade, the world has watched a single lesson take root: that lies work, cruelty wins, corruption pays, and no consequence comes. Trump may not have broken democracy, but he broke the Republican Party. Or rather—he finished the job. The party had already abandoned majority rule and moved toward suppression, obstruction, and deflection. What Trump brought was a formula: be shameless, be corrupt, lie, be loud, never defend but attack, and if cornered or caught, deny, defy, delay—and you will rise. That message has now been absorbed as the party's future. The next leader is already watching. Already preparing. Already practicing. And what he has learned is chillingly simple: the jackpot is real. All you have to do is play without conscience, without honor. When in doubt, do what's good for you and your donors, the country be damned.

We are already seeing it.

Because Trump paid no price, others have followed. Governors attack their own health departments. Legislators refuse to certify valid elections. Cabinet officials openly campaign from their offices. The standard has shifted: not what is right, but what can be gotten away with. That shift did not begin with Trump, but he made it doctrine. What once brought shame now brings applause. What once prompted resignation now prompts promotion. There is no longer a presumption of apology—only of defiance. Without honor at the top, there is corrosion at every level beneath. The office sets the tone. And the tone now is decay. And corruption. And greed. And—more than any of them—a hunger for permanent power.

Can it be restored? Not easily. Tradition cannot be legislated.

Honor cannot be mandated. Service cannot be compelled. But all of them can be expected—and rebuilt. First, by naming what was lost. Second, by refusing to forget. And third, by reforming what must now be law. The presidency must no longer depend on the conscience of the officeholder. It must be constrained by rules that do not assume good faith. Mandatory tax returns and medical disclosures. Required transparency. Enforceable ethics. A structural wall between private profit and public duty. Public commitments to oversight, access, and transition. What was once a matter of trust must now be a matter of code.

We cannot legislate decency. But we can demand visibility. We can make decisions traceable. Finances accountable. Appointments confirmable. Actions reviewable. We can restore the expectation that power must justify itself—that those who govern must explain. These are not radical demands. They were once routine. They were honored across parties, across decades. Across generations. Their loss is not a new chapter. It is a regression. What Trump destroyed is not just the presidency of Obama, Bush, or Clinton. It is the moral inheritance of Washington, Lincoln, and Roosevelt. We do not restore that by longing. We restore it by law.

But law alone is not enough. If the public shrugs, the damage is permanent. If the press adapts to outrage and pressure, dishonor becomes background noise. If parties defend their own but not the office, then no office remains. A presidency without shame is not a strong presidency. It is a hollow one—power wrapped in image, not bound by duty. If we want that to end, we must stop laughing, stop excusing, stop waiting. We must say clearly: this is not normal. This is not acceptable. And this is not survivable—if we want democracy to last. Honor may be voluntary. But it is not optional.

The Framers feared tyranny. But they never imagined shamelessness—ambition divorced from honor, power devoid of restraint. Their system presumed some boundary between self and office. Between private interest and public role. Between appetite and restraint. That boundary was once guarded by conscience. It is now guarded by nothing at all. And until we replace that nothing with something—law, pressure, vigilance, memory—the collapse will continue. Not always with spectacle. Sometimes in silence. One tradition at a time. But make no mistake: if we do not constrain the presidency, democracy does not survive. Not in form, not in function. Not even in name. There will be nothing more to erode. Nothing left to remember. No loss left to grieve.

We know what that presidency looks like. We have lived it. We are living it still. It is not style. It is not tone. It is strategy—designed to punish dissent and reward obedience. A blueprint for power without responsibility. For grievance without service. For rule without listening. For greed without limit. It is a presidency that treats criticism as treason and obedience as loyalty. That consumes the institutions meant to constrain it. That exploits tradition, law, and office until none remain. And that demands, in return, not respect—but submission.

Correction must begin with elections—but it cannot end there. Voters can remove a man, but not erase the damage. That work belongs to us. To lawmakers, to journalists, to watchdogs, to historians, to citizens. It requires rebuilding what was broken, codifying what was ignored, and expecting what was once assumed. It means asking: what should we be ashamed of? What must never happen again? And how do we stop it—not just from returning, but from remaining?

Making these corrections has to matter. That the President is mocked abroad instead of feared or respected. That Canadian friends stay home. That a daughter won't return to her country because of the guns. That Australian shoppers are putting products back on the shelf if they say "Made in the USA." That NATO allies now prepare for a future without us. That in Denmark, Americans are asked about Greenland and cannot answer. That U.S. car sales fall overseas—not from competition, but from contempt. That the portraits of former presidents and Black war heroes were removed from public view. That truth no longer binds a party, and lies no longer break it. It all has to matter. Because if it doesn't matter to us, it won't matter at all. Not to history. Not to the world. Not even to our children.

Every thread torn must be tied again. Every breach answered. Every silence replaced with record. That is the work of restoration. It does not glorify the past. It does not long for civility alone. It insists on function. It insists on constraint. It insists that the presidency is not a person, but a duty. Not a spectacle, but a trust. Not a brand, but a bond. If honor is no longer inherent, then it must be enforced. If tradition cannot bind, then the people must.

We will be told this is petty. That it is performance. That it doesn't matter. But it does. Because children are watching. Because allies are watching. Because enemies are watching. Because history is watching. A presidency without honor does not merely embarrass the nation. It endangers it. The next collapse will not come from the absence of law. It will come from the absence of shame. Unless we act. Unless we rebuild. Unless we say clearly: the office will have honor again—not because one man chooses it, but because a free people demand it.

Because history is watching. A presidency without honor does not merely embarrass the nation. It endangers it. The next collapse will not come from the absence of law. It will come from the absence of shame—and from a people who stop expecting better. The office will not have honor again *unless* we act. Unless we rebuild. Unless we make it undeniable. Not because we trust the powerful, but because we have bound them, watched them, and refused to look away.

11

CONSTRAINT WITHOUT EXCEPTION
WHEN LAW, TRADITION, AND STRUCTURE FAIL, ONLY THE PEOPLE REMAIN.

"The price of apathy towards public affairs is to be ruled by evil men."
— Plato

The presidency was not meant to run on goodwill. It was meant to be bound. The Framers feared power uncontained, ambition unanswerable, and tyranny cloaked in public office. So they built a structure—three branches, checked and balanced, designed not for efficiency but restraint. For a time, it held. The separation of powers prevented monarchy. The veto and impeachment restrained excess. But none of it was foolproof. None of it was final. The Constitution could divide power. But it could not guarantee character. It could not imagine shamelessness. And it could not survive a generation willing to obey the letter while erasing the spirit. Trump revealed just how little structure alone can hold.

Laws were meant to supply what structure could not. Ethics rules. Oversight statutes. Inspectors General. Special counsels. The

Hatch Act. Whistleblower protections. Each new law was a patch sewn into the fabric of government—none perfect, all essential. Together, they formed a legal web of restraint. But that web only held if defended—by agencies, by Congress, by the courts. Especially the Court. Trump tested each one. He delayed, denied, and defied. He fired those who enforced, ignored those who summoned, and punished those who exposed. And the system let him. Some courts tried. But when it mattered most—when the Supreme Court was asked whether the President could act with impunity—it did not defend the Constitution it was sworn to protect. It gave the President the one thing the Framers built an entire system to prevent: power without constraint.

The third realm of restraint was never written. It was lived—and it grew over time in response to failure. Tradition restrained what law could not reach. It held when presidents believed the office demanded humility, dignity, and service. Every president brought some measure of that belief—until Trump. He arrived with no shame, no reverence, no willingness to be bound by anything but self-interest. And when a presidency built on tradition met a man with no use for it, the entire structure collapsed. There were no visitor logs. No press briefings. No disclosures. No concession. No acceptance of oversight. No sense of public trust. Honor had no place in him—and so the traditions built upon it lost their place in a government that still desperately needs them.

The system was not destroyed by Trump. It was destroyed by the test he brought. A man who would lie, defy, delay, and erase—at once and without apology. And it failed that test. The Constitution did its job building structure. The law did its job defining restraint. Tradition did its job modeling it. But the courts failed to enforce. The party failed to object. And the people, too many of them, failed to refuse. What must be restored is not just law. It is consequence. It is expectation. It is memory. Honor cannot be legislated—but dishonor can be disqualified. And no man who scorns the oath should ever again be trusted with the office it binds.

Trump did not break the presidency. He proved how breakable it already was. He did not find a flaw. He found a blueprint. A formula for permanent impunity: violate every boundary at once, and the system cannot keep up. Defy the law. Ignore tradition. Overwhelm the courts. Politicize the process. Deny the evidence. Punish dissent. The process was not brilliant. It was shameless. And it worked—not because the Constitution is weak, but because it assumed the office-holder would care whether it survived. Trump showed how easily that assumption could be erased. And how quickly others would follow.

There are only two paths forward. We can codify what was once assumed—enshrine norms into law, close every loophole, and compel enforcement without exception. We must do both. But the second is more urgent. Restraint does not begin with statute. It begins with character. Honor cannot be compelled. Integrity cannot be codified. No law can restrain a man who serves only himself. And no system can function when that man holds its highest office. The most effective constraint on power is to deny it to those who will not be bound.

Constraint must be real, not symbolic. It must bind the powerful, not flatter them. No judge should be unanswerable. No justice above the law. No senator, secretary, or elected official should be exempt from consequence. The people must have the right to recall. To remove. To refuse. Because if honor can be bought, it is not honor. And if laws can be ignored, they are not laws. The legitimacy of a republic does not rest on ceremony or seniority. It rests on service. And when service ends—when it is betrayed, perverted, or sold—the people must be able to end it themselves. That is not defiance. It is fidelity. Not revolution. But repair. And responsibility. Both to the people—and of the people.

Two truths must now be made non-negotiable. First: no one—

not the President, not a general, not a billionaire donor—can ignore a lawful order. Not without arrest. Not without consequence. Second: no justice on the Supreme Court may invent law, grant immunity, or shield lawlessness from accountability. To do so is to break the oath they swore—and breaking that oath must come at a cost. Not in editorials. In impeachment. In removal. We cannot legislate virtue. But we can insist that those who swear to uphold the Constitution be bound by that oath—and removed when they violate it.

Constraint does not begin in Washington. It begins in culture—in the expectation that truth will be spoken, laws followed, power explained, and betrayal punished. Republics do not endure because they are designed perfectly. They endure because they are maintained. Constraint is not a single act. It is a civic habit—practiced daily, by millions who may never meet, but who each carry a share of its defense.

That defense is not passive. It is not thought. Or blame. Or hope. It is action. Quiet, ordinary, and constant. By the people. By us. By me. By you.

You will never know what made the difference. It may be a sentence you say. A lie you answer. A sign you hold. A postcard you send. A phone call you make. A vote you cast even when it feels like it won't count. The restoration of this republic will not come all at once. It will come in moments. Acts. Words. Silences broken. Truths repeated. There is no map for what will matter. But everything matters. So act. Not because you know it will work. But because you know what happens if you do not.

You may not like this part. But you don't need permission to act. Not from your family. Not from your workplace. Not from your town, your neighbors, or the country. You are the only one who sees exactly what you see. Who hears what you hear. Who carries what you carry. And those who expect your silence are not asking you to obey. They are asking you to disappear. Don't. If you must go, go loudly. Go kicking. Go screaming. Scream until your voice breaks—and then one scream more. You may think no one hears you. But someone will. Maybe it's your voice that breaks the silence. That tips the scale. You won't know. That's not your burden. Your burden is only this: to keep going until you don't have to scream anymore. Or until someone hears—and joins you.

Live. Love. Hope. Act. Repeat. That is the rhythm of a free people. That is how a republic is restored—not in slogans, not in spectacles, but in habits. In refusal. In belief. In daily choices made for the common good. If silence is how democracies die, then repetition is how they live. Repetition of care. Of courage. Of consequence. You do not need permission. You need only to start.

The Founders dreamed beyond the possible. They did not inherit democracy. They invented it. And they knew it would last only as long as the people demanded it. They built a presidency to serve, not to rule. A court to interpret, not to dominate. A Congress to answer, not to hide. That dream is now endangered. But it is not gone. Not yet. It can still be saved. Not by them. By us. Starting now.

PART III. A JUDICIARY THAT UPHOLDS LAW, NOT LOYALTY

THE CONSTITUTION GAVE JUDGES INDEPENDENCE. REFORM MUST NOW GIVE THEM ETHICS, TRANSPARENCY, AND ACCOUNTABILITY.

"Judges were never meant to be kings in robes."
— JP Vincent

The Constitution does not create a democratic government. It creates a framework for one. Article III is the shortest of its three founding branches, vesting the judicial power of the United States in one Supreme Court and such inferior courts as Congress may establish. It guarantees life tenure during "good Behaviour," and prohibits reductions in judicial salaries. These were protections—not privileges—meant to insulate the courts from monarchs, mobs, and manipulation. But judicial independence was never meant to become judicial impunity. The courts were to be impartial, visible, and bounded by law. Today, they are increasingly partisan, opaque, and untouchable. That transformation is no accident. It is design, delay, and decay—engineered, permitted, and sustained.

From Britain, the Framers inherited courts that stood apart from executive power—but reimagined them as true arbiters of law, not enforcers of royal will. Unlike judges under George III, American judges were to serve during good behavior, not at the pleasure of kings. Yet even in their innovations, the Framers underestimated the fragility of restraint. They did not require the Supreme Court to explain its rulings. They assumed Congress would regulate ethics. They imagined judicial independence as a shield for integrity, not a loophole for lifelong partisanship. They built a structure, but left it unfinished—relying on the honor of those who would later inhabit it. In doing so, they left it vulnerable to those with no honor at all.

The need for reform is not a repudiation of the Constitution. It is a recognition that structure is not enough. What the Framers could not imagine was a political party that would see the courts not as guardians of balance, but as targets for capture—and a man who would treat judicial protections not as tools of justice, but as shields for corruption. The Republican Party delayed confirmations to hold vacancies open, blocked hearings for nominees, and remade the lower courts through volume and ideology. Then came Trump, who did not invent the strategy—he perfected it. He turned delay into defiance, loyalty into appointment, and the courts into battlegrounds for executive power. Under his second term, those same courts now face daily attacks—some resist, others submit. But the system as a whole is no longer functioning as designed.

Judges are now assigned to cases not for their competence, but for their outcomes. Venue shopping and single-judge divisions have allowed partisan actors to handpick ideologues to rule on questions of national law. Ethics standards vary by level and are largely unenforceable. The public cannot see or hear many of the trials that shape their lives. Rulings of enormous consequence emerge unsigned, unexplained, and unreviewed. Some courts uphold the law. Others shield those who break it. And all of them are operating under rules that were built for a different era—an era of good faith. That era is over.

This part of the book is not a condemnation of the judiciary. It is a defense of its purpose. We do not seek to politicize the courts. We seek to depoliticize what has already been captured. The six reforms that follow do not weaken the judiciary. They rescue it. They do not attack judicial independence. They rebuild its foundations. They are not ideological—they are institutional. And they are urgent. Because without public trust in the courts, law is no longer binding. It is performative. And without reform, the courts will not save democracy. They will bury it.

The following chapters detail six essential reforms: Judicial Assignment and Accountability; Judicial Ethics Reform applied uniformly to all federal judges; Court Transparency and Shadow Docket Reform; Supreme Court Term Limits; Lower Court Expansion; and FOIA and Administrative Transparency. Each addresses a different failure—venue manipulation, ethical impunity, procedural secrecy, generational capture, structural understaffing, and administrative concealment. Together, they are not radical. They are the bare minimum required to ensure that courts serve law, not power—and justice, not party.

It is not enough to complain of what Trump has done or what Justices have allowed. If we do not act to fix what has failed, we are complicit in its collapse. The Framers gave us a structure. Trump revealed its limits. This is our test—and our task. Not to tear down the courts, but to restore them. Not to punish judges, but to protect justice. Not to preserve an illusion, but to rebuild a reality where the rule of law still holds.

In a functioning legal system, cases are assigned randomly, heard impartially, and decided based on law. But in today's federal judiciary, venue selection and ideological placement have replaced neutrality with orchestration. In single-judge divisions like Amarillo, Texas, litigants can all but guarantee a particular judge will hear their case. The result: handpicked rulings on abortion access, immigration, and executive power—not by chance, but by design. This is not jurisprudence. It is judicial capture through geography. And it is made possible by outdated rules, unchecked discretion, and the absence of a national standard for assignment integrity.

We must reform case assignment to prevent abuse. First, Congress should require that all federal cases involving constitutional questions or national injunctions be assigned by random draw from a pool of judges across the district or circuit, not a single courthouse. Second, any case with nationwide impact should be heard by a multi-judge panel, preventing single-judge rulings from rewriting national policy. Third, create an Office of Judicial Integrity to track assignment patterns, review outlier rulings, and publish reports on reversals, recusals, and procedural anomalies. Judicial power is not license. It is service. And when that service becomes predictable by ideology, the courts lose the very neutrality on which their legitimacy depends.

Unlike every other judge in the United States, the nine Justices of the Supreme Court operate without a binding code of conduct. But ethical impunity does not end at the top. Across the federal judiciary, disclosure violations, conflicts of interest, and recusals are governed by guidance, not enforcement. The result is a system where trust depends on personality, not principle. And in a democracy, trust cannot be optional. It must be earned, reviewed, and enforced.

A single, enforceable code of ethics must apply to all Article III judges—district, appellate, and Supreme Court. Gifts must be disclosed publicly, financial interests reported in real time, recusals tracked and enforced, and violations investigated by an empowered body under the Judicial Conference. Justices must be held to the same standards they expect from the attorneys and citizens who appear before them. Ethics are not cosmetic. They are constitutional. When judges rule on laws that affect millions, they must be held to standards visible to all. The robe cannot shield corruption. It must symbolize trust.

The right to a public trial is foundational. But in today's federal system, the public is often locked out. Key proceedings occur without video or audio access. Dockets are hidden behind paywalls. And some of the most consequential Supreme Court decisions are issued unsigned, unexplained, and unreviewed. This "shadow docket"—once reserved for routine orders—has become a venue for reshaping national law without scrutiny. In Trump's second term, it has delayed cases, created legal ambiguity, and granted de facto immunity—all in the dark.

Reform begins with light. Require real-time video or audio access to all federal trials of national consequence. Overhaul the PACER system to eliminate fees and ensure all documents are publicly accessible. End the abuse of the shadow docket: any decision that alters rights, policy, or constitutional precedent must be accompanied by a full hearing, signed opinion, and public explanation. Courts derive power not from secrecy, but from visibility. Justice cannot be trusted if it cannot be seen.

The Founders did not write term limits into the Constitution, but they did not envision justices serving for thirty or forty years either. The average life expectancy in 1787 was under 50. Today, Justices can time their retirements to partisan advantage, stay on the bench into extreme old age, or die in office after decades of unchecked influence. The stakes of each appointment have become apocalyptic, distorting our politics and freezing the Court in generational amber.

Eighteen-year term limits, staggered by design, would restore balance. Every president would appoint two Justices per term. After their active service, Justices would retain their title and salary but rotate into senior status, available for temporary panels or procedural review. This does not abolish life tenure—it redirects it. And it ensures that the Court reflects a living democracy, not a partisan relic of past majorities. Balance requires rhythm. The Court must return to it.

The federal judiciary has not grown in proportion to the population, the caseload, or the complexity of modern governance. Strategic understaffing—especially in ideologically targeted circuits—has created bottlenecks that delay justice, increase costs, and encourage political manipulation. Litigants wait months or years for rulings. Watchdog cases stall. Venue shopping thrives because understaffed courts cannot absorb demand. This is not neutral inefficiency. It is structured neglect.

Congress must authorize new judgeships—not to alter ideology, but to match the scope of federal law and the expectations of equal access. Prioritize districts with high reversal rates, long delays, or consistent ideological manipulation. Expand clerical and research capacity to reduce backlog. This is not court-packing. It is constitutional maintenance. If law is to be timely, courts must be equipped to deliver it.

The Freedom of Information Act (FOIA) was designed to make government accountable by making it visible. But loopholes, delays, and privatization have turned it into an obstacle course. Exemptions are abused. Timelines are ignored. And when public functions are outsourced to private contractors, transparency disappears entirely. In the judicial context, this means secretive enforcement contracts, concealed data systems, and vanishing trails of accountability.

Reform FOIA to shorten response deadlines, narrow exemptions, and apply public standards to any entity performing a public function—especially in law enforcement, court administration, and federal oversight. Mandate timely publication of contracts, decisions, and review timelines. Transparency is not just a right. It is a safeguard. And in the age of executive overreach and judicial concealment, it is our last line of defense.

Together, these six reforms do not seek to punish the judiciary. They seek to fulfill its purpose. We ask judges to be impartial, ethical, visible, modern, accessible, and accountable. None of these is radical. All of them are overdue. If the courts are to protect the rule of law, we must protect the integrity of the courts. The republic cannot survive without them. And it will not survive if we let them fall.

The Framers built a judiciary designed to be independent of monarchs—not beholden to them. Yet today, Trump and the Republican Party have reshaped the courts into something the Constitution was written to prevent: a tool of executive will. Justices rule not as guardians of principle but as instruments of the president who appointed them. Lower court judges are selected to deliver outcomes, not apply law. Some courts now shield insurrectionists, delay justice, and suppress scrutiny—not by accident, but by design. This is not the evolution of law. It is its inversion. The courts no longer check power. They serve it.

These reforms do not reject the Constitution—they restore it. They complete the structure the Framers began, fortify it against modern sabotage, and renew its legitimacy in the eyes of the people. To trust the courts, the public must be able to see them, understand them, and believe that no man—not even the president or a justice—is above them. That belief is vanishing—and it will not return unless we act. If we want courts that stand independent, we must build them so. Because when judges bend to the throne, the republic ends. And when they stand upright, so does the Constitution.

12

JUDICIAL ASSIGNMENT REFORM AND CASE INTEGRITY

HOW ONE JUDGE CAN STOP THE NATION: VENUE MANIPULATION AND THE QUIET CAPTURE OF FEDERAL POWER

---◆---

"Justice is not served when outcome is a matter of address."
— Learned Hand

Courts are not supposed to be battlegrounds for ideology. They are meant to be sanctuaries for law—where argument is judged on merit, not loyalty. But today, the location of a courthouse can determine the outcome of a case before it's even heard. In single-judge divisions—rural jurisdictions with only one sitting judge, created for logistical reasons but now used for strategic gain—plaintiffs handpick not just their arguments but their adjudicator. These are not flukes. They are designs. And what emerges is not jurisprudence, but power masquerading as neutrality. This quiet sabotage is one of the least understood crises in American governance. When litigants can choose their judge for ideological outcomes, what we call a court is no longer a legal forum. It becomes a political weapon—disguised in robes.

The U.S. Constitution grants judges lifetime tenure not to

elevate them above accountability, but to protect them from political pressure. Article III created an independent judiciary so that law would be decided without fear or favor. But the Constitution is silent on how cases are assigned. That discretion was left to Congress and, later, to the courts themselves. The assumption was that impartiality would guide procedure. But in the absence of national standards, assignment rules became vulnerable to partisan abuse. The Founders envisioned judicial independence as fidelity to law, not loyalty to party. Yet what now prevails in federal courtrooms is a system where proximity to power determines which judge will rule—not the merits of the case. Fixing this will require national standards for assignment, multi-judge panels for consequential cases, and public oversight of assignment trends.

In the early days of the republic, case assignment was shaped by necessity. Judges rode circuits, sharing dockets across wide regions. Geography mattered less than logistics. But as population centers grew and courts became stationary, divisions hardened. In rural districts with low caseloads, Congress permitted single-judge assignments—out of practicality, not ideology. Over time, however, these districts became traps: fixed locations where certain judges would receive every case filed there. What began as a logistical compromise became a strategic loophole. No national reform followed. As the stakes of litigation grew, so too did the incentive to manipulate jurisdiction. And with no uniform standard to prevent it, manipulation flourished—especially where partisan benefit aligned with procedural control.

For most of American history, lawyers filed where their clients lived or were harmed. But that changed with the rise of nationwide injunctions and regulatory lawsuits. Litigants learned that certain venues—especially single-judge divisions—offered predictable results. No draw. No diversity of judicial voice. Just a chosen bench. Republican legal groups turned this into an art form, targeting locations where ideological alignment could be counted on. The rule of law became the rule of venue. In time, case law itself became distorted—not through appellate precedent, but through an ecosystem of lower-court rulings never designed to be representative. These rulings then delayed enforcement, triggered appeals, and fractured legal norms. Manipulation wasn't just possible. It was professionalized.

No example illustrates this distortion more vividly than Amarillo, Texas. That division of the Northern District has only one sitting judge: Matthew Kacsmaryk, a Trump appointee with a record of far-right rulings. Every case filed there—no matter how sweeping its implications—is heard by him. This is not a matter of chance. It is an engineered outcome. Conservative groups routinely file in Amarillo not because it's relevant to the case, but because Kacsmaryk is. He has become a one-man veto on national policy, issuing injunctions on immigration, abortion, LGBTQ+ rights, and regulatory authority. It is venue manipulation elevated to a doctrine (often called forum shopping). And every time it works, it teaches others how to manipulate the courts.

In 2023, plaintiffs sued the FDA to revoke approval for mifepristone, a medication used in over half of U.S. abortions. They filed in Amarillo, knowing Judge Kacsmaryk would hear the case. He ruled the FDA lacked authority to approve the drug—overturning 23 years of scientific consensus and federal regulation. At the same time, a judge in Washington issued a contradictory ruling, preserving access. Two federal courts, two opposite outcomes, both claiming authority. Legal coherence fractured. Confidence in fairness broke.

What amplifies the danger of venue manipulation is the unchecked rise of nationwide injunctions. Once rare and carefully reasoned, they have become tools for unilateral disruption. One judge in Texas now has the power to suspend policy for the entire country. No deliberation. No appellate consensus. Just a signature. These injunctions are not inherently unconstitutional—but they were never meant to function this way. They were intended as remedies for specific harms, not preemptive strikes against federal governance. When used selectively and ideologically, they override elected branches and paralyze executive function. The problem isn't just the ruling. It's the premise: that one person, in one courthouse, should speak for 330 million.

Under Donald Trump, judicial manipulation became strategy. Legal challenges were funneled to sympathetic venues. Lawsuits were filed not to test legal merit, but to secure injunctions that blocked policy. His administration praised judges who ruled in his favor and attacked those who did not—conditioning the public to see courts as extensions of power, not law. But the deeper damage outlives any presidency. It lies in how the judiciary itself was transformed: not through lawbreaking, but through the meticulous exploitation of rules never designed to be defended. And unless those rules are reformed, the next administration will do the same —only more efficiently.

Efforts to repair this system have been met with silence or sabotage. Congressional Republicans blocked reforms to case assignment and injunction limits, knowing the current structure favors them. The Judicial Conference, which could set internal standards, deferred action. Democrats raised alarms but lacked the numbers— or will—to force change. And through it all, the legitimacy of the courts eroded. When the outcome of a case can be predicted by geography, the institution ceases to command trust. Justice, once presumed to be blind, now appears scripted. Without reform, that perception calcifies into reality.

At the heart of judicial authority is not force, but consent. The public must believe that judges decide law—not that law is chosen to suit the judge. That belief cannot be rebuilt by rhetoric. It requires visible reform. Cases with national consequence must no longer hinge on courthouse selection. No judge, however principled, should preside in a system that permits such manipulation. What we restore is not only fairness. It is unpredictability—the best evidence of a court chosen by law, not by design.

Congress must mandate random assignment for cases with national reach. Not within a single division—but across an entire district or circuit. This would apply to constitutional challenges, federal agency suits, or attempts to halt national policy. It would remove predictability from venue selection and dilute ideological capture. Fairness doesn't begin at the verdict. It begins at the assignment. And if that assignment is random, the outcome—whatever it may be—regains its authority.

Some rulings are too consequential for one voice. When a single injunction can halt federal programs or redefine national rights, the burden must be shared. Three-judge panels—already used for redistricting—should be the standard for nationwide injunctions. Not to suppress bold rulings, but to ensure they reflect more than one mind. When one judge can bind 330 million people, deliberation is not excess. It is duty.

We also need institutional oversight. A Federal Office of Judicial Integrity would review assignment trends, outlier rulings, and recusal failures. It wouldn't dictate verdicts—but track patterns that corrode trust. If a courthouse with one judge issues 90% of a nation's injunctions, that's not justice. That's a loophole exploited. Oversight must match authority. If we grant lifetime power, we must expect lifetime transparency.

Currently, Supreme Court justices are bound by no binding ethics code. Lower courts technically are—but self-policed. Recusal is often left to the conscience of the judge. That is no system. We need codified, enforceable ethics standards: mandatory recusal for financial entanglements, reporting of gifts and benefits, disqualification for prior political advocacy on a case's subject. When trust is earned, ethics is the result. But when trust is exploited, ethics must be the rule. A judge with lifetime power and no binding code is not a neutral actor. He is a sovereign. And we did not elect a nobility in robes.

Many of the most damaging cases aren't filed as constitutional disputes. They're framed as regulatory or administrative challenges—against the FDA, the Department of Education, or Homeland Security. This framing evades random assignment triggers. It pretends small impact while delivering national effect. The Amarillo abortion pill case was argued as an FDA procedural failure, but its goal was the national revocation of reproductive rights. If reform applies only to declared constitutional questions, the abuse will continue unchecked. What matters is not the label. What matters is the consequence. If a case could alter national policy, affect millions, or suspend agency action—it must be assigned without favor, not by design.

This is no longer litigation in good faith. It is sabotage dressed as law. When ideological actors exploit procedural loopholes to dictate national policy through one judge, they are not participating in justice. They are dismantling it. A republic governed by law cannot survive the manipulation of its legal system. And yet that is what we now face: lawsuits designed not to win through merit, but to paralyze through geography. Decisions not reached by weighing argument, but by targeting a judge. This is not law. It is procedural siege. And the longer it continues, the more it becomes precedent for the next administration, the next party, the next erosion.

Some will argue that these reforms are partisan. But what is truly partisan is the refusal to fix a system because it currently serves one party's ends. If courts are truly neutral, then randomization and transparency pose no threat. If judges are impartial, then oversight will affirm their integrity, not undermine it. The resistance comes not from principle, but from advantage. And that is the clearest evidence that the system is broken. We are not asking for loyalty from the bench. We are asking for law. If a judge fears review, fears sunlight, fears random assignment—then the danger is not in the reform. It is in what it reveals.

The judiciary does not enforce its own authority. It survives by consent—by public belief that courts offer fairness, not force. But that consent is thinning. When rulings are shaped by venue, when outcomes are foregone conclusions, when law bends to loyalty, people stop believing. And when belief goes, so does legitimacy. Then the very rulings courts issue will be ignored. That is the cliff edge we approach. Judicial authority rests not on robes or gavels, but on trust. And if we lose that, we lose the last place in government meant to rise above partisanship. We lose the final refuge of the law.

The goal is not to punish. It is to restore. A judiciary where no one knows which judge will get the case. Where national policy is not blocked by a single courthouse. Where judges recuse themselves not because they must be forced, but because they are bound. Where data is public. Ethics are codified. And decisions—though controversial—are at least credible. This does not require revolution. It requires legislation, will, and the courage to admit we let something vital decay. We do not need perfection. We need integrity. And it starts with process.

The judiciary is where Americans go when every other institution fails them. It must be better than politics. It must be better than loyalty. That begins with restoring process, shielding assignment from abuse, and rebuilding a culture where law outweighs favor. We can pass the reforms. We can randomize the assignments. We can monitor the patterns. But we must also reclaim the meaning of justice. It cannot mean "who you know" or "where you file." It must mean the same rule, applied to all. That was the promise. If we still believe in democracy, it must be the promise once more.

13

JUDICIAL ETHICS REFORM AND FEDERAL ACCOUNTABILITY
FROM DISCRETION TO DISCIPLINE: ENFORCING TRUST IN THE FEDERAL JUDICIARY

"Trust is not what frees power from oversight. It is what makes oversight necessary."
— *J.P. Vincent*

Judicial independence is one of the Constitution's most powerful ideas—but it is not the same as judicial impunity. Article III grants lifetime tenure and salary protection to federal judges to shield them from political pressure. But it does not exempt them from scrutiny. Nowhere in the Constitution is there mention of a separate standard of integrity for the judiciary. Nor is there language forbidding Congress from setting rules to preserve public trust. The Framers assumed virtue in those who would wear the robe—but they also designed checks and balances in every direction. The idea was not to elevate judges above accountability. It was to protect their rulings from influence. And today, that protection is being misused.

The Framers had seen what unchecked judicial power looked

like under monarchy—and they wanted no part of it. In Britain, judges served at the pleasure of the Crown, often appointed as rewards and removed for disloyalty. The courts were instruments of royal will, not legal principle. The American Constitution broke from that tradition deliberately. It gave federal judges life tenure and salary protection—not as privilege, but as insulation from political coercion. Independence was a shield against partisan interference, not against ethical restraint. Alexander Hamilton, in Federalist 78, warned that the judiciary would wield "neither force nor will, but merely judgment"—a modest role that demanded trust. But power without constraint invites its own undoing.

After Watergate, Congress moved to limit the quiet corridors where power could be traded without consequence. The 1978 Ethics in Government Act imposed financial disclosure rules on executive and legislative officials—and, with some adaptation, the judiciary. The Judicial Conference adopted the Code of Conduct for U.S. Judges in 1973, but made it apply only to lower courts. The Supreme Court, citing its constitutional independence, excluded itself. For decades, the fiction held that Justices would police themselves. The Constitution did not grant this exemption. The Court claimed it. And the claim became practice. The more the public learns about undisclosed travel, gifts, and conflicts, the more it becomes clear: self-regulation is not a system of accountability. It is an excuse for inaction.

The divide between lower courts and the Supreme Court has become a fault line. District and appellate judges operate under a published code of conduct, submit annual disclosures, and can be reviewed by judicial councils. But these systems depend on peer enforcement—not public oversight—and even here, compliance is uneven. Judges have ruled in cases involving companies they own stock in. Recusals are rare, and consequences rarer still. Yet at the Supreme Court, the system simply does not exist. There is no code. No process. No penalties. The public sees what follows: secret trips, undisclosed gifts, activist spouses, and no accountability. This is not an oversight. It is abandonment. And in a democracy, it cannot last.

When Congress asked the Court to voluntarily adopt a binding code, the Justices declined. In 2011, Chief Justice Roberts argued that the Court "does not sit in judgment of one another's recusal decisions." In 2023, the Justices issued a statement of "Ethics Principles," but it had no enforcement mechanism, no disclosure timeline, and no penalties. It was a gesture of optics, not obligation. Lawyers arguing before the Court face stricter ethical rules than the Justices deciding their cases. No other court in the nation operates on trust alone. This is not a flaw of design. It is a failure of will. And the longer it continues, the more damage it inflicts.

What rules exist are partial, opaque, and toothless. Judges are required to file annual financial disclosure forms, but the process is cumbersome, often delayed, and difficult for the public to access. The Judicial Conference sets advisory standards but has no authority to investigate Supreme Court Justices or enforce compliance. Recusal decisions are left to each judge's discretion. There is no system for tracking violations, no independent review, and no consistent mechanism for public complaint. While lower court judges can theoretically be disciplined, those processes are rarely invoked—and nearly impossible to initiate without insider cooperation. We've built a judiciary that values the appearance of trust over the reality of enforcement.

What's missing is not advice. It is enforcement. A credible system of judicial ethics must have four elements: mandatory, real-time disclosures; independent investigation of violations; clear and enforceable penalties; and equal applicability across all Article III judges—including the Supreme Court. Today, none of those conditions are met. Instead, the judiciary operates on a culture of deference, silence, and personal discretion. This was manageable in a time of higher public trust. It is unsustainable now. A judge with undisclosed financial entanglements cannot be trusted to rule impartially. A court that shields itself from review cannot command confidence. The risk is not just perception. It is actual injustice—delivered with the false stamp of neutrality.

Recusal is the most visible failure—and the most corrosive. Judges who have financial interests in a party before them, or whose family members are directly involved in relevant political causes, are expected to step aside. But expectation without enforcement is etiquette, not ethics. In case after case, Justices have refused to recuse despite glaring conflicts. Justice Thomas ruled on cases involving his wife's efforts to overturn the 2020 election. Justice Alito failed to disclose luxury travel from parties with business before the Court. Lower court judges have made similar violations without consequence. In any other profession, this would trigger an investigation. In the judiciary, it triggers press coverage—and little else.

Congressional Republicans have blocked every serious attempt at reform. In 2023, the Supreme Court Ethics, Recusal, and Transparency (SCERT) Act passed out of the Senate Judiciary Committee. But Republican senators—led by Chuck Grassley and others—refused to advance it. They dismissed calls for accountability as partisan attacks. Even modest proposals—like requiring online publication of disclosure forms—were filibustered or tabled. Meanwhile, GOP donors with cases before the Court have given lavish gifts to sitting Justices without disclosure or penalty. This is not principled conservatism. It is protection of power. And it confirms what millions now understand: the rules apply only to those who cannot afford exemption.

The judiciary is now an instrument of Republican consolidation. From the Federalist Society's vetting of judicial nominees to coordinated resistance against ethics reform, the Republican Party has treated the courts not as neutral arbiters but as ideological allies. When judges act in partisan interest, Republicans defend them. When they rule against GOP power, they are attacked. Ethics is no longer treated as a constitutional necessity but as a political liability.

And that is the clearest sign of institutional rot: when integrity becomes a threat to be neutralized, rather than a standard to be upheld.

Trump's second term has already accelerated the dismantling of judicial accountability. In early 2025, his Department of Justice halted cooperation with Judicial Conference ethics initiatives, citing "executive discretion." Proposed DOJ funding for federal ethics monitoring was zeroed out in the revised budget. Internal agency lawyers were told not to enforce recusal tracking or conflict disclosures—unless directed by the White House Counsel's Office. At the same time, Project 2025 architects moved to weaken the Administrative Office of the U.S. Courts—pressuring it to drop transparency proposals. This is not reform. It is retaliation. And it confirms the real goal: not a neutral judiciary, but a loyal one.

This dismantling of ethics finds its most blatant expression in two Justices now beyond scrutiny. Thomas's conduct is plainly transactional: undisclosed gifts, private school tuition, real estate deals, luxury travel—all from wealthy conservatives with interests before the Court. His rulings have aligned with their agenda, and his refusal to recuse from Trump-related cases despite his wife's direct involvement in the 2020 coup effort reveals the price of access. Alito's motivations are murkier but no less troubling. He has taken private jet travel and accommodations from partisan billionaires, waved away ethical concerns, and publicly defended the Court's conservative bloc against criticism. Whether chasing prestige, power, or patronage, both men have abandoned the standard they swore to uphold.

Selective recusals reveal a deeper truth: the Court is no longer above politics—it is inside it. In recent years, we have seen a consistent pattern. Justices recuse when cases involve their personal finances but not when they involve their ideological patrons. Recusal has become image management—not ethics. The appearance of impartiality—once the bedrock of judicial trust—is now filtered through partisan lenses. Lower courts mirror this pattern: judges shield themselves from scrutiny by appealing to vague standards and complex disclosure loopholes. This is not an accident. It is a design failure that has become a political opportunity. And it is why Congress must act—not against the courts, but to protect them from corrosion.

The cost of inaction is already measurable—and growing. Public trust in the Supreme Court has fallen to historic lows. In 2023, Gallup found just 40% of Americans trusted the Court to act impartially. And that loss of trust cascades. When the highest court is seen as biased, every court below it inherits suspicion. For civil rights cases, electoral disputes, and presidential accountability, this is catastrophic. Rulings may still have legal force, but they lose democratic legitimacy. And in a nation built on the idea that law binds us equally, that loss is existential. A democracy cannot function if the people believe its referees are rigged.

The erosion of judicial trust leads not just to cynicism—but to civil danger. When citizens no longer believe in lawful resolution of conflict, they turn to other means. We saw it on January 6. We see it in threats against judges, jurors, and prosecutors. We see it in the rising tide of political violence, from statehouses to school boards. The courts were once the buffer against that chaos. Now, in too many cases, they are seen as participants. If the courts lose their moral standing, then laws become instruments of faction. And when law is factional, it becomes fragile. What breaks next is not the rulebook. It is the republic.

Judicial capture does not require the removal of courts. It only requires the removal of boundaries. When judges are placed above enforcement, above review, above consequence, they no longer serve justice. They serve power. That is how authoritarian regimes preserve the illusion of legality while consolidating control. Opinions are still issued. Dockets still move. But they no longer speak with the voice of the law—they echo the will of power. America is not there yet. But every exemption, every unpunished violation, every failure to recuse brings us closer. Reform is not a matter of optics. It is the precondition of legal democracy. We do not need courts that rule for one side. We need courts that answer to none.

The path forward is clear: one enforceable code for all Article III judges, applied without exception. That code must require public, real-time disclosure of gifts, travel, financial interests, and outside income. It must mandate recusal from any case involving those interests. It must establish an independent oversight body with the power to investigate violations, compel testimony, and recommend discipline—including public reprimands and impeachment referrals. Supreme Court Justices must no longer exempt themselves. The same standards they demand from attorneys must govern their own conduct. This is not forbidden by the Constitution—it is required by it. The Framers intended to guard the courts from political influence, not elevate judges to unchecked power. Congress not only has the authority to act. It has the duty. Because the question is not whether they can be trusted. The question is how we verify it—and who decides when that trust is broken.

Judicial ethics are not ornamental. They are constitutional. The robe is not a relic. It is a trust—granted by the people, bound by law, and answerable to both.

That trust holds only if accountability is real, enforceable, and equal. In this moment of deep national division, the courts must be more than symbols. They must be safeguards. But they cannot serve that role if they answer only to themselves. A judge who cannot be questioned is not a judge. They are a sovereign. And the United States does not recognize sovereigns. It recognizes the rule of law. And that law must now speak—clearly, publicly, and for all.

14

COURT TRANSPARENCY AND SHADOW DOCKET OVERSIGHT

HOW SECRECY AND THE SHADOW DOCKET TURNED THE SUPREME COURT INTO A TOOL OF UNACCOUNTABLE POWER—AND WHY VISIBILITY IS THE ONLY REMEDY

―――― ✦ ――――

"People in an open society do not demand infallibility from their institutions. But it is difficult for them to accept what they are prohibited from observing."
— Chief Justice Warren Burger, *Richmond Newspapers v. Virginia* (1980)

The Constitution does not require justice to be swift, infallible, or even popular. But it does require that it be seen. The Sixth Amendment guarantees the right to a public trial in criminal cases—not as ornament, but as safeguard. It reflects a deeper principle woven through the American system: that power, to be trusted, must remain visible. Article III grants judges life tenure to shield them from political winds, but in exchange, it places them under the expectation of public scrutiny. Judges serve not during pleasure, but during "good Behaviour"—a phrase that presumes accountability. And in a self-governing republic, accountability begins with access. The courtroom is not merely a legal forum. It is a public stage where law and legitimacy meet. When the doors close, both are put at risk.

This was not just a textual idea, but a civic one. In *Richmond Newspapers v. Virginia* (1980), the Supreme Court held that the public has a First Amendment right to attend criminal trials. Writing for the majority, Chief Justice Burger noted that openness is not incidental to justice—it is intrinsic to its operation. "People in an open society," he wrote, "do not demand infallibility from their institutions. But it is difficult for them to accept what they are prohibited from observing." That principle applies even more urgently today. The Constitution does not define "public" narrowly. It does not say that justice must be seen only by those able to sit on a bench inside a courthouse. In an age of digital governance and national consequence, justice must be visible in practice, not just in theory. The courtroom must remain a public square—accessible not just in geography, but in truth.

American justice was not always so distant. In the early republic, trials were public to the point of spectacle. Courtrooms were not hushed temples of procedure but civic gathering places—visible symbols of law in motion. Citizens filled benches, pressed into aisles, and stood in doorways to hear evidence and verdicts. Judges did not retreat behind closed chambers; they presided under the gaze of neighbors, rivals, and the press. The law spoke aloud. Its language, its reasoning, and its contradictions were part of public life. There was no mystery in its operation. And for all its exclusions and imperfections, the early courtroom affirmed a simple truth: justice was not hidden. It had to account for itself.

That began to change in the twentieth century—not through conspiracy, but through institutional caution. In 1981, the Judicial Conference of the United States restricted cameras in nearly all federal courtrooms, citing concerns over decorum and distortion. At the time, the shift felt narrow: a pause against the growing glare of television. But the effect was profound. With no audio, no video, and increasingly restricted physical access, the federal judiciary began to slip beyond view. Around the same time, PACER—the Public Access to Court Electronic Records system—was introduced as a digital archive. But instead of becoming a public good, it was treated as a revenue stream. Records were placed behind login screens and page fees, charging ten cents per page to read the rulings written in the public's name. For a nation that once conducted trials in town squares, this was an astonishing reversal: the courtroom became a portal, and the portal became a tollbooth.

By the 2000s, the drift was complete. Court filings were digital but paywalled. Hearings were public but inaccessible. And the workings of federal law had become functionally invisible to all but the professionally credentialed or institutionally funded. What began as caution hardened into exclusion. What had once been democratic ritual was reduced to a private exchange between judge and advocate. The public had not been pushed out with force. It had simply been forgotten. Or remembered that it had cash. And in the space it left behind, new powers learned how to operate without being seen.

Republican legal strategists did not create judicial secrecy. But they were the first to see its full potential. What began as caution they recast as opportunity. Over the last three decades, the conservative legal movement—led by the Federalist Society and reinforced by Republican judicial appointments—learned to use opacity as a weapon. They did not simply seek favorable rulings. They reshaped the machinery through which rulings were delivered. Emergency stays, unsigned orders, per curiam decisions without opinion—all once rare, all now routine. These were not errors of haste or necessity. They were instruments of design. A ruling issued without authorship cannot be challenged. A decision without explanation creates no precedent. A pattern of silence, repeated over time, becomes a method of rule.

Legal scholars call this system of unsigned, unexplained, and expedited rulings the "shadow docket." The term refers to decisions made outside the Court's regular process—without oral arguments, without full opinions, and often without public scrutiny. Unlike the Court's formal docket, which proceeds with transparency and deliberation, the shadow docket operates in haste and silence. Once rare, it has become the preferred channel for power without explanation.

This strategy matured in the early 2010s, when the Court began intervening in high-profile cases not with argument, but with disappearance. In *Herbert v. Kitchen* (2014), the Court halted marriage equality in Utah with a single unsigned order, issued without explanation and over no recorded dissent. The lower court had ruled that the state's ban on same-sex marriage was unconstitutional. The Supreme Court did not yet overrule it. It simply paused the outcome—leaving the law in limbo and the public in confusion. It was a tactical silence. And it marked the moment when procedure became substance. Republican-aligned lawyers and judges understood what that silence could do: allow contested policies to take effect while litigation ground on, shield controversial positions from public scrutiny, and enforce ideological outcomes without the constraint of legal reasoning. They were not abusing the law. They were bypassing it.

It was this new architecture of invisibility that Trump inherited. But what had been a backstage tool for conservative legal maneuvering became, under his leadership, a blunt instrument of governance. In his first term, Trump's administration filed more emergency applications to the Supreme Court than any in modern history. These were not cautious appeals for last-minute relief. They were calculated efforts to secure legal advantage before public resistance or judicial review could catch up. Immigration restrictions, asylum bans, abortion limits, and executions were all pushed forward under the guise of emergency. The goal was not deliberation—it was preemption. To act before the law could speak. And the Court, with a conservative majority in place, opened the door.

In case after case, Trump's lawyers asked the Court to overturn lower court injunctions on urgent grounds, and the justices complied—without oral argument, without written opinion, and often without even disclosing who had requested the relief. These unsigned orders carried immediate consequence: reinstating bans, canceling protections, greenlighting punishments. In substance, they changed the law. In form, they denied that any law had changed. No author. No rationale. Only orders issued in silence—and left to stand. It was a presidency that governed not through legislation or persuasion, but through procedural momentum, powered by a Court willing to decide without speaking. The law became not a process, but a reflex.

Trump's second term has turned the shadow docket from a weapon into a shield. In his first term, it was used to impose policy. In his second, it is being used to evade accountability. His legal team now floods the courts with emergency filings—not just to advance legislation, but to block investigations, freeze prosecutions, and silence subpoenas. Since January 2025, the administration has filed at least 13 emergency applications with the Supreme Court, with five more pending. These filings are not meant to win. They are meant to stall. Each motion buys time. Each delay prevents consequence. And in case after case, the Supreme Court has responded not with clarity, but with silence—granting stays, declining to intervene, or allowing lower court confusion to persist. The result is legal suspension. The law does not fail. It simply stops.

In one instance, the Court issued an unsigned order to pause enforcement of a contempt ruling against a Trump official who refused to testify before Congress. In another, it stayed a state prosecution related to election interference—pending review that has since been postponed three times. There is no explanation. No timeline. No dissent. Just a procedural pause that functions as indefinite immunity. Trump has not overcome the rule of law. He has simply parked it at an abandoned bus stop. When rulings arrive without signature or schedule, there is no one to answer for delay—and no one to hold accountable for what that delay enables.

The shadow docket, once a narrow tool for urgent relief, now serves as a mechanism for executive impunity. Trump's defenders call it prudence. But delay, in law, is never neutral. When power acts while the courts wait, justice does not hang in balance—it disappears. The longer it remains hidden, the harder it is to restore. And in that silence, a new precedent takes root: that a President can govern without law, so long as the Court remains silent. And silence, repeated, becomes power.

That silence is not just procedural—it is physical. It is built into the walls of our courthouses, coded into access systems, and embedded in the public inaccessibility of justice itself. Power not only hides in silence. It hides in architecture. Courtrooms remain closed to cameras. Transcripts arrive late, if at all. Audio is often restricted, redacted, or retroactively edited. And the official record—the PACER system—is an outdated archive riddled with missing metadata, inaccessible formats, and absurd costs. A single page download can cost as much as a paperback. For ordinary citizens, journalists, and researchers, the barriers are not just technological. They are financial. And they defy the constitutional principle that justice must not only be done—but be seen. What was meant to be the public record of justice has become a gated domain, open to the few who can pay, and opaque to the many it was meant to serve.

The consequences are both practical and philosophical. Investigative journalism becomes harder. Legal advocacy becomes slower. Public trust erodes. In criminal cases, the Sixth Amendment guarantees a public trial—but in civil and administrative cases, no such access exists. And even where access is permitted, the tools of understanding are withheld. There is no centralized portal. No unified index. No requirement for courts to make reasoning easily discoverable. Instead, there is fragmentation by design. Every obstacle blurs the lines of responsibility and shields the workings of power. In an era when the executive branch floods the courts with lawsuits, refuses cooperation, and claims immunity from consequence, that silence is not procedural—it is protective. And in the absence of transparency, the burden of democracy falls on a press that cannot see, and a public that cannot know.

This is not incidental. It is the goal. Republican leaders have spent decades building a judicial system that rules without being seen. They would sooner embrace a public outbreak than a public record. Court reform efforts—bipartisan, modest, and overdue—have been buried without debate. Legislation to modernize PACER, expand livestreams, or require audiovisual access has been repeatedly blocked in committee, often without a hearing, without a vote, and always without a trace. The stated concern is decorum. The true motive is control. A system this opaque becomes a sanctuary for shadow rulings, for unsigned decrees, for influence with no fingerprint. It is not caution. It is concealment. And in concealment, democracy does not simply dim. It gets lost.

Restoring visibility begins with removing the barriers to it. The judiciary cannot be exempt from the standards of transparency already expected across public life—from live-streamed legislative sessions and televised executive briefings to public university governance and local council meetings. It is time to rebuild the architecture of access around three pillars: public hearings, public records, and public reasoning. First, Congress must mandate real-time audio and video access for all federal hearings of national significance—including appellate arguments and emergency motions. Second, the PACER system must be abolished or rebuilt as a free, searchable, fully transparent public infrastructure. The law belongs to the people. Its records should not be behind a paywall.

Third—and most urgent—Congress must end the use of the shadow docket as a tool of silent rule. Any judicial action that alters rights, blocks enforcement, or suspends policy must meet public standards: signed authorship, stated reasoning, and timely full review. No more silent law. No more unsigned reversals. Emergency powers may still exist—but their use must be visible, accountable, and constrained by democratic principle. These reforms do not limit the courts. They limit those who exploit opacity to bypass Congress, evade oversight, and rule without consent. The Constitution demands law by process—not by ambush.

These reforms are not radical. They are minimal. They do not seek to strip judicial power, but to demand that it answer to the people in whose name it is exercised. Every one of these proposals affirms a principle as old as the Republic: that law gains its authority not from secrecy, but from legitimacy. A ruling seen is a ruling understood. A ruling understood is a ruling answerable. And only a ruling answerable belongs in a democracy.

A Court that rules in silence does not speak for the law. It speaks only for itself. And if left unchecked, it will continue to do so—on matters of war, rights, punishment, and power—without consent, without clarity, and without consequence.

That is the danger we now face—not the collapse of the judiciary, but its quiet withdrawal from public life. A justice system that hides its workings cannot be trusted to defend the Constitution. And a democracy that accepts that silence will not remain one for long. This is not merely a question of access or aesthetics. It is a question of authority. The law does not compel obedience by force. It earns it—by reason, by fairness, and by being seen.

We must remember what is at stake. When emergency rulings replace due process, when unsigned orders silence debate, the foundation of public trust begins to erode. Judicial restraint becomes judicial evasion. Tradition becomes excuse. What the Constitution demands, we must now defend: courts that are independent and visible; powerful and principled; protected from politics but accountable to the people in whose name they govern.

The courts are not immune to failure—but they remain the last functioning barrier against authoritarian rule. Under Trump's second term, they are swamped, defied, and increasingly silenced. Yet even now, amid procedural sabotage and political pressure, they preserve narrow channels of accountability. That is why they are being targeted. The shadow docket is not just a quirk of judicial process. It is a weapon of minority rule—engineered in secret and wielded without scrutiny. It must be dismantled before it becomes the new normal. The judiciary must not only be fair. It must be seen to be fair. In this fight, visibility is not a virtue. It is a shield. And in a democracy under siege, it is the only way to prove that the rule of law still rules.

In the end, law should not be a mystery. It is a promise, made visible. Most judges still honor that promise. But the system now rewards those who would break it—through delay, through silence, through power wielded without name or reason. If we want justice to survive, we must make it visible again—before the darkness becomes law.

15

SUPREME COURT TERM LIMITS AND GENERATIONAL BALANCE

REFORM IS NOT FORBIDDEN BY THE CONSTITUTION. IT IS REQUIRED BY IT.

───── ◆ ─────

"Laws are not made to last forever, but to endure until they no longer serve justice."
— Montesquieu

The Supreme Court no longer reflects the rhythm of a living democracy. Appointments are rare and apocalyptic. Vacancies arrive by death or strategic retirement. Once confirmed, Justices serve not for a season, but for a generation. The result is an institution locked in the past—one that interprets the present through an ideology anchored in a vanished era, imposes doctrine decades out of date, and enforces the will of a long-expired majority. This is not the natural consequence of constitutional design. It is the deliberate perversion of it. The Court, once a check on power, now guards the fortress of those who seized it. Democracy demands rotation. This is entrenchment.

The Framers included no term limits, but they did not imagine Justices sitting for forty years. In 1787, the average life expectancy was under fifty. Judicial service rarely exceeded fifteen years. The judiciary was designed to be independent, not immortal. Its authority was meant to evolve with the Republic. But life tenure, once a shield for judicial courage, has become a weapon of judicial entrenchment. Locked into the bench by ambition or ideology, modern Justices pass judgment on generations they no longer understand. They shape the lives of citizens whose realities they neither share nor recall. This is not continuity—it is calcification.

For much of the Court's history, turnover was steady. Justices often retired after a decade or two, their health or age cutting short any notion of dynastic power. Appointments reflected the politics of the moment, but not with the ideological permanence we now endure. The average tenure through most of the 20th century was under 17 years. Justices came and went with less fanfare. There were bitter confirmation fights—Brandeis, Fortas, Bork—but most nominations were confirmed by broad margins. The Court was respected, even when contested. And while its decisions shaped the nation, it did not overshadow it. The Court had weight. It did not have permanence.

What changed? The rise of a judiciary-as-legacy strategy, pioneered by conservatives but now practiced across the political spectrum. Presidents seek youthful nominees with extreme views and long lives. Confirmation battles become political wars. Merrick Garland is denied a hearing. Amy Coney Barrett is confirmed days before a national election. Justices now outlast entire political movements, casting votes shaped by decades-old ideologies. The goal is not legal excellence, but ideological dominance. Every seat becomes a stronghold, every ruling a campaign victory. The Court becomes the prize of a permanent campaign. And in that battle, its legitimacy bleeds out, case by case, term by term.

Three of the six conservative Justices now sitting were appointed by a president who lost the popular vote. Two were confirmed by a Senate representing a minority of Americans. One was installed just days before an election by the same party that denied its predecessor even a hearing. This is not democratic legitimacy. It is procedural conquest. The rules change depending on who holds power. The result is a Court increasingly seen not as an impartial guardian of rights but as a political weapon. Its decisions do not reflect democratic consensus—they reflect partisan strategy and generational lock-in. And its aim is enduring: to rule from the bench when the people will no longer consent to be ruled at the ballot box.

Behind this conquest stands the machinery of manipulation. The Federalist Society handpicks the nominees. Leonard Leo curates the bench. Dark-money networks fund the campaigns, advertisements, and influence operations. The goal is not fairness—it is permanence. Justices in their 40s are selected not for wisdom, but for longevity. Their votes will shape law long after the presidents who appointed them are gone. In every meaningful sense, this is not judicial service. It is ideological entrenchment masquerading as neutrality. The Court has become an outpost of minority rule, protected from the winds of change by the illusion of restraint and the shield of life tenure.

Donald Trump did not invent this strategy. But he accelerated it and weaponized it. Three appointments, all confirmed at record speed. All young. All partisan. None centrist. His Supreme Court is not merely conservative—it is compliant. He speaks of it as his Court. He seeks from it the power he cannot gain from Congress or public approval. Immunity from prosecution. Deference to executive orders. Validation for authoritarian policy. The Court, once a check, now becomes a tool. What began as judicial independence has curdled into judicial loyalty, wielded not for justice, but for self-preservation.

The danger is not only in who sits, but in how long. Clarence Thomas has served more than thirty-three years. Samuel Alito is past eighteen. These men are not neutral arbiters of law—they are architects of ideology. Their entanglements—familial, financial, ideological—no longer remain hidden. And yet the robe remains. Because without term limits, there is no end but death, disgrace, or the rare decision to step down. Democracy, meanwhile, remains at their mercy. They cast binding votes on matters that will shape the next century while being tethered to the grievances of the last.

Trump's second term strategy depends on that mercy. His policies, his immunity claims, his attacks on the administrative state—all are designed to pass through a court he helped build. He trusts it to protect him. And he's often right. Every ruling that favors him becomes a weapon in his arsenal, a rebuke to his critics, a green light for greater defiance. The Court is no longer above politics. It is inside them. And with no term limits, it cannot leave. It becomes, in essence, a captive institution, delivering permanence to a presidency that could not otherwise endure.

But the Constitution is not the obstacle to reform—it is the foundation. Article III guarantees life tenure, not life service on the Supreme Court. Congress may regulate judicial duties, as it has done for centuries. It has restructured the lower courts, reassigned jurisdictions, and altered roles. It created the current federal appellate system in 1891 and reshaped the circuits multiple times since. What it has done before, it can do again. It can limit active Supreme Court service to 18 years—while preserving lifetime judicial status and full pay. Life tenure ensures independence from politics—not an entitlement to a specific judicial seat.

Every two years, the president would appoint one Justice. Every Justice would serve 18 years of active duty before rotating to senior status. Their title and salary would remain. They could serve on lower courts, administrative panels, or emergency cases. This is not removal—it is redirection. It fulfills the promise of life tenure while ending the harm of perpetual power. And it restores what the Court has lost: rhythm, renewal, and relevance. Just as laws must be revisited, so too must the institution that interprets them. The Court must live in time, not above it.

Such legislation has already been proposed. The Supreme Court Term Limits and Regular Appointments Act, introduced by Rep. Ro Khanna and Sen. Sheldon Whitehouse, creates precisely this system. No constitutional amendment required. No elimination of tenure. Just a recognition that a republic must change, or it will rot. The Justices would leave the bench as they came to it—not by death or disgrace, but by design. The dignity of judicial service would be matched by the dignity of departure. This is not a partisan dream. It is a constitutional repair.

The transition could begin immediately. Every two years, the longest-serving Justice rotates out. No one is removed. No appointment is wasted. Over time, the bench resets. A new Justice arrives with each Congress. A Court that once stood still begins again to move with the people it serves. And the legitimacy of its rulings is no longer a matter of partisan luck, but public trust. The cycle of panic and manipulation ends. What remains is predictability, fairness, and a return to deliberative law.

Why now? Because time is the disease. The Court, locked in the past, cannot serve a changing country. A frozen bench rules from an extinct world, imposing old fears and vanishing values on a restless public. This is how democracy dies—not in a coup, but in a coma. The old guards the gates, and nothing new can enter. When law no longer adapts, it no longer protects. When judges refuse to move, justice becomes static. And the people, seeing no change, lose faith in the system itself.

We are alone among democracies. Canada mandates retirement at 75. Germany limits terms to 12 years. India, the UK, and Australia all require retirement. These nations demonstrate that term limits and judicial independence can coexist. Only the U.S. treats the highest court as a lifetime monarchy. This is not constitutional fidelity. It is institutional inertia. And it endangers everything the Court was meant to protect. The Founders envisioned independence, not immortality. We have allowed the robe to become armor. That must end.

Most Americans agree. A majority across parties supports term limits. They know that power must circulate, or it decays. But lawmakers fear retaliation, and presidents fear losing the weapon. Reform will not come from those who benefit from the freeze. It must come from those who have nothing left to lose but the illusion of restraint. The call must come not from the Court, but from the country it claims to serve.

The stakes are not judicial. They are civilizational. A nation that changes but cannot change its court becomes a hostage to its past. We cannot build a democracy on permanent imbalance. And we cannot preach justice while locking the scales in one direction forever. The Court is not sacred. It is human. And humans must yield to time.

The rhythm of democracy is not silence. It is pulse, change, return. The Court must have that rhythm again. Term limits are not a threat to the Constitution. They are its renewal. Because in a republic, no one—not even a Justice—should rule until death. Let the robe be passed, not preserved. That is how balance is restored—across generations, through service, not possession.

This is not a revolution. It is a restoration. Let the Justices serve. Let them depart in honor. So the Court may live—and democracy with it. To preserve legitimacy, we must rediscover rhythm. To defend the future, we must let go of the past.

16

LOWER COURT EXPANSION AND ACCESS TO JUSTICE

HOW WE REBUILD A JUDICIARY THAT SERVES THE PEOPLE—NOT PARTY. NOT POWER.

———✦———

"No institution serves the people by accident. It does so by design, or not at all."

— JP Vincent

The Constitution vests Congress with the power to create and shape the lower courts—not as a privilege, but as a responsibility. Article I, Section 8 grants the legislative branch authority "to constitute Tribunals inferior to the Supreme Court," while Article III, Section 1 reaffirms that all federal courts beyond the Supreme Court exist only as Congress ordains. This framework reflects the founders' understanding that justice must be present and accessible—not theoretical. Together, these provisions form a constitutional expectation: that as the republic grows, so must its judiciary. To withhold that growth is not restraint. It is failure. When justice outgrows its structure, delay becomes denial, and silence becomes injustice. That is where we find ourselves today.

Throughout American history, Congress responded to that

responsibility with regular judicial reform. From the Judiciary Acts of 1789, 1801, and 1869 to the Evarts Act of 1891 and the Omnibus Judgeship Act of 1978, Congress expanded the courts roughly every 30 to 50 years—each time to meet the needs of a growing, modernizing nation. These were not radical acts. They were bipartisan maintenance. Population increased. Law grew more complex. Caseloads rose. And the judiciary was scaled to match. That rhythm broke after 1978. For nearly half a century, despite the immense expansion of federal jurisdiction and public demand, Congress failed to act. What was once routine became paralyzed.

The paralysis was not confusion—it was strategy. Beginning in the 1980s, the Republican Party embraced a long-term plan to capture the judiciary not to preserve balance, but to impose its agenda through the courts regardless of electoral outcomes. With the founding of the Federalist Society, the right built a pipeline of ideologically vetted judges—trained to dismantle civil rights protections, gut regulatory authority, and shield corporate power. These judges were not chosen to interpret law neutrally, but to enforce a political doctrine: that markets outrank democracy, and that hierarchy is order. Expansion of the courts was blocked not to delay justice, but to ensure that when justice arrived, it served its political purpose. The goal was not neutrality. It was control.

This obstruction became infrastructure. Under Newt Gingrich and later Mitch McConnell, Republicans turned the judicial appointment process into a weapon of minority rule. Dozens of vacancies—some with bipartisan support—were left open for years. Merrick Garland was denied a hearing. Senate rules were rewritten or ignored to accelerate loyalists and block moderates. The power to confirm judges was no longer used to preserve legal continuity—it was used to entrench one party's dominance over the courts. When Republicans held power, confirmations moved at unprecedented speed. When they did not, the process froze. The result was a judiciary increasingly skewed: ideologically extreme, demographically narrow, and structurally imbalanced. Justice slowed for ordinary people, but power moved swiftly through favored channels, hand-picked venues designed to deliver conservative outcomes.

While Trump did not create this system, he understood its potential—and used it with surgical efficiency. With McConnell guiding Senate rules and Leonard Leo coordinating nominations, Trump filled over 200 federal judgeships in his first term alone. Many were selected not for experience or even competence, but for their allegiance to a worldview: deregulatory, anti-democratic, and fiercely partisan. The bench became younger, more extreme, and more willing to distort precedent for political ends. Trump did not view the courts as neutral arbiters. He viewed them as instruments of personal power. Rulings in his favor were expected. Rulings against him were treated as betrayal. He didn't build the weapon—he loaded it, he picked the targets, he aimed it and, confident of the outcome, he fired it.

His second term deepened the damage. Once back in office, Trump refused to request additional judgeships despite mounting litigation across nearly every federal domain: civil rights, immigration, whistleblower protections, regulatory collapse, environmental deregulation, and economic sabotage. He knew that delay served his interests. His legal teams targeted circuits with known ideological leanings—especially the Fifth Circuit, in Texas—to obtain favorable injunctions or obstruct oversight. Venue shopping became his governing strategy. Cases that threatened executive power or revealed corruption were quietly assigned to judges who had already signaled their loyalty. Trump's first term was judicial weaponization. His second is judicial manipulation by design.

The failure to expand the courts was not a passive oversight. It was a structural collapse. As the republic grew more populous, more complex, and more governed by federal law, the judiciary remained fixed in size—too small to enforce accountability, too fragile to resist manipulation. Judges faced dockets they could not clear, timelines they could not honor, and areas of law they could not meaningfully oversee. In that vacuum, power became selective. Large corporations, powerful political actors, and executive allies found ways to move swiftly through a bottlenecked system. For everyone else, justice slowed, stalled, or vanished. What survived was not the rule of law—but a caste system of access.

We now rebuild from that neglect. Judicial expansion is not a radical demand. It is the next chapter of constitutional maintenance—a renewal once routine, now long delayed. Just as previous generations responded to postwar growth, territorial expansion, and industrial transformation, we must respond to the twenty-first century realities of digital governance, global interdependence, multinational commerce, real-time information, and increasingly complex law. Congress must authorize new judgeships—not all at once, but through a decade of scaled appointments guided by caseload, reversal rates, and delay. This is not court-packing. It is capacity restoration. By spanning administrations, fairness is not guaranteed—but it is possible. The Constitution does not prescribe a number of courts. It prescribes a judiciary purpose. And that purpose, equal justice under law, can and must be restored.

But numbers alone will not save us. A functioning court requires more than judges—it needs the people who make rulings possible: clerks, researchers, translators, schedulers, and support staff who move each case forward. Without them, dockets back up, errors multiply, and delay becomes default. But people cannot succeed without tools. Many courts still lack modern filing systems. Hearings go unrecorded. Rulings are delayed not for lack of law, but for lack of infrastructure. Entire decisions remain locked behind PACER, a paywalled system that charges the public to access its own legal record. A judiciary worthy of a democracy must be staffed, equipped, and transparent. That requires investment in both the hands that do the work and the systems that make that work endure.

We must also ask: where will the additional judges come from? The legal profession holds the answer—but only if we widen the pipeline. For too long, judicial appointments have favored prosecutors, corporate litigators, and ideologically-groomed clerks. That must change. We need civil rights lawyers, public defenders, legal aid attorneys, and immigration advocates on the bench—judges who understand not only precedent, but the lived experience of those the law often forgets. Expanding the courts gives us the opportunity to diversify not just demographically, but professionally and philosophically. A truly representative judiciary is not ornamental. It is constitutional. It reclaims what was denied.

But absence is not just a matter of exclusion. It is also the product of discouragement. Many who spend their careers defending the vulnerable never see the federal bench as a path they are meant to pursue. The confirmation process penalizes advocacy. The culture of judicial prestige favors corporate polish over public service. The clerkships, mentors, and institutional endorsements that ease the way for one kind of lawyer are often closed to others. And even those who could rise may hesitate, believing—often rightly—that entry requires the soft betrayal of one's principles. If we want judges who come from public service, we must build a judiciary that honors it.

The courts must not only grow. They must grow in ways that reflect the nation they serve. For decades, judicial imbalance has been geographic as well as ideological. Districts with diverse populations and heavy caseloads—California, New York, Illinois, Arizona—have faced persistent understaffing, while conservative strongholds such as Texas have received disproportionate judicial appointments. Nowhere is this clearer than along the southern border, where the federal judiciary oversees an enormous volume of immigration-related litigation—yet not one federal district in California, Arizona, New Mexico, or Texas includes a judge with a background in immigration defense. This imbalance is not incidental. It was engineered. A true restoration of justice requires rebalancing this map—not for partisan gain, but to restore fairness. Equal justice cannot exist if access depends on geography or if litigants are rewarded for knowing which courtroom to shop.

Restoration also demands that we repair the timeline of justice. Courts must not only deliver rulings—they must deliver them in time to matter. Legal delay, once rare, has become routine—at times, a strategy. Whistleblower complaints stall for years. Immigration appeals linger unresolved. Civil rights violations go unanswered while lives move on or fall apart. When justice arrives too late, it does not restore. It cannot repair the job lost, the home foreclosed, the child deported, the truth buried. It merely documents the damage. Expanding judicial capacity allows courts to respond within meaningful timeframes—to prevent harm, not just record it. A working judiciary is not one that eventually speaks. It is one that speaks in time.

But even justice delivered on time is meaningless if the doors are closed. Access to justice does not begin in the courtroom. It begins with the ability to enter. For millions of Americans, that access is constrained by distance, language, cost, or digital exclusion. Rural communities face court deserts where travel to hearings requires days off work. Low-income litigants navigate complex procedures without legal aid or face filing fees they cannot afford. Language barriers remain widespread, and disability accommodations uneven. These are not marginal problems. They are structural denials—policy choices that define who may speak and who must remain silent. A restored judiciary must embrace universal e-filing, remote hearing access, multilingual resources, and the expansion of legal aid as democratic infrastructure. The right to be heard must not depend on wealth or geography. It must depend only on being an American.

Critics will call this court-packing. They will argue that adding judges threatens judicial independence. But independence is not defined by austerity. It is defined by function. A court that cannot act in time, cannot hear the people, and cannot serve the law is not neutral—it is broken. Paralysis does not protect democracy. It enables its slow undoing. The founders never intended the judiciary to be frozen in size or ideology. They empowered Congress to adjust it—to ensure the courts could serve a growing republic, a power used for two centuries. It stopped only when expansion no longer served one party. What we propose is not rupture. It is necessary resumption. The true anomaly is not expansion. It is the refusal to expand while justice fell out of reach for all but the privileged, the wealthy, and the well-connected.

To make reform durable, we must codify it as a democratic norm. Judicial expansion should not depend on partisan will or crisis moments. Congress should establish a nonpartisan Judicial Capacity Review Commission empowered to assess caseloads, reversal rates, and systemic delays every ten years—and to recommend expansions, redistributions, or realignments accordingly. Its proceedings must be public, its metrics standardized, and its authority grounded in data, not ideology. The judiciary must evolve as the nation does, not as power permits. This model draws on the Census and the military base review process: regular, transparent, and protected from partisan capture. If the courts are to serve democracy, they must be structured to withstand it.

Just as we expand the courts, we must also protect the process by which judges are nominated and confirmed. Over the last two decades, partisan abuse of the Senate's advice-and-consent role has eroded public confidence in judicial legitimacy. Never again can a Supreme Court seat be held vacant for ten months, nor filled in three weeks. The selection, nomination, vetting, and confirmation of judges must neither be rushed nor delayed for partisan gain. To restore legitimacy, Congress must enforce time-bound confirmation procedures, require transparency in the nominee pipeline, and eliminate procedural tools designed to obstruct without accountability.

The public has a right to see how judges are chosen—and to ensure that merit, not loyalty, defines the process. Reforming the pipeline is not an attack on independence. It is how independence is made real again.

But even these safeguards are not enough. We must confront the deeper truth: that any system can be corrupted if the public ceases to defend it. Courts are vulnerable not only to bad law and partisan strategy, but to quiet neglect. Once public faith collapses, illegitimacy follows. To prevent this, the judiciary must not remain isolated. Judges, courts, and cases must be visible, accountable, and integrated into the civic life of the nation. Public legal education must go beyond explaining court procedure. It must teach people how to use the law—how to file, to challenge, to appear, to appeal. An accessible court system means nothing if people believe it exists only for the rich, the corporate, or the connected. An informed people do not fear the law. They claim it. Use it. And ultimately, trust and respect it.

Some will say this is futile—that the next authoritarian will simply undo it all. But that is the logic of surrender. True reform builds not perfection, but resistance. If Republicans attempt another judicial hijacking, let them face not a weakened institution but a fortified one: expanded, transparent, balanced, and supported by the people it serves. Let the cost of corruption rise. Let the structure be so visible, so just, and so broadly supported that to attack it is to expose one's own illegitimacy. We cannot make democracy immune to sabotage. But we can make it resilient.

This is our task now. Not to punish the past, but to honor what has worked—and to prevent its collapse from ever repeating. We expand the courts not because we lost faith in them, but because we believe they can still serve the nation they were designed to protect. We do it not to seize power, but to return it to the people—by restoring timely, fair, and meaningful access to justice in every region, for every person, under every law. This is not a partisan cause. It is constitutional stewardship. If democracy is to survive, the courts must be strong enough to carry it. And strong enough to defend it.

The last few generations built a judiciary that could be captured—and now is. We must now build one that cannot be. That means embedding reform into law, practice, and public expectation. It means acknowledging past mistakes and correcting them with care. And it means abandoning the fantasy that courts are self-correcting. No institution is. They function because we sustain them. They serve because we insist upon it. But above all, they endure because Congress fulfills its constitutional duty to maintain a fair, functioning, and independent judiciary. The republic we rebuild will be known, in part, by the quality of its judges—and by whether they were empowered to serve justice or perverted to serve private and political interests. This will be our legacy to choose.

A broken judiciary cannot be repaired by sentiment. It must be rebuilt with precision. The collapse we face is not the result of one failure but of many: judicial scarcity, professional imbalance, geographic distortion, procedural delay, and civic exclusion. The courts did not fall behind by accident. They were allowed to wither —starved of resources, captured by partisans, shielded from scrutiny, and sealed from the public they were meant to serve. Restoration is not a return to some lost golden age. It is a conscious act of national repair.

We must expand the courts to meet the scale of modern law and life. We must open the judiciary to public defenders, legal aid attorneys, immigration lawyers—those who have stood beside people the law forgets. We must rebalance judicial geography, accelerate proceedings so justice arrives in time, and fund the full architecture of access: remote hearings, multilingual services, and universal e-filing. We must institutionalize periodic, nonpartisan review to adapt capacity to need. We must fix the nomination pipeline—so no court seat is stolen by delay or filled in a rush. And we must teach the public not just what the law says, but how to use it.

Each of these reforms is vital. Together, they form a single commitment: that justice in America will not be ornamental, inaccessible, or reserved for the few. It will be lived. It will be functional. And it will be fair. But for these reforms to take root, we must elect those who believe in the purpose of the courts—not as weapons of ideology, but as engines of equality. The American people are not powerless in the face of legal decay. Through those we choose to represent us, we write the laws. We structure the courts. We decide whether justice is a promise or a performance.

For too long, we chose leaders who served the powerful and left the public with delay, denial, and decay. That, too, was a choice—and now we choose differently. Let future generations look back and see not the era when the courts collapsed, but the moment they were rebuilt. Let them inherit not our paralysis, but our resolve. A republic of laws must be equipped to deliver them. Justice must not be what survives the system. It must be what the system guarantees—swiftly, fairly, and without exception.

17

TRANSPARENCY REFORM AND PUBLIC ACCESS TO INFORMATION
HOW SECRECY, PRIVATIZATION, AND SILENCE ARE DISMANTLING THE PEOPLE'S RIGHT TO KNOW

---◆---

"Justice must not only be done, but must also be seen to be done."
— Lord Hewart, *R v Sussex Justices, Ex parte McCarthy* (1924)

Justice in America was meant to be visible. Not as performance, but as principle. From its inception, the legal system stood apart from the monarchy it replaced: not shrouded in secrecy, not enforced in silence, but conducted in public, for all to see. Trials were open. Verdicts were explained. Arguments were made aloud, in the presence of the people. This was not just a matter of custom. It was a declaration of legitimacy. A nation that would govern by law must first prove that law is real and rightful—to friend and critic alike—not behind closed doors, but in the full light of day.

The Constitution, as first ratified, contained no guarantee of transparency. Article III established a Supreme Court and permitted Congress to create inferior courts, but said nothing about public access, published opinions, or accountability to the people. It created institutions, not rights. The powers to tax, enforce, and adjudicate were enumerated—but no freedoms were named. This omission sparked alarm. Americans who had lived under British repression knew that power unchecked by visibility would inevitably turn abusive. Without public speech, public press, and public oversight, liberty becomes performance—not practice. In the years between ratification and the Bill of Rights, critics warned that the new government could jail dissenters, silence the press, and enforce laws in darkness. They were not imagining a threat. They were remembering one. The First Amendment, added in 1791, was not an ornament. It was a barricade. It guaranteed not just the right to speak—but the right to see, to know, to challenge, and to judge. It was the antidote to monarchy in 1791. And it remains our clearest protection against its return—disguised not in crowns, but in secrecy, silence, and unchecked power.

Nowhere was this protection more essential than in the courtroom. From the start of the republic, trials were presumed open. Courtrooms were places not only of judgment but of public witness. Early state constitutions codified the right to observe legal proceedings. Newspapers printed full accounts of cases, and citizens came to listen, not just to verdicts but to arguments. Even when the law was unjust, its delivery had to be public. That visibility did not guarantee fairness, but it made injustice visible—and thus challengeable. The public record was not just a tool of accountability. It was a declaration that democracy was active, watchful, and alive in the hands of the people.

Over time, this tradition deepened. The requirement that judicial decisions be explained in writing, the emergence of appellate review, and the legal doctrine of stare decisis—the principle that courts must follow prior rulings—together reinforced a basic expectation: that the law must show its work, and that each judgment must be traceable to the reasoning and record that produced it. Even in complex systems, this visibility endured. Judges published opinions. Dockets were available for review. The people could trace the logic of justice, or at least interrogate its failures. Transparency was not a nicety. It was the only assurance that justice meant more than obedience.

But the balance between authority and access has always been unstable. Even as transparency norms spread, power pushed back. In times of war, protest, or unrest, courts closed ranks. Journalists were barred. Records were sealed. And over the course of the twentieth century, legal transparency came to depend less on tradition and more on statute. The most important of these statutes was the Freedom of Information Act of 1966 (FOIA)—a law passed not in comfort, but in the shadow of Vietnam and institutional secrecy.

FOIA was an answer to a growing democratic crisis. It created a legal right to access the workings of the federal government, including the justice system. It forced agencies to explain decisions, release records, and justify denials. It was strengthened after Watergate, resisted by every administration since, and gradually weakened by reinterpretation and neglect. Even so, it remained one of the last tools available to citizens trying to understand how they were governed—and by whom.

While every administration chafed against FOIA, Republican administrations—from Reagan onward—made weakening it a governing priority. What began as reluctance to obey became strategy to weaken. National security became a pretext for silence. Proprietary data, a shield for privatization. By the time of George W. Bush, the Department of Justice was encouraging agencies to withhold information preemptively and promising to defend those decisions in court. The legal standard shifted from "access unless prohibited" to "secrecy unless forced."

Trump did not simply resist transparency. He reversed it. During his first term, the DOJ allowed political appointees to screen FOIA requests involving controversial matters—a practice that subverted the legal obligation to disclose information based on law, not political sensitivity. Requests were delayed, narrowed, or denied not because they failed statutory standards, but because they might embarrass senior officials or expose misconduct. Immigration hearings were held in privately owned spaces that barred press access. Federal court functions, from detention to case management, were handled through opaque contracts with firms that refused to disclose even the terms of engagement. The justice system became a private service, selectively illuminated—and easily concealed.

But it was his second term that marked the true break. With the creation of the Department of Government Efficiency (DOGE), Trump built a new architecture of state power—an agency that combined legal enforcement, surveillance coordination, and administrative control, all beyond the reach of the public. DOGE, now likely defunct, never disclosed its contracts, identified its vendors, or complied with transparency laws. For months, it managed surveillance systems, directed interagency enforcement, accessed sensitive data, and influenced court scheduling—all without oversight, review, or redress. Its existence was not merely a violation of transparency. It was a rejection of the foundational principle that government must answer to the people it governs.

Transparency was never accidental. It was a design—a system of visibility built to constrain power. That design is what the Republican Party dismantled, and what Trump discarded entirely. No institution serves the people by accident. It does so by design, or not at all. When courts operate in shadow and enforcement is outsourced to secrecy, the result is not merely corruption. It is submission without recourse.

The remedy begins with law. Congress must strengthen FOIA to apply to any entity performing a public function—including contractors, subcontractors, and intermediaries executing federal judicial operations. There must be fixed response timelines, enforceable penalties for delay, and automatic publication requirements for contracts, audits, surveillance protocols, and administrative rules. Exemptions must be narrowed, and claims of national security must undergo independent review. The burden of secrecy must be on government to justify, not the public to overcome.

But statutes alone are not enough. The judiciary must reform its own practices. Every federal court should maintain a public registry of administrative decisions, contract awards, recusal notices, and docket changes. Courts must disclose how technology is used to schedule, prioritize, or flag cases. Where judicial processes are digitized, the public must retain access. Paywalls on opinions and docket searches must be abolished. The people should not have to pay to see the law that governs them.

Yet even a fully reformed transparency system cannot prevent the deeper threat: the dismantling of government itself. In Trump's second term, DOGE was not merely a secrecy machine. It was a liquidation platform. Agencies like NOAA, the National Weather Service, the NIH, the Department of Education, and even Social Security were rumored to be on the chopping block—not to be reformed, but to be sold. Enforcement powers and life-sustaining services were marked for transfer to contractors, data firms, and partisan allies. This was not privatization in the classic sense. It was the auctioning of the republic.

Privatizing government functions does not merely change how services are delivered—it changes who they serve. It removes accountability, rewards abuse, fragments responsibility, and conceals harm. It normalizes secrecy, weakens democratic control, and erodes constitutional rights. It drains public institutions, encourages corruption, and betrays the very purpose of self-government. These are not theoretical concerns. They are structural consequences. When profit governs power, justice becomes a commodity. And when public functions are auctioned off, democracy is not reformed—it is replaced.

We have seen what happens when those dangers are realized. Health care became a for-profit industry—and a cured patient became a lost customer. Prisons became private—and high recidivism rates drove shareholder returns. Education was turned into a profit center—where cutting faculty, inflating class sizes, and eliminating needed programs improved the balance sheet but degraded the public trust. In each case, the system was re-engineered to reward harm. Profit flowed not from serving the public, but from failing it. That is the wrong end of the javelin. And it did not benefit patients, inmates, or students. It enriched investors—those least affected by the damage, and most rewarded by its continuation.

Some services may be privately delivered but must remain publicly regulated: utilities, communications, infrastructure. Others must remain directly accountable to Congress and the people: veterans' care, public health, prisons, the military, food and drug safety, Social Security, and the machinery of justice itself. These are not market functions. They are democratic obligations.

True transparency does not mean absolute exposure. It respects boundaries where real harm would result—when naming minors, revealing trade secrets, disclosing national security operations, or exposing private identifying details. But those exceptions must be rare, temporary, and reviewable. They must not become the rule. The aim of transparency is not exposure for its own sake, but accountability through visibility. Secrecy may sometimes be justified. Silence, never.

Transparency is not just a policy that abolishes this silence. It is a posture—a declaration that those in power remain answerable to those who granted it. It is how a self-governing people exercises civic sight: the ability to see who governs, how, and for what purpose. Without that sight, oversight becomes fiction, and freedom becomes theater. Transparency is not what makes democracy easy. It is what makes democracy possible.

To defend democracy, we must see how it is being taken. We must see who profits from concealment. We must see which institutions function in truth, and which only pretend. A free people cannot hold accountable what they cannot witness. And they cannot protect the rule of law if the rule of law retreats behind locked doors.

What we call transparency is not about data. It is about power. The courts do not govern by force. They govern by consent. And consent depends on trust—trust that cannot survive what the eye cannot verify. If we cannot see how justice works, then we cannot know whom it serves. And if we do not know whom it serves, it does not serve justice at all.

18

THE RULE OF LAW IS WHAT WE BUILD IT TO BE

WHY JUDICIAL REFORM IS NOT AN ATTACK—IT IS THE CONSTITUTION'S COMPLETION.

"A government of laws, and not of men."
    —John Adams

Law without legitimacy is not law—it is theater cloaked in precedent. The judiciary was never meant to rule the people but to serve the republic—to stand as the final check when every other institution bent. Yet today, Americans increasingly see the courts not as guardians of the law, but as instruments of power. A judge's ruling no longer commands consent by its reasoning, but instead, suspicion by its source. And that collapse of trust is not perception alone. It is rooted in design defects, strategic manipulation, and the unchecked corruption of power cloaked in robes.

The most dangerous moment for any institution is when the public ceases to believe in its purpose. That moment now looms for the courts. From the manipulation of case assignment in Amarillo, to the ethical impunity of Justices Thomas and Alito, to the shadow docket's silent reversals of national law, the judiciary has become a maze of secrecy, loyalty, and delay. The promise of impartial justice is still spoken. But what is seen, again and again, is deference to power, protection of privilege, and rulings whose impact arrives without explanation, without attribution, and without shame.

The Framers designed a judiciary of independence—but they assumed virtue. They left no binding code of ethics. They imagined life tenure would protect conscience, not entrench ideology. They never conceived of single-judge districts issuing national decrees or lifetime appointments weaponized for partisan rule. The blueprint was brilliant—but unfinished: brilliant in aspiration, but incomplete in constraint. It trusted in the honor of future judges and the vigilance of Congress. Today, both are in crisis. And what that unfinished design left vulnerable, bad faith actors have learned to exploit without limit.

The modern Republican Party did not simply capture the courts. It redesigned the path to capture. It blocked expansion, delayed confirmation, and rewrote Senate rules to guarantee control. It denied a hearing for Merrick Garland, then rushed Amy Coney Barrett through confirmation days before a national election. It empowered the Federalist Society to select nominees and ensured those appointments would outlast public opposition. This was no accident of judicial evolution—it was the goal. The result is not judicial conservatism. It is judicial domination—structural, strategic, and generational.

Trump inherited that apparatus and made it personal. In his first term, the courts were tools of advance—delivering injunctions, suspending oversight, and validating ideology. In his second, they are tools of evasion—stalling prosecutions, shielding cronies, delaying justice until accountability fades. His filings flood the docket not to win, but to exhaust—a strategy to delay justice until the cost of continuation outweighs the hope of resolution. His loyalists are not confirmed for integrity, but for obedience. And every unsigned order from the Supreme Court that bends to his will is taken not as law, but as loyalty confirmed.

The effects of this sabotage are measured not just in rulings, but in consequences deferred. Federal dockets are overwhelmed. Whistleblower cases stall. Immigration proceedings vanish into administrative backlog. The Fifth Circuit and Amarillo courts deliver sweeping injunctions without oversight. Meanwhile, Americans are denied timely hearings, accessible records, and judges drawn by impartial procedure. Delay becomes denial. Secrecy becomes normal. And the ideal of equal justice recedes into illusion.

What defenders of the status quo call "judicial independence" is, too often, impunity by design. A judge who cannot be investigated is not protected—he is unbound. A system that hides dockets, delays opinions, and operates in silence is not cautious—it is captured. And when courts become predictable by geography, immune to ethical review, and permitted to rule without signature or reason, the question is no longer whether justice is done. It is whether law itself still governs at all.

The six reforms we propose do not threaten the judiciary—they rescue it. They do not politicize the courts—they shield them from politics already inside. Judicial Assignment Reform ends venue manipulation and restores randomness. Judicial Ethics Reform applies the same code to every federal judge, including the nine with the most power. Court Transparency and FOIA Reform dismantle secrecy, abolish paywalls, and make the workings of law accessible in fact, not just theory. Term Limits for Generational Balance end lifetime lock-in. Lower Court Expansion restores capacity and fairness. Each reform is necessary. Together, they are urgent.

We group these not as isolated fixes, but as pillars of democratic function. Visibility and access are restored through transparency, public hearings, and open records. Structural integrity returns through assignment randomization and lower court expansion.

Generational legitimacy is repaired through eighteen-year term limits—ensuring no Justice governs from the grave. And trust—the core of all judicial power—is rebuilt through enforceable ethics, recusal rules, and a return to law as a service—not as a spectacle.

This is not rebellion against the Constitution. It is fidelity to its purpose. The document does not forbid reform. It demands it. Article III created the courts but left Congress the responsibility to shape them. It is not judicial overreach we fear—it is legislative neglect that allowed this decay. The oath taken by every senator, every representative, and every judge is to the Constitution. Not to the president. Not to the party. And not to power.

If we do not act, law will not hold. The courts will not save democracy. They will bury it—beneath delay, behind curtains and without name. Already, rulings arrive unsigned. Evidence vanishes into sealed dockets. Billionaires vacation with Justices while cases await review. The public watches, not in outrage, but weariness. And that weariness is what authoritarianism feeds upon. Not belief. Not resistance. But collapse into resignation.

Yet the courts cannot be saved from within. No robe will rise to demand less power. No bench will volunteer for oversight. Reform must come from Congress. And Congress will only act if the public demands it—loudly, persistently, and without apology. Judges are not monarchs. The robe is not sacred—it is a symbol of trust, not supremacy. And the laws they interpret were written by the same people who empowered us to correct what fails. It is our duty now to finish what the Framers began.

Let us remember: what the Constitution gave us was not a final design, but a living structure. It anticipated growth, adaptation, and repair. And it trusted us with the task of completing it. That task cannot wait. The courts now stand at the edge of irrelevance. What remains is either a restoration of trust—or its irreversible loss. And with that loss, the rule of law does not collapse in one blow. It bleeds out—silently, invisibly, and then suddenly, permanently, it is gone.

To hold the courts is to hold the line between governance and tyranny. But we do not hold it with reverence. We hold it with action —with reform, with legislation, with the unyielding insistence that public power serve public good. If we want judges who answer to law, we must build courts that cannot be captured. If we want rulings that bind the powerful, we must expose those who would rule in silence. This is not optional. It is urgent. It is the foundation on which democracy stands.

The republic we inherit will be defined by the judiciary we allow. Let us no longer allow what we know to be broken. Let us finish the structure. Let us demand transparency, restore trust, and pass laws that end impunity before it becomes permanent. In this chapter of American history, the courts will either become the last defense of democracy—or the first casualties of its collapse. The choice is ours. And the time is now.

We are not powerless. We are the authors now. And the integrity of the law will rise—or fall—by what we do next.

PART IV. REBUILDING AN INFORMED PUBLIC

HOW DISINFORMATION, MEDIA COLLAPSE, AND CIVIC NEGLECT BROKE THE PUBLIC—AND WHAT IT WILL TAKE TO REBUILD AN INFORMED DEMOCRACY

"Freedom is the freedom to say that two plus two make four. If that is granted, all else follows."
— George Orwell, *1984*

A democracy does not begin at the ballot box. It begins in the mind. Self-government requires more than freedom—it requires understanding of institutions, laws, and facts. The Framers placed their faith in "We the People" not because the people were always wise, but because wisdom could be cultivated: by access to facts, by free discussion, by civic education. The First Amendment was never meant to sanctify chaos, nor the press to profit from its debris. These freedoms were designed to make knowledge a public good. When that knowledge collapses, so does the republic built upon it.

The collapse is now. Americans are no longer divided by ideology alone but by incompatible realities. A single event—an election, a pandemic, a protest—can generate two entirely separate universes of explanation, neither of which can speak to the other. This is not the result of too much speech. It is the result of speech weaponized—stripped of trust, detached from verification, and driven through systems that reward outrage, not truth. The tools we built to inform the public now fracture it. And the consequences reach beyond opinion: they threaten the very possibility of consent.

Without a shared baseline of truth, negotiation, governance, and even disagreement become impossible. The law once recognized this danger. The Fairness Doctrine, the Red Lion ruling, public interest broadcast requirements—these were not constraints on liberty but conditions for democracy. They acknowledged that when communication channels are few and powerful, truth must be protected structurally. But since 1987, the legal architecture that once defended shared reality has been dismantled. Section 230 gave platforms immunity without responsibility. Campaign transparency was gutted by dark money loopholes. And the courts, while upholding the letter of free speech, abandoned its democratic function.

The history of American disinformation is long, but never before has it been so fast, profitable, and intractable. Lies are not new. But the speed at which they travel, the systems that reward them, and the structural inability of truth to catch up—these are uniquely modern. The Founders worried about faction. They did not foresee algorithm. What once moved by pamphlet and rumor now circulates globally in seconds, curated by artificial intelligences that optimize for engagement, not enlightenment. This is no longer a story of bad actors. It is the architecture that enables them.

And yet those bad actors have learned exactly how to exploit the breakage. The Republican Party, facing demographic decline and ideological rejection, has made disinformation a central pillar of its survival. From the repeal of the Fairness Doctrine to the amplification of election lies, from state censorship of history classrooms to digital threats against social media moderation, the strategy is clear: saturate the field with falsehoods, destroy the possibility of verification, and rule through confusion. A democracy without truth cannot hold a majority. And that, for a party unable to win one, is the point.

No one proved this more than Donald Trump. He did not lie in shadows; he lied as spectacle—relentlessly, shamelessly, and on record. He understood that in an unguarded information ecosystem, contradiction is not weakness. It is dominance. He lied to dominate headlines, flood channels, and drown rebuttal. His lies were not personal defects. They were tools of power—repeated until they replaced memory, belief, and trust. He governed through distortion because the systems meant to correct him—media, education, platform, party—had already failed. He was not the collapse of truth. He was its revealer.

But the greater betrayal did not come from the saboteurs. It came from the sentries who stood aside. The legacy press, the platform billionaires, the institutions charged with safeguarding public understanding—many walked away. Some for profit, as clicks replaced credibility. Some for protection, seeking access to power rather than accountability. Some out of fear, confusing neutrality with neutrality toward lies. They claimed objectivity while giving oxygen to authoritarian spin. And in their silence or their cynicism, they let the public drift—confused, exhausted, and increasingly ashamed of not knowing what was real. Or worse, convinced they did know—certain their vision was reality, and that all others must be lies.

The result is not just political polarization. It is epistemic collapse. The average citizen now swims through noise, mistaking performance for principle, opinion for proof. Misinformation is not merely annoying. It is disabling. It undermines civic confidence, depresses turnout, radicalizes belief, and erodes the shared space in which democratic negotiation can occur. There is no path to renewal that does not pass through the reconstruction of public knowledge. And yet the work will be hard. Because the problem is not just what people believe—it is the systems that shape belief.

These reforms will not be easy. There will be ferocious resistance—by those who profit from lies, by those who mistake accountability for censorship, and by those who have built their identity around grievance and suspicion. The platforms will object. The pundits will cry foul. The partisans will threaten legal retaliation. And the exhausted center, unsure whom to trust, will hesitate. We do not promise to fix everything. We cannot address every failure. What we offer in the chapters ahead are three structural reforms—platform transparency, media fairness, and civic education—without which nothing else can endure.

Truth is not a luxury. It is the scaffolding of democracy. And today, that scaffolding is broken. Rebuilding it will not restore every fracture, but it will give us ground to stand on. Without it, we are not debating policy. We are debating reality. And if we cannot agree on what is real, we cannot defend what is right. These reforms do not silence speech. They strengthen consent. They do not tell us what to think. They make it possible to think together. That is what a republic requires. That is what we must now rebuild.

To rebuild an informed public, we begin with visibility. The algorithms that shape thought and behavior must no longer operate as trade secrets immune from public oversight. These systems determine what we see, what we trust, and who we believe. That power—concentrated in a handful of private platforms—rivals the authority of any government. And yet unlike the press, they have no editorial board. Unlike utilities, they have no regulatory framework. Unlike public schools, they are accountable to no community. If they continue to shape our reality, they must be made visible to it.

What these platforms optimize for is not truth. It is time. The longer a user remains on the feed, the more ads they see—and the more fractional payments flow to shareholders and billionaires.

Engagement is currency. Rage is profitable. Lies that keep you scrolling are worth more than facts that let you walk away. Every second of attention is another fraction of a cent to the platform's owners. That is the economy: not of information, but of extraction—pulling not oil or ore, but attention, behavior, and belief.

But engagement does more than make money. It builds precision maps of the human soul. These platforms know more about you than your mother does. Dog person or cat person. Romance or true crime. Gay, straight, or still deciding. Apartment or house. Married, single, conservative, radical, vaccinated, grieving, angry, alone. This is not advertising metadata. It is identity intelligence, and it is sold—openly or covertly—to anyone who pays. Campaigns, corporations, foreign states. This data determines who can be persuaded, converted, enraged, or recruited. Not just for sales. For power. And we give it away freely, with every click, swipe, and share.

Transparency is not censorship. It is the minimum standard of democratic infrastructure. When decisions about truth, content, or amplification are made by algorithms, those algorithms must be auditable. When false political ads are sold, they must be disclosed. When coordinated disinformation campaigns are detected—foreign or domestic—they must be exposed in real time, not years later through congressional subpoenas. Platforms must be required to share how they decide what is promoted, what is demoted, and who decides. In a self-governing society, the information infrastructure must be subject to the public it shapes.

Broadcast media, too, must return to its public role. For decades, conservative talk radio and partisan cable news have operated without constraint—not because the First Amendment demands it, but because regulation was dismantled. The repeal of the Fairness Doctrine was not inevitable. It was a choice. And the results are plain: networks built not to inform but to inflame, anchors who trade journalism for propaganda, audiences cultivated to distrust everything but the feed. Fairness, disclosure, and truthfulness are not violations of liberty. They are conditions for it.

As citizens in a democracy, we demand a media system in which public resources carry public obligations. If broadcasters profit from the public airwaves, they owe the public honest content. If cable monopolies carry networks of deceit, they must be held to standards of disclosure and correction. If streaming platforms become dominant news sources, they must adopt clear policies to distinguish journalism from manipulation. These are not infringements on speech. They are frameworks for civic survival.

But even if platforms were transparent and broadcasters were fair, the work would remain incomplete without a public able to interpret what it sees. That is the work of civic education—not as sentimental enrichment, but as essential civic infrastructure. A republic cannot function if its citizens do not understand how it works. And yet in state after state, civics is underfunded, distorted, or replaced by ideologically sanitized curricula that teach grievance, not government. Other nations confront their past to protect their future. In Germany, students study the Holocaust and the Final Solution—not for shame, but for vigilance. In Australia, broadcasters and cultural institutions routinely acknowledge the First Peoples of the land. The United States, by contrast, erases slavery, softens segregation, and buries its long record of exclusion and hate. We do not teach students how power works. Then we are surprised when power is misused.

Civic education must be reimagined for an era of epistemic warfare. This means not just teaching how a bill becomes a law, but how an idea becomes a belief—and how that belief can be tested, challenged, and changed. It means equipping students to identify disinformation, to recognize manipulated media, to ask who benefits from the lie. It means restoring pride not in blind patriotism, but in democratic participation—in voting, speaking, organizing, and protecting the republic. We cannot expect democracy to renew itself if we do not teach what democracy demands.

And we cannot stop with students. The damage inflicted by disinformation is not limited to the young. It has fractured families, isolated communities, and created entire cohorts of adults who feel ashamed of what they do not know. That shame breeds silence. That silence breeds manipulation. We need public campaigns—not of judgment, but of re-engagement. Public service announcements, civic workshops, adult education programs, or cross-partisan town halls must be funded and invited to take part. Libraries, universities, unions, and even faith communities must be enlisted. Civic knowledge must be lifelong, not front-loaded. And truth must be made welcoming again.

This is not cultural nostalgia. It is national defense. A public that cannot recognize propaganda is a public that can be ruled by it. A citizen who cannot distinguish evidence from assertion, fact from opinion, truth from spin, cannot defend their rights. An electorate trained to distrust every institution is ripe for capture by the one that promises to destroy them. The crisis of misinformation is not a glitch. It is the precondition for authoritarian rule. And the only answer to that crisis is structural, persistent, and public.

> "Those who can make you believe absurdities can make you commit atrocities." — Voltaire

We will be told this is too much. That regulation is censorship. That civic education is indoctrination. That transparency is a threat to innovation. These are not principled objections. They are tactics—deployed by those who profit from the collapse of public reason. But we do not need to control what people think. We need to restore the conditions under which thinking is possible. And we need to do it before democracy becomes not just uninformed—but undefended.

These reforms are only the beginning. They are not comprehensive. They do not address every platform, every media conglomerate, or every pathology of public discourse. But they are foundational. Without them, nothing else holds. Without transparency, we do not know what is shaping us. Without media fairness, we cannot discern who is lying. Without civic education, we have no tools to resist. Truth is not a relic. It is the infrastructure of consent. And rebuilding it is not a luxury. It is a moral and democratic necessity.

That work begins with education—but not only in textbooks or classrooms. Civic education must also restore the idea of public service—not as performance, but as principle. In a healthy democracy, two of the most meaningful paths a citizen can choose are military service and elected office. Yet both have been distorted. Public office is too often treated as the preserve of dynasties, celebrities, or the wealthy, when in truth it should be open to anyone of sound judgment and steady character. Nothing is more humbling—or more sacred—than to be entrusted by a community to speak and act on its behalf. We do not need the richest, the smartest, or the loudest. We need those who are willing to live their lives in service—to uphold the Constitution, advance the public good, and deliver, by their own hand, the blessings of liberty.

The same is true of military service. Its purpose may be national defense, but its byproducts—discipline, teamwork, courage, humility, and a purpose beyond self—are democratic virtues. We should speak of both forms of service not as sacrifice, but as contribution. Young people should be taught not only how government works, but how to join it. Not only what power is, but how to wield it with honor. A republic requires such citizens. And democracy cannot renew itself unless it deliberately forms them.

A republic cannot be rebuilt on fractured ground. The reforms we have outlined—platform transparency, media fairness, civic education—are not discrete fixes. They are the foundation of a shared reality. Without them, no policy endures, no vote is fully informed, and no truth can be trusted long enough to bind a people together. Democracy is not self-sustaining. It must be taught, renewed, defended, and made visible in the lives of those who serve it and live in it. If we fail to rebuild the public mind, no institution will save us. If we succeed, the republic does not merely survive. It begins again—on firmer, shared ground.

19

DISINFORMATION AND PLATFORM TRANSPARENCY

HOW DISINFORMATION BECAME INFRASTRUCTURE—AND WHAT WE MUST DO TO REBUILD THE PUBLIC MIND

---◆---

"If liberty means anything at all, it means the right to tell people what they do not want to hear."
— George Orwell

Democracy cannot survive without truth, yet the Constitution offers no guarantee that the truth will be heard. It presumes a people capable of reasoning, deciding, and governing—but leaves the architecture of their understanding to the nation itself. The First Amendment protects citizens from government censorship, not from being deceived. It safeguards dissent, not distortion. When private platforms—bigger than any newspaper, more engineered for compulsion than any public medium before—shape public knowledge by profit rather than principle, the people no longer govern with their minds. They react. And reaction is not self-government. It is how tyrants rise.

The liberty to speak is not the same as the power to amplify. A whisper in the park is not the same as an AI-fueled image of Kamala

Harris devouring puppies, reaching a million screens in an hour. Nor is a conversation between neighbors the same as a child's face twisted into synthetic pornography and circulated globally while platforms delay action, citing policy ambiguity. A republic must protect not only the right to speak but the right to not be destroyed by lies. When virality outweighs veracity, the informational commons collapses—and with it, the shared world democracy requires.

For most of American history, public speech carried public responsibility. Newspapers could be sued for defamation. Broadcasters were licensed under obligations to serve the public interest, to present opposing views, and to avoid false claims. Commercial speech faced regulation from the FTC, FDA, and FCC. Platforms that carried information—telephones, telegraphs, radio—were classified as common carriers or utilities. But in 1996, Section 230 of the Communications Decency Act changed that. It granted immunity to online platforms for content posted by users, even if the platform profited by promoting it.

That immunity was intended to encourage moderation, not to absolve responsibility. Platforms were supposed to be neutral hosts with the freedom to remove harmful content. But as traffic became profit and outrage became strategy, moderation declined. In the early 2010s, platforms like Facebook and Twitter did attempt to limit disinformation. They flagged false stories, worked with fact-checkers, and removed known lies. But political pressure mounted. After Trump's election, Facebook dismantled its integrity teams. By 2025, it had contributed more than one million dollars to Trump's second inauguration and quietly relaxed its moderation policies—not for ideology, but for protection: from regulation, from retribution, and from the wrath of a President who had made enemies of facts.

This decline was not technological. It was moral. These platforms once proved that moderation at scale was possible. They simply chose to stop. Facebook could suppress false vaccine claims in 2016. It now permits AI-generated images of miscarriages blamed on shots that never happened. X, formerly Twitter, once removed coordinated harassment campaigns. It now amplifies them—elevating rage, repackaging cruelty, and calling it "freedom." Platforms are not failing to act because they lack the tools. They are refusing to act because the lies now serve power and profit—and punishing truth is safer than risking access, ad revenue, or presidential revenge.

The erosion of platform responsibility coincided with the Republican Party's long campaign to delegitimize moderation itself —a campaign documented in congressional hearings, executive orders, and platform correspondence revealed in lawsuits and leaks. Fact-checking was framed as partisan bias, community standards as tyranny, and content warnings as censorship. In internal Facebook emails from 2017 to 2020, executives acknowledged altering moderation algorithms to avoid triggering conservative backlash, a shift reinforced by Republican threats of regulation and public accusations of bias. Right-wing media outlets like Fox News, Breitbart, OANN, and Truth Social built a narrative ecosystem rooted not in fact but grievance—linking conspiracy, resentment, and white identity politics into a self-reinforcing feed. By the mid-2010s, GOP-aligned firms such as Cambridge Analytica were harvesting Facebook data without consent and deploying it to suppress turnout among Black voters and manipulate belief through precision-targeted fear. The shift was no longer cultural. It was strategic. Disinformation had become infrastructure.

As the pressure escalated, tech platforms were no longer just bending to avoid conflict—they were being reshaped as tools of minority rule. By 2025, Facebook contributed over one million dollars to Trump's second inaugural committee and quietly eased its moderation policies—reducing visibility for independent journalism, withdrawing from fact-checking partnerships, and shifting internal priorities away from integrity enforcement. This was not business as usual. It was appeasement. The message to other platforms was unmistakable: compliance would buy survival, and integrity would invite retaliation. In a system where lies now served the state, truth became the liability.

Republicans now champion legislation against "deepfakes," but these laws increasingly appear designed not to protect the public, but to insulate the powerful. Under vague definitions, parody can be mistaken for impersonation, satire for defamation. Critics across the political spectrum have warned that such laws—while marketed as safeguards—may be used to shield political figures like Trump from ridicule, while leaving women, teens, and marginalized users exposed to AI-driven harassment, impersonation, and synthetic abuse. When laws prioritize reputational defense for elites over real harm suffered by the vulnerable, the result is not a safer digital public square. It is one where cruelty flows unchecked and power becomes untouchable.

But even without legislation, Trump's allies have found other ways to dominate speech—by taking over the platforms themselves. Elon Musk's transformation of Twitter into X has weaponized the largest town square on Earth. The reinstatement of banned accounts —white nationalists, conspiracy theorists, and harassment groups— was not random. It was a declaration: moderation is weakness, and anything short of total amplification is suppression. Musk's alliance with Trump is not commercial. It is ideological. Together, they have turned platform impunity into governance strategy—using algorithms to destroy private lives and drown dissent in targeted digital flood.

Truth Social completes the circuit. It is not a public square—it is a presidential broadcast channel disguised as social media. Trump no longer needs the White House briefing room. He governs through Truth Social, issuing policy signals, market nudges, holiday messages, and retaliatory threats from a platform he owns and controls. Tariffs are announced there. Easter messages appear only there. Market watchers decode cryptic posts for insider cues. There is no press pool, no follow-up, no correction. It is the purest form of unaccountable speech: a head of state speaking to his base, while the rest of the country listens in—helpless to verify, respond, or resist.

Together, Truth Social and the major platforms form a closed-loop amplification system. Trump does not need mass users on his own site. All it takes is one follower—ally or critic—to repost, and the message ricochets across Facebook, Instagram, X, Bluesky, Reddit, and beyond. Truths become tweets, memes become headlines, and every outrage—no matter how fringe—reaches tens of millions within hours. The result is a digital environment where no lie is ever isolated, and no truth ever catches up. When unaccountable speech is launched by a head of state and rebroadcast across platforms without challenge, disinformation is no longer a side effect. It becomes the infrastructure of uncontained power.

In this environment, Trump did not simply spread disinformation. He reorganized power around it. In 2016, he weaponized lies. In his first term, he punished truth. In 2020, he incited violence through falsehood. In 2024, he promised to silence dissent—and in his second term, he is doing it. He has codified the machinery of digital unaccountability, ensuring that what was once viral is now official. He has reinstated banned propagandists, sidelined investigative scrutiny, criminalized parody, and partnered with private platforms to remake public reality in his image—and worse, in his voice. This is not free speech. It is coerced illusion.

Trump's first term laid the groundwork: he issued executive orders against Section 230, threatened to revoke broadcast licenses, and pressured Facebook and Twitter to stop fact-checking his lies. He slashed funding for scientific communication, erased climate data, and dismantled pandemic warning systems—while spreading falsehoods about masks, bleach, and vaccines. He accused journalists of treason, sued his critics, and fostered an atmosphere where truth became not just inconvenient, but dangerous. By 2020, his campaign was deploying manipulated video, disinformation influencers, and state-linked botnets. He wasn't trying to win arguments with better facts. He was trying to make it impossible to know what's true at all. By flooding the public sphere with lies, distortions, and distractions, he wore people down—confusing them, exhausting them, and making truth seem like just one opinion among many. This wasn't a debate. It was a strategy to sever the public's grip on reality—so power could operate without resistance. Reality wasn't just contested. It was crowded out.

The 2020 campaign culminated in catastrophe. "Stop the Steal" wasn't a slogan—it was a pretext. The lies of electoral fraud were spread across every platform, boosted by official channels and algorithmic preference. Twitter flagged the claims. Facebook debated them. But neither stopped the spread. The insurrection on January 6 was born in these feeds, organized in private groups, and incited by a President who knew what he was doing. This wasn't the failure of platforms. It was their use-case. Trump had trained the system to reward the very content that democracy cannot survive.

By 2024, disinformation wasn't an accessory to Trump's campaign. It was the campaign. He ran not on policy but on retribution—promising to silence the liars, imprison the leakers, pardon the loyal, and purge the unfaithful. He shared AI-generated videos smearing Kamala Harris, Gretchen Whitmer, and Joe Biden with fabricated quotes, manipulated audio, and deepfake images. He praised efforts to crack down on memes and hinted at prosecuting parody as impersonation. Behind the scenes, bot networks linked to his PACs flooded the digital commons with fake headlines posing as local news. It wasn't a campaign of persuasion. It was an all-out war on truth. And it worked.

In his second term, Trump institutionalized the digital autocracy. Facebook, having donated $1 million to his inauguration, was rewarded with hands-off treatment as it quietly relaxed its moderation guidelines. DOJ loyalists investigated critics under vague pretexts of disinformation, fraud, or national security violations. Public media was gutted: NPR and PBS were stripped of funding, dismissed as biased relics of a liberal era. In their place, a federally subsidized "truth channel" was launched—disguised as news but designed for obedience—while Fox News retained its status as the President's favored platform, rewarded with early access, exclusive interviews, and policy leaks. Civil servants were monitored for ideological loyalty. Platforms were pressured to boost MAGA content, remove dissenters, and amplify AI-generated praise. This wasn't policy drift. It was the strategic erasure of reality.

Once, Americans turned to The New York Times and The Washington Post to refute the lies of social media. Today, those papers no longer stand outside the storm—they bend to it. Under pressure, they changed editorial policies, softened headlines, narrowed investigations, and allowed their most principled voices to leave or be silenced. Their mottos—All the News That's Fit to Print and Democracy Dies in Darkness—are now the stuff of late-night satire and foreign cartoonists. What remains of the gold standard is now overseas. The BBC World Service, The Guardian, and Reuters—all based in London—still practice verification without fear. In the U.S., only ProPublica and the Associated Press continue to report with integrity, though both are under constant attack. They are still holding—for now. The rest have surrendered neutrality, or were stripped of it.

Trump's defenders cite "free speech." But under his regime, truth is punished and flattery rewarded. Children are tormented by AI-generated images—mocked, stalked, and shamed—and some die by suicide while platforms delay action. But post a meme mocking Trump, and Republican lawmakers threaten prosecution under new deepfake laws. Under these vague laws and platform immunity, the state protects the powerful from embarrassment while abandoning the powerless to abuse. This is not speech. It is surveillance. Not liberty, but control. A republic cannot be rebuilt on such terrain. It must be cleared.

This is not the free speech our laws were meant to protect. It is the infrastructure of uncontained power—where cruelty spreads faster than care, and the price of growing up online can be death. Children are stalked, women are targeted, private citizens are broken—and those responsible walk free because the law was written for another age. The result is not liberty, but abandonment. And as the powerless are abandoned, the powerful exploit that same freedom to punish parody, criminalize dissent, and redraw the boundary between public truth and personal power.

The remedy begins with law. Section 230 must be rewritten to reflect twenty-first century harms. Platforms that amplify lies for profit must be held accountable for that choice. Safe harbor should depend on real moderation, real transparency, and measurable standards. Those who knowingly profit from coordinated disinformation or AI fakery—whether political or personal—must lose protection. There is no freedom in a space where the powerless suffer unchecked and the powerful silence all dissent in the name of that same freedom.

But the line must be drawn carefully. We must defend criticism, humor, and satire—even of Presidents and power. A meme is not a crime. A joke is not defamation. Takedown laws must distinguish between parody and impersonation, between harm and discomfort. And enforcement must be independent, appealable, and transparent. Because a tyrant's first move is to criminalize mockery—and a coward's is to let him. We cannot claim to defend children from harm while punishing artists and critics for telling the truth slant.

Protection must extend where it has long been denied: to children, women, vulnerable minorities, and private citizens destroyed by synthetic abuse. Age verification must be real. Cyberstalking must be federally recognized and prosecuted. Platform moderation must become as urgent for bullying and AI defamation as it once was for copyright infringement and bot removal. What's needed is not technical discovery—it already exists—but political will. A republic that cannot protect its children cannot claim to govern in their name.

This will require oversight. A new federal body must be empowered to enforce platform transparency, audit algorithms, review takedown procedures, and issue public reports on bias, error, and abuse. It must defend the right to dissent and the right not to be erased. It must ensure public knowledge remains a civic structure—not a commodity to be bought, sold, or destroyed. No more shadow moderation. No more silent takedowns. No more algorithmic reward for cruelty, fear, or deception. If the system will not correct itself, the people must.

A republic cannot be rebuilt on fractured ground. The reforms we have outlined—platform transparency, media fairness, civic education—are not discrete fixes. They are the foundation of a shared reality. Without them, no policy endures, no vote is fully informed, and no truth can be trusted long enough to bind a people together. Democracy is not self-sustaining. It must be taught, renewed, defended, and made visible in the lives of those who serve it and live in it. If we fail to rebuild the public mind, no institution will save us. But if we succeed, we do more than repair. We rekindle the power of a people who know who and what is real—and choose to govern themselves with that power.

20

FAIRNESS IN BROADCAST MEDIA

WHEN THE RULES FOR TRUTH WERE DISMANTLED, DEMOCRACY LOST ITS FOUNDATION. THIS IS HOW WE REBUILD IT.

---◆---

"It isn't what I don't know that gets me in trouble—it's what I know for sure that ain't so."
— Mark Twain

The First Amendment protects the freedom to speak—but it does not grant the freedom to deceive with impunity. Nor does it guarantee the right to dominate public discourse through private platforms built on public airwaves. The Constitution is not silent on broadcasting. It entrusts Congress with regulating interstate commerce, authorizes agencies to act in the public interest, and demands a system in which consent is informed, not manipulated. Free speech is not a license for disinformation. It is a protection for the conditions of truth-seeking. And when those conditions collapse—when lies are louder, cheaper, and faster than facts—it is not liberty that expands. It is power, unchecked and shameless.

The legal foundation for fairness in broadcasting is deep, deliberate, and bipartisan—until it was dismantled. The Radio Act of 1927 established that the airwaves belong to the public. The Communications Act of 1934 created the FCC and affirmed that licenses could only be granted if content served "the public interest, convenience, and necessity." The Fairness Doctrine, adopted in 1949, required coverage of controversial issues and demanded balance—not truth, but a reasonable representation of opposing viewpoints. These were not censorship schemes. They were democratic guardrails—rules of engagement for pluralism in a landscape where bandwidth was scarce, and power could too easily be abused. The system worked, for decades—until political will and corporate influence broke it.

In 1969, the Supreme Court upheld the Fairness Doctrine unanimously. In *Red Lion Broadcasting v. FCC*, the Court declared that "it is the right of the viewers and listeners, not the right of the broadcasters, which is paramount." That sentence has never been overturned. But the doctrine it defended was destroyed. In 1987, the FCC—under Reagan appointees—repealed the Fairness Doctrine by administrative fiat. Reagan then vetoed congressional legislation that would have restored it. This was not the result of new technology. It was an ideological project: to weaken oversight, empower corporate speech, and dismantle the shared reference points of American political life. It worked. And the collapse began.

The repeal of the Fairness Doctrine triggered the rise of a new media architecture—built not to inform, but to inflame. Rush Limbaugh turned grievance into a business model. Fox News, launched in 1996, did not merely lean conservative. It redefined news as entertainment, facts as opinion, and loyalty as truth. This shift was not balanced by counterweights. Progressive talk radio withered. Local newsrooms shrank. The market rewarded rage, not reason. Deregulation did not democratize information. It consolidated it—into louder, narrower, more partisan empires. By the early 2000s, what passed for journalism in millions of households was scripted outrage, masquerading as news and unbound by fact.

The Telecommunications Act of 1996, signed by President Clinton but shaped by Republican lawmakers, accelerated the collapse. Ownership limits were lifted. Cross-platform consolidation soared. A handful of companies—Sinclair, iHeartMedia, Comcast—absorbed hundreds of local outlets. National content replaced community reporting. Public interest standards vanished. In city after city, local anchors read scripts dictated by corporate headquarters—sometimes pushing coordinated, partisan talking points. Diversity of ownership was replaced by uniformity of message. Viewers saw their hometowns but heard only the party line. This was not journalism. It was political branding—delivered in familiar voices, wrapped in false objectivity, and protected by a gutted regulatory system.

By the 2010s, disinformation had matured into a governing weapon. It no longer spread by accident—it was deployed by design. Republican operatives, think tanks, and billionaires built a self-reinforcing loop: defund public media, deregulate private media, then attack whatever truth remained as "liberal bias." Every attempt to restore standards was cast as censorship. Meanwhile, entire voter blocs were radicalized not through argument, but through engineered distortion—fed narratives that could not be questioned, facts that could not be verified, and identities shaped more by loyalty than learning. The Fairness Doctrine was gone. In its place stood a doctrine of domination.

Trump did not invent this system. But he saw its potential—and made it his primary tool of rule. In his first term, he attacked journalists as "enemies of the people," tried to yank press credentials, and threatened regulatory retaliation against disfavored networks. Fox News became his shadow cabinet, elevated to state propaganda. OANN and Newsmax became audition pipelines for administration posts. When fact-checkers corrected him, he doubled down. When platforms flagged falsehoods, he threatened legislation. He governed not by controlling the media, but by flooding it—overwhelming truth with performance, and training his base to believe only those who praised him. This was not propaganda on the margins. It was strategy at the core.

We have seen this before. Authoritarians do not begin by banning opposition—they begin by flooding the public square with so much distortion that opposition loses its footing. Mussolini co-opted the Italian press long before he seized absolute power. Hitler's rise was aided by newspapers and radio networks that amplified conspiracy and silenced dissent. Putin shuttered independent outlets and replaced them with loyal oligarch-owned media. Orbán in Hungary rewrote media laws to make state-friendly coverage mandatory. The pattern is always the same: attack truth, reward flattery, and define reality from above. Trump did not borrow their uniforms. But he studied their methods—and he used American institutions to enact them.

America has faced this danger before. In the lead-up to World War II, powerful voices used radio and print to soften the image of Nazi Germany—arguing for neutrality, excusing fascist expansion, and warning that war would cost too much. Charles Lindbergh blamed "foreign influence" for rising tensions, while the America First Committee amplified isolationist propaganda dressed as patriotism. During the McCarthy era, broadcasters and studios blacklisted dissenters under pressure from congressional hearings. In the 1960s, civil rights protesters were branded as agitators by local media trained to equate order with justice. Disinformation does not always wear a uniform. Sometimes it arrives wrapped in the flag, voiced by celebrities, and funded by those who profit from silence.

In the 1850s and 60s, the country was torn apart by one issue that allowed no middle ground. It forced citizens to choose between their values and their relationships, between moral clarity and national unity. Today, we face not one such division, but many: immigration, taxation, public health, housing, identity, truth itself. But unlike the 1860s, we now live in separate realities—engineered and amplified by networks, platforms, and channels that no longer see fairness as a duty but as a barrier. Conflict is not clarified. It is distorted, even sought. Common ground is not debated. It is not even possible. We cannot resolve what we are prevented from seeing clearly. And when disagreement is manufactured for profit, division becomes permanent by design. And, as surely now as when Lincoln first said it, divided we fall.

This division continues today, now as presidential focus. In his second term, Trump has escalated that strategy into structure. He has installed loyalists at the FCC with records of opposing public interest regulation. He has signed executive orders to defund media outlets deemed hostile—PBS and NPR—while protecting those aligned with him, like Fox and OANN, from scrutiny. He has called for laws that would mandate right-wing curricula and punish dissent as disloyalty. Transparency rules have been rolled back. Fairness has been redefined as bias. Access—to the pressroom, on-air interviews, and the Oval Office—is now granted only to those who serve the narrative, or those whose legitimacy he seeks to appropriate through spectacle. The message is unmistakable: reality is what Trump says it is. And when truth disagrees, it must be silenced, discredited, or reclassified as entertainment.

The consequences are not theoretical. Millions of Americans now consume a sealed information environment. Facts that contradict the narrative are dismissed without examination—and with disdain. Entire states are governed by leaders who campaign against imaginary enemies and legislate against fabricated threats: the "invasion of immigrants," the "fraud in elections." When lies dominate the airwaves, democracy cannot function. Consent loses its meaning. And when half the electorate cannot distinguish between journalism and manipulation—between Fox and fact—the collapse is not political. It is a collapse of shared reality. We are no longer debating policy. We are debating reality. And no republic can survive on that ground. None ever has.

Reform is not optional. The remedy begins not with silencing voices, but with rebuilding standards. Broadcasting is not private property. It is licensed access to a public resource. The public has the right to demand accountability from those who use it. That means instituting a modern standard—adapted for today's channels but rooted in the same principle: that when platforms shape public understanding, they owe the public transparency, balance, and verifiability. This is not censorship. It is democratic infrastructure. The goal is not to decide what people think. It is to make it possible to think clearly, together, in a world where facts are visible and lies are named.

The Fairness Doctrine need not be resurrected. But its principle must return: if you profit from public infrastructure, you carry public obligations. The goal is not to restore a bygone policy for a bygone medium—but to build a new standard for all mass-reaching platforms, whether free-to-air, cable, satellite, streaming, or whatever emerges next. That means covering controversial issues with integrity. It means labeling opinion as opinion, not smuggling it through under the banner of news. It means disclosing conflicts of interest, correcting falsehoods, and ensuring that citizens hear more than a single voice echoed back at them. If a network will not meet that threshold, it should not receive the privileges of public licensing. There is no constitutional right to mislead at scale. And there is no republic that survives when deception becomes a business model.

The Federal Communications Commission must be rebuilt—not politicized, not captured, but restored to its original mission: to protect the public interest. That means appointing independent commissioners committed to transparency and nonpartisanship. It means banning appointees with direct ties to the industries they regulate. It means funding investigative arms, reasserting regulatory authority, and enforcing meaningful standards—not just for content, but for ownership concentration, local accountability, and access. The FCC was created to prevent domination of the airwaves. For too long, it has stood by while domination took hold. That must end. Oversight is not government control. It is democratic defense.

No less urgent is the breakup of media monopolies that distort the civic landscape. When one corporation owns the network, the cable infrastructure, and the digital platform, it doesn't just distribute content—it decides what the public sees, hears, and believes. Cross-ownership laws must be reinstated. Market caps must be reimposed. Exclusive carriage agreements that suppress competition must be banned. Public interest obligations must be enforced, especially for companies with local news dominance. Journalism is not just about what's reported. It's about who gets to report it—and who decides what disappears before it can be seen.

Transparency is essential. Every political ad must be traceable—who paid for it, who placed it, who promoted it, and who benefits. Platforms and broadcasters alike must maintain public archives of political content, flag coordinated disinformation campaigns, and report algorithmic promotion standards. Sponsorship must be disclosed. Fabricated stories must be corrected in real time. And platforms must be held to the same disclosure rules as broadcasters when they carry political content at national scale. The goal is not to filter belief. It is to illuminate the infrastructure behind it—so that persuasion cannot hide behind anonymity or algorithmic fog.

Public journalism must also be revived. Independent local newsrooms have collapsed under the weight of consolidation and clickbait economics. We must create a national public media fund—firewalled from political interference—to support investigative reporting, civic education, and local accountability. Universities, libraries, and public broadcasters must be empowered, not threatened. Community-based media must be funded to reflect the voices of those most often silenced. If we leave journalism to the marketplace alone, we will get the journalism the marketplace rewards: outrage, tribalism, and distortion. Democracy requires something better—an information commons that serves citizens, not shareholders.

None of this will be easy. The resistance will be immediate, loud, and cynical. Corporations will call it censorship. Partisans will call it bias. Those who have built their fortunes and followings on distortion will scream that democracy is under attack—when in truth, it is their monopoly on unreality that is being challenged. But the First Amendment does not require us to protect lies at the expense of truth. It requires us to preserve the possibility of informed judgment. And no society can do that while its loudest voices are unchecked and shameless, shielded from scrutiny, and unbound by consequence.

We must be ready. The backlash will not just be rhetorical—it will be legal, financial, and sustained. But clarity is not cruelty, and accountability is not oppression. To defend democracy, we must reject the idea that truth is neutral and verification optional. We do not silence dissent. We set standards for those who speak with institutional power. These reforms will provoke fury because they strike at the ecosystem of impunity and profit. That fury is not a reason to hesitate. It is a signal that we are finally confronting the architecture of deception where it lives.

And we must speak plainly to the millions for whom partisan media is not just information but identity. For many, Fox News is not a source—it is a sanctuary. It confirms belief, shields against contradiction, and offers moral clarity in a life marked by uncertainty. In a world of disappointment and despair, Fox names the target to hate. We cannot shatter that bond with scorn. But we can insist that if a network claims to be news, it must behave as such—or face reclassification. Fox itself has argued in court that its programming is entertainment, not fact. Fine. Then license it accordingly. Truth is not a loyalty test. It is a civic standard. And if broadcasters abandon it, they abandon their right to speak with institutional authority.

Some have proposed even more radical ideas: barring foreign

ownership of U.S. broadcast networks if those owners control media overseas, or revoking the citizenship granted only to enable such ownership. These are not authoritarian proposals. They are sovereignty questions. No democracy should be required to cede its public discourse to foreign oligarchs with no allegiance to its people. Others have argued for clearer legal distinctions between journalism and political entertainment—a civic truth-in-labeling standard. None of these reforms would silence a single voice. But they would expose the ones that lie—and prevent them from masquerading as truth.

The goal is not to dictate what Americans believe. It is to restore the conditions under which belief is informed, tested, and shared. Truth must be verifiable. Lies must be labeled. And public discourse must be structured to serve the republic, not those who seek to break it. This will not come from market incentives or algorithmic tweaks. It will require law, regulation, funding, and courage. The Constitution protects speech. It does not protect the corporate capture of reality. The Founders did not fight a revolution for liberty only to see that liberty twisted into the freedom to deceive without consequence.

A democracy cannot endure on fractured ground. Without fair broadcasting, there is no shared fact. Without shared fact, there is no consent. And without consent, there is no republic. The reforms we have outlined will be attacked as radical. But the radical act was dismantling them in the first place. We do not need to control what people think. We need to restore the systems that make thinking possible. The truth is not fragile. But the institutions that protect it are. And if we fail to defend them, we will live not in freedom, but in fiction—governed not by consent, but by spectacle.

21

CIVIC EDUCATION AND DEMOCRATIC LITERACY

WHAT LIBERTY DEMANDS HAS BEEN LOST, BUT MUST BE RESTORED

"Surely we can teach each other how to stay free."
— JP Vincent

The Constitution does not mention civic education. It does not prescribe textbooks, mandate curricula, or establish a national civics council. And yet the survival of democracy depends on what the public understands. No document can enforce itself. No government of the people can endure without a people who know what they are governing. The Framers did not include civic education as a clause because they assumed it as a condition. They believed a republic required not just liberty, but literacy in liberty—an electorate that could read, reason, debate, and decide. Self-government, to them, was not instinctual. It was learned. Or at least taught.

This assumption saturates the Constitution. It is why power begins with "We the People," not with landowners, monarchs, or clerics. It is why the Bill of Rights protects the press, assembly, petition, and dissent—tools not of obedience, but of understanding. It is why elections recur, not to amuse the populace, but to train it—to habituate judgment, to compel reflection, to test trust. The entire structure rests on one quiet belief: that ordinary people, if educated and equipped, can govern themselves better than any ruler could govern them. That belief is not naive. It is constitutional.

And we are losing it.

The American commitment to civic education once matched its constitutional faith. From the founding through the Cold War, public schools taught not only how laws were made but why freedom mattered. Students learned the structure of government, the limits of power, and the responsibilities of citizens in a republic. After World War II, this mission intensified. The defeat of fascism—and the rise of Soviet propaganda—made civic understanding a national defense priority. President Eisenhower championed civic virtue. John F. Kennedy called for civic action. Public education was not just a ladder of opportunity. It was the bedrock of a functioning democracy.

By the 1960s and 1970s, civic instruction expanded beyond the mechanics of government to include the fuller context of American power: civil rights history, labor movements, immigration, and global conflict. Students were taught not just how institutions functioned, but how they could be improved. Participation meant voting, petitioning, speaking at meetings, running for office. Protest was part of the toolkit—but so were deliberation, debate, and service. Court rulings like *Tinker v. Des Moines* affirmed that students did not check their citizenship at the schoolhouse door. Meanwhile, the rise of science and engineering education—driven by Cold War urgency—channeled investment away from civics, not by design but by competition. By the 1980s, civics was left exposed. Reagan's culture war reframed it as ideological. Public school programs were defunded. And civics—still the foundation of self-rule—was treated as a distraction, or a threat, but no longer a necessity.

Other nations moved in the opposite direction. In Germany, students study their history: the rise of fascism, the collapse of the Weimar Republic, and the Final Solution—not as guilt, but as preparation. In Australia, Indigenous history and civic structure are taught together, forming a shared national narrative. Scandinavian countries integrate media literacy and political participation from early grades onward. These countries do not treat civic knowledge as nostalgia. They treat it as infrastructure—as vital to survival as energy or water. They do not expect democracy to perpetuate itself. They teach what it can provide, what it demands, how to be part of it, and what happens when it fails. Finland ranks among the highest in civic literacy and trust in government. That is not coincidence.

The United States once led these efforts. American civic outreach helped design postwar institutions, supported transitional democracies, and exported models of public education rooted in constitutional principles. But today, the U.S. does not export understanding. It exports confusion. Its media fragmentation, political disinformation, and decaying public trust now radiate outward through the very platforms it built. From Hungary to Brazil to the Philippines, America is no longer the case study in how democracy works. It is the proof that democracy unravels. Not because the system failed, but because the citizens were not taught how to sustain it.

This unraveling did not happen by accident. It was engineered. Over the past two decades, Republican-led legislatures have attacked civic education with surgical precision. They have defunded public schools, censored curricula, and passed laws forbidding the honest teaching of race, gender, and power. In Florida, the Stop WOKE Act bans discussions that cause discomfort—rendering civic inquiry all but impossible. In Texas and Oklahoma and elsewhere, history standards have been rewritten to obscure slavery and suppress social justice movements. These are not educational reforms. They are education sabotage, designed to leave voters ignorant, exhausted, and misled.

The Republican goal is not neutrality—it is obscurity. It is obedience. In place of civics, Republican leaders offer patriotic indoctrination: programs like the 1776 Commission, which portray right-wing America as infallible and dissent as disloyal. These efforts whitewash genocide, romanticize empire, and recast protest as chaos. They do not prepare students to participate in democracy. They train them to accept authority, defer to hierarchy, and fear the complexity of truth—and ultimately, to be told, when government fails to serve, who to blame. A citizen who cannot recognize injustice cannot fight it. A student who cannot question power cannot limit it. That is the point. And that is why these programs exist.

The damage is not theoretical. It is political. Voters stripped of civic understanding are easily manipulated by false claims of fraud, persecution, and absolute power. They are taught to fear their neighbors, not hold their leaders accountable. They become susceptible to conspiracy, blind to corruption, and hostile to institutions that preserve law. When civic education collapses, so does constitutional consent. The people may still vote—but they no longer know what they are voting for, what powers they are granting, or what rights they are losing. That is not democracy. It is misrule by confusion. And it is spreading.

The collapse of civic education did not merely weaken democracy. It exposed its weakness. A public that no longer understands how government works cannot defend itself against those who would break it. It cannot recognize violations, challenge falsehoods, or distinguish governance from performance. Not knowing what a democracy is meant to provide allows the public to be satisfied with whatever it gets. And into that vacuum stepped a figure who did not seek to inform the public, but to exploit its confusion—to turn civic ignorance into political advantage, and misinformation into method. He did not need to dismantle institutions. He only needed a people no longer trained to recognize when their institutions were already failing.

Donald Trump did not invent civic ignorance. He revealed and took advantage of how easily it could be weaponized. In his first term, he mocked the Constitution, claimed powers it did not grant him, and relied on a public too uninformed—or too exhausted—to distinguish spectacle from sovereignty. He called the press the enemy of the people. He demanded loyalty from the Justice Department. He refused oversight, defied subpoenas, and celebrated those who did the same. He once referred to "Article XII" of the Constitution—a document that has only seven articles. It was not a joke. It was a glimpse into a political strategy that no longer required understanding, only allegiance. The line became symbolic: not just of Trump's ignorance, but of how little such ignorance seemed to matter to his supporters—and how civic illiteracy had become politically irrelevant, or even a badge of anti-elitism. These were not slips of the tongue. They were blatant signals: that knowledge was no longer required, and that ignorance, even in a president, could be a kind of power.

Beyond his own ignorance, Trump's administration treated civic understanding as an obstacle. The 1776 Commission was its answer —a whitewashed history designed not to educate, but to pacify. It was not a neutral call for patriotism. It was a state-sponsored attempt to rewrite American history, downplaying systemic injustice and recasting dissent as disloyalty. Historians condemned it as propaganda, but its purpose was never academic. It was strategic. It modeled how authoritarians use education to control public memory and suppress democratic inquiry. Meanwhile, real civic infrastructure eroded. Public media lost funding. Universities faced political scrutiny. Agencies once tasked with education and transparency were absorbed into partisan messaging machines. And when Trump lost re-election, he tested what that erosion would allow. He told the public the election was stolen. That he could not lose. That their vote was meaningless unless it crowned him again. And for millions, stripped of the knowledge to know otherwise, that lie became truth.

The January 6 insurrection was not only an assault on the Capitol. It was a final exam in civic illiteracy. Millions believed the Vice President could overturn the results. That electors could be replaced. That state legislatures could nullify the people's will. These were not just lies—they were lies that only worked in the absence of civic education. Trump's effort failed in 2021. But the test results were clear: too many Americans no longer knew how their government worked. And too many in office no longer felt bound to teach them. Ignorance had become strategy. And the second term would prove it.

In his return to power, Trump did not waste time. He slashed funding to civic education initiatives, purged staff from the Department of Education, and expanded the reach of Project 2025 into schools, universities, and local districts. Textbooks were rewritten. College accreditation became a political tool. Grants were withheld from institutions that taught "divisive concepts," including race, climate science, and democratic decline. The message was unmistakable: teach what he approved, or lose everything. And beneath the surface, the deeper project continued—the cultivation of a public that did not understand power, did not question authority, did not believe in democracy, and simply believed what they were told.

That is the crisis we now face—not just disinformation, but disempowerment. Not just lies, but engineered ignorance. Civic education is no longer about passing a test. It is about ensuring that democracy remains possible. Without it, elections become performances, offices become prizes, and law becomes spectacle. Without it, the public cannot hold its leaders accountable, because it no longer knows what accountability requires. This is not a cultural loss. It is a constitutional one. And if civic knowledge collapses, so does the legitimacy of consent. You cannot meaningfully authorize what you do not understand—or demand more than you are given.

The remedy begins where the damage began: with education. We must reestablish civic instruction as public infrastructure—as essential to a functioning democracy as roads, electricity, or clean air and water. Every student in every state must be taught what government is, how it works, what it owes, and how to participate in it. This is not indoctrination. It is preparation for self-government. Civic education must be rooted in fact, protected by law, and open to scrutiny. It must teach not just how a democracy works, but the rights, responsibilities, and moral imagination it demands.

And it must extend beyond the classroom. The damage done by disinformation does not disappear at graduation. We need adult civic education—funded, accessible, and woven into the institutions people already trust. Public libraries, universities, unions, and houses of worship all have a role to play. Public broadcasting must be resourced and revived. Fact-checking must be mainstreamed, not marginalized. And civic knowledge must be reclaimed as a common good—lifelong, nonpartisan, and necessary. This is not an academic reform. It is democratic defense. A public trained to think critically, to spot lies, and to engage with complexity is not just harder to fool. It is stronger, freer, and more capable of building the democracy we have not yet achieved.

We must also elevate civic participation itself. Public service must no longer be the realm of the wealthy, the ambitious, the connected, or the theatrical. It must be reclaimed as honorable democratic labor: humble, accountable, and rooted in the trust of the governed. Young people should be encouraged—not just to vote, but to run. To staff polling places, serve on commissions, and shape the systems they inherit. Military service, too, must be reframed—not as sacrifice, but as shared commitment, as citizenship made visible. Both forms of service teach discipline, solidarity, and responsibility. Both can anchor the habits of self-government. Both must be valued—and made accessible to all who are ready.

None of this will be easy. There will be resistance—from those who benefit from ignorance, from those who equate education with control, from those who prioritize private gain over public good, and from those too invested in rage to allow reconciliation. But we must not mistake that resistance for reason. Civic education is not the enemy of liberty. It is its foundation. When people understand their power, they do not give it away lightly. When they recognize their rights, they do not surrender them easily. When they see clearly, they do not follow blindly. That is why authoritarianism attacks education first. And that is why we must rebuild it now.

American citizenship is, for many, a birthright taken for granted. But for millions around the world, it remains a prize—fought for, prayed for, risked for. Some walk through a thousand miles of jungle and danger for a chance at the freedom it promises. They dream not just of safety or opportunity, but of belonging to a democracy—of one day holding a passport that still opens doors and declares dignity. And all we ask of those born to that privilege is that they participate. But without civic education, even that is too much. We have left millions unable to grasp what they never learned to reach for. We have cheapened what it means to be American. And for what?

We are not born democratic. We become so—by learning, by failing, by trying again, then passing what we know to our children. Over and over. The Constitution assumes nothing about the next generation except this: that it can be taught. That it can understand. That it can govern. If that assumption fails, the republic follows. Civic education is not a luxury. It is not a favor. It is the mechanism by which liberty renews itself. We have taught each other how to fly, how to split atoms, how to reach the stars. Surely, we can teach each other how to stay free. That is the work. That is the hope. That is what must come next.

22

THE SIX THAT HOLD
WHAT MUST BE SECURED, OR ALL WILL BE UNDONE

―――― ✦ ――――

"The republic survives not on trust, but on design—on checks that withstand betrayal."
— Learned Hand

Every reform we propose—every measure to restore fairness, dignity, and self-government—will be seen by someone as a threat. Not a correction. Not a remedy. A threat. These are not minor adjustments to a functioning system. They are structural repairs to a broken one. And those who have profited from that brokenness will not surrender their advantage easily. Some will call it overreach. Others, vengeance. But do not mistake outrage for principle. These reforms disrupt wealth, ideology, impunity, and control. They will bruise reputations. They will end careers. They will obliterate entire business models. And that is why they are essential.

We should be clear-eyed about who will oppose them. Right-wing legal groups that gerrymandered the judiciary. Billionaire networks that bought their way into Cabinet appointments. Partisan secretaries of state who purged voter rolls. Social media executives who built fortunes on outrage. Think tanks that turn white papers into weapons. Media empires that treat distortion as a business model. This is not abstract resistance. These are organized, well-funded, deeply entrenched power blocs. And they will respond to reform not with argument, but with attack.

They will try to undo what we pass. Not just at the ballot box, but through the courts, through regulatory sabotage, through media disinformation, and through electoral retaliation. Any reform that threatens their hold on power will face lawsuits, delays, defunding, and repeal. This has happened before. It is already happening now.

Some reforms must come first—not because they are easier, but because they shield the rest. They are not just reforms. They are protections. They are the six that hold. Thus, we begin not with what is popular or easy—but with these six.

1. Supreme Court Reform

The first reform must be Supreme Court expansion. Without it, every other safeguard—especially campaign finance reform—will be struck down by a Court designed to entrench minority rule. Four justices must be added without apology. Not someday. Not after debate. Immediately. Not to tip the balance, but to restore it. Anything less, and we will lose the fight before it begins.

The current Court is not a check on tyranny. It is its shield. Appointments were stolen, rushed, and confirmed under open partisan manipulation. The Court has blocked voting protections, allowed dark money to flood elections, and granted sweeping immunity to those who defy the law. It has abandoned precedent to serve ideology, delayed justice to protect allies, and refused ethical constraint. A captured Court will dismantle every major reform—on climate, labor, education, equality—no matter how constitutionally grounded. The solution is not gradual. It is immediate: expand the Court by four justices and impose binding ethical rules. This is not a power grab. It is a rebalancing.

The opposition will be ferocious. The Federalist Society, Republican leadership, conservative media, and elite law schools will declare the republic dead. They will call it illegitimate, lawless, unprecedented. But the precedent has already been broken—by them. What they fear is not imbalance. They fear loss of control. Court expansion will provoke outrage because it threatens their last unbreakable stronghold.

But the Constitution is on our side. It does not fix the number of justices—Congress does. The Court has ranged from six to ten justices in its history, and the current number is not sacred law but legislative choice. Expanding the Court by four is not only constitutional, it is necessary—and historically justified.

That is why it must come first.

2. Campaign Finance Reform

Campaign finance reform must be next, done immediately, done before the next election cycle begins. If billionaires can buy seats, nothing else matters. Campaign finance reform is the firewall between democracy and oligarchy. Every policy—from taxes to healthcare to housing—is vulnerable to repeal if the wealthy can purchase a majority. We need publicly funded elections, real-time disclosure of donations, hard limits on outside spending, and a ban on corporate PACs. This isn't just a fairness issue. It's a survival issue. We cannot outvote dark money. We must banish it.

Expect immediate backlash. The donor class will not give up power quietly. The Koch network, crypto billionaires, hedge funds, energy giants, and defense contractors have all shaped legislation with their checkbooks. Media companies will claim it's censorship. Candidates who thrive on super PACs will call it an assault on free speech. Legal groups tied to corporate lobbies will sue in every federal court they've packed. But this is not about silencing opinion —it is about ending purchase. Until we sever the link between wealth and representation, no law is safe, no voter is equal, and no democracy is secure.

3. Voting Rights and Fair Maps

The vote is the foundation of consent. If it is manipulated, democracy becomes a simulation. We must end partisan gerrymandering, restore the Voting Rights Act, standardize early voting, and make registration automatic. No reform survives if voters cannot protect it. And no democracy survives if its elections are rigged in advance.

This threatens dozens of state power structures. Governors, secretaries of state, and redistricting commissions in GOP-controlled states will resist. They will claim federal overreach. They will pass voter ID laws, close polling places, and purge rolls to retaliate. But we've seen what happens when we let them decide who votes. They decide who governs. And who governs decides who counts. That must end.

4. Presidential Accountability and Emergency Powers

The presidency now commands extraordinary power—budgetary, military, regulatory. In the wrong hands, it is a weapon. We have seen executive power used to withhold aid, fire watchdogs, silence agencies, and punish dissent. It must be constrained. Emergency powers must be time-limited, subject to congressional review, and stripped of immunity. No President is above the law—not now, not ever.

Trump's defenders will call this revenge. Conservative media will warn of executive paralysis. But what they fear is exposure. They fear a system where the President cannot act with impunity. If we do not lock the presidency back into the Constitution, we are not a republic. We are a monarchy in denial.

5. Oversight Independence and Protection

Without oversight, power rots. Inspectors General must be protected from political firing. Whistleblowers must be shielded from retaliation. Congressional subpoenas must be enforceable. Agencies must report not to the President, but to the public through law. These are not bureaucratic reforms. They are democratic life support.

Corrupt officials, partisan loyalists, and corporate contractors will resist. They fear oversight because it exposes what they've hidden. Without protection, they will erase records, silence witnesses, fire examiners. Oversight is not a partisan issue. It is what keeps democracy from becoming autocracy in a suit and tie.

6. Disinformation and Platform Accountability

Democracy cannot function if the people are lied to at scale. The Constitution protects speech. But the truth must still have a fighting chance. Platforms must disclose algorithms, label synthetic content, regulate political advertising, and face penalties for amplifying falsehoods that lead to harm. This is not censorship. It is the defense of a shared reality.

Big Tech will resist. So will political campaigns that rely on outrage and lies. So will media outlets whose business model is distortion. But if we cannot agree on what is real, we cannot govern.

And if we cannot govern, we do not have a democracy. We have an open-air illusion.

THESE ARE the six that hold. They are not glamorous. They won't fit on a bumper sticker or in a thirty-second ad. But without them, nothing else endures. They are the shield. If we pass them, every other reform gains a fighting chance. If we delay them, we risk losing everything before it can take root. They do not need to come in a single bill—but they must all be enacted within the first four years. This is not optional. It is not idealism. It is strategy. It is defense. It is the foundation on which everything else depends.

There will be protests. There will be lawsuits. There will be filibusters, defiance, bad-faith outrage, and calls for calm. But reform is not measured by comfort. It is measured by permanence. If we want American Restoration to last beyond the next election, these six reforms must be the steel in its frame.

The work ahead will be hard. Some of it will be unpopular. But this is what democracy requires: not just hope, not just vision, but the courage to protect what we build before it is taken from us again. Restoration is not just about what we repair. It is about what we refuse to lose.

And that will depend on who we choose to lead it. These reforms cannot be carried by the timid, the calculating, or the ambitious. They demand something rarer—leaders who measure their success not in attention, but in consequence. Public servants who do not flinch when the backlash comes. Officials who understand that restoring democracy may end their careers, cost them friendships, or brand them as radicals. But who do it anyway, because the alternative is worse.

These are not the leaders the system selects. They are the ones we must find. They will not look like what we're used to. Some may already be quietly serving—uninvited to the greenrooms, unwelcomed by donors, unmoved by self-preservation. Finding them will be difficult. Supporting them will take risk. Electing them will take strategy and speed. But it must begin now.

This is not a search for stars. It is a search for spine. The kind of person who sees a collapsing republic and does not ask what it will cost them to act—but what it will cost everyone else if they do not.

23

IF WE ARE TO LAST

THE FINAL TEST OF DEMOCRACY IS WHETHER WE CHOOSE TO REBUILD IT

---✦---

"We were not given a future. We were given the tools to build one."
— JP Vincent

Democracy in the United States did not shatter in a single year or under a single man. It eroded slowly—through judicial decisions that hollowed the Voting Rights Act, deregulation that unleashed dark money, propaganda that blurred fact and fiction, and political strategies designed not to persuade but to suppress. For decades, power was consolidated while the public was distracted. Rights were revoked by attrition, not decree. Warnings were ignored. The engine of democracy was quietly rerouted to serve those who already owned its levers.

When Donald Trump took office—first in 2017, and again in 2025—he did not break democracy. He proved it was already broken. He exploited every weakness the system allowed. He did not invent executive overreach, disinformation, voter suppression, or judicial capture; he inherited them. But unlike his predecessors, he wielded those tools without shame, without pretense, and without pause. What had been creeping became explicit. What had been constrained by reputation was now fueled by impunity. The second Trump presidency was not the origin of our crisis. It was its confirmation.

The courts did not stop him. Congress would not. The press tried to sound the alarm, but was drowned out by a flood of performative outrage and bad-faith noise. As protections collapsed, what remained was the raw question of will—whether citizens would tolerate, enable, or resist the dissolution of their own power. And even that question was blurred by confusion: Was this still democracy? Or merely a simulation, sustained only by ritual and stagecraft?

What we witnessed was not a surprise. It was the final consequence of what we refused to confront. There was no single cause. There will be no single cure. But if we are to last, we must start by telling the truth: we saw the fire rising, and for too long we called it warmth.

But collapse was not the only force at work. Alongside the unraveling came something else: resolve. In the absence of federal leadership, cities, states, and ordinary citizens began to push back. They filed lawsuits, organized boycotts, ran for office, built alliances, and told the truth even when it cost them. Voter protection efforts became national movements. Civic education, long neglected, began to return to classrooms and town halls. Whistleblowers came forward. Journalists dug in. Public servants refused to yield to unlawful orders, even when their jobs were on the line.

American Renewal was born not in a party headquarters but in protests, petitions, and planning sessions across the country. It did not seek to resurrect the past. It aimed to repair what had been deliberately broken. *American Restoration* now goes further—laying out the long-term blueprint for a democracy built not on tradition alone, but on fairness, accessibility, transparency, and inclusion.

These are not just policies. They are lines in the sand. And though progress has been uneven, the work has begun.

But some reforms matter more than others—not because they are better, but because they are protective. Without Supreme Court reform, every law can be struck down. Without campaign finance reform, every seat can be bought. Without voting rights, no majority can govern. Without executive constraint, no rule is stable. Without oversight, no abuse is checked. Without truth, no consent can be given. These six form the shield. Without them, everything else is vulnerable—now and again.

Law alone is not enough. No statute can compel honor, and no regulation can substitute for truth. The collapse we lived through was not merely institutional. It was moral. Leaders lied to the public and to themselves. They excused cruelty, rewarded loyalty over competence, and treated power as an entitlement, not a responsibility. What eroded was not just oversight, but conscience.

You could see it in the water crisis in Flint, Michigan—where officials failed to act for months while families drank lead-contaminated water, and accountability came only after national outrage.

You could see it when federal agents denied that family separations were happening while parents slept on concrete floors, not knowing where their children had been taken. These were not accidents. They were failures of basic decency masked by technical legality.

To restore democracy, we must recommit to principles that precede and undergird the law. Truth must matter—not as tactic, but as foundation. Transparency must be assumed, not requested. Fairness must be measurable. Power must be constrained. And when officials fail to uphold the dignity of their office, there must be consequence—not someday, but now. These are not lofty ideals. They are the baseline. If we treat them as optional again, they will vanish, and with them, democracy in America.

We are not trying to return to 2015 or 2008 or 1965. We are trying to build what has never fully existed: a functional, multiracial, pluralist democracy in which power is earned, rights are protected, and government answers to the governed. That means universal and equal voting access. It means campaign finance reform with real limits, enforced in real time. It means a judiciary that serves justice rather than ideology. It means digital platforms regulated for truth, not optimized for outrage.

It also means dignity in policy: care that reaches every family, education that prepares citizens not just for work but for self-government, and media systems that inform rather than inflame. These are not fringe ideas. They are the infrastructure of democratic survival. Most developed democracies already provide them. The fact that we do not is not a mark of freedom. It is a measure of our failure.

If we are to last, democracy must no longer be a performance. It must be a practice—visible, tangible, and built into the lives of every citizen, every day. What comes next is not just about laws and institutions. It is about design. And we must build it deliberately, before others finish dismantling it.

This work will not be led by saviors. It will be carried by public servants—people who act before the polls move, who speak when silence would be safer, who build not for credit but for consequence. Some of them are already among us. But most are still hidden—uninvited by donors, unwelcomed by party hierarchies, unwilling to posture when the moment calls for risk. They will not emerge by accident. We must find them. We must choose them.

They are not always the names we know. Leadership may come from school boards, labor unions, tribal councils, local media, or neighborhoods that national politics has ignored. They will not be perfect, and they must not pretend to be. But they will need clarity, resilience, creativity, and above all, courage—more courage than most of our elected leaders have shown. Protesters have gathered again and again since the second inauguration. Inside, we have seen too many strongly worded letters, too many hearings with "hard questions," too much hesitation dressed as propriety. Merrick Garland waited 600 days to begin a real investigation of Trump's crimes. President Biden remained silent for fear of seeming improper while democracy bled beneath him. The people have moved. The leadership has not kept pace.

This must change now. We do not have until 2028. We do not have until 2030. If we do not identify, support, and elect new leaders now—leaders who understand both the scale of the threat and the urgency of the remedy—then the majorities we win may be revoked before they can ever govern. Power will not wait for consensus. Neither can we.

Every democratic era reaches a point of inflection. Ours has arrived. The choices we make in the next four years, and the five years after that, will not just decide laws or budgets. They will decide whether self-government remains possible—or becomes a memory dressed in ceremony. This generation did not ask for that responsibility. But it holds it now.

The young are not obligated to admire what we built. But they may yet decide to repair it. They understand climate collapse, algorithmic manipulation, and economic precarity not as abstractions but as daily realities. If they do not lead, democracy will not be led. If they do not vote, democracy will not hold. If they do not organize, democracy will not evolve. They are not the last hope. But they are the current one.

The promise of democracy is not secured by elections alone. It is secured by habit. By showing up. By listening, demanding, resisting, voting, organizing, running, and holding. It is not a moment. It is a discipline. And like any discipline, it weakens when ignored.

We are often told that democracy depends on trust. But that is not quite true. It depends on participation. Trust may follow—but action must come first. We cannot expect justice without presence. We cannot expect dignity without noise. We must do more than watch and wait. We must do more than vote and hope. We must practice democracy even when it is exhausting—especially then.

Across the world, billions have never known what we risk losing. They have never cast a vote that mattered, never spoken without fear, never read a press that could challenge power and survive. And yet they watch us—not because we are perfect, but because we once showed what was possible.

They see a country letting go of its own promise. Not all at once, but year by year—through neglect, denial, delay. What they long for, we discard. What they are still fighting to build, we are letting slide into memory. We are not just breaking faith with ourselves. We are breaking faith with those who believed we might last.

If we are to last, we must stop pretending that democracy will fix itself. It is not self-sustaining. It is not self-healing. It is not permanent. It must be renewed, restored, rebuilt, and reimagined—year by year, generation by generation, law by law, voice by voice. The systems we inherited were not designed for permanence. They were designed for amendment, expansion, and moral reckoning. If we cannot meet that standard, we do not deserve the name republic. If we do not act, it is already lost.

But if we do—if we build a democracy that is fair, functional, transparent, and truly inclusive—then we will have done something rare. We will have learned from collapse. We will have earned the future. We will have refused cynicism and chosen construction. And we will have handed down a nation not as mythology, but as mission. To our children. To their children. And theirs.

This is not the end.

It is the handoff. What happens next is up to us.

APPENDIX A - EIGHTEEN ITEMS IN THE REFORMATION AGENDA

———✦———

"Power must be made visible before it can be held accountable." — JP Vincent

American Restoration is not a theory of governance. It is a repair manual. These reforms are not designed to tilt the system toward any party or ideology. They are the structural foundations a democracy cannot survive without: fair elections, real constraints on power, functional institutions, and public trust in the idea of consent. Each one addresses a vulnerability that has already been exploited. None can be deferred again.

We do not present this list as aspiration. It is a minimum viable democracy. Without these reforms, the system remains rigged—by money, manipulation, delay, and inherited impunity. With them, we begin to build a republic worthy of its promise: one that earns consent, restrains corruption, functions transparently, and rebuilds the public trust it has so carelessly lost.

I. Consent – Restoring the Right to Choose Government

No democracy is legitimate without fair elections, equal representation, and access to power

1. **Campaign Finance Reform** - Restore legislative authority to regulate money in politics. Enact real-time transparency, advertising limits, public financing pilots, and a new national framework for election truth and integrity.
2. **Voting Rights Protection** - Guarantee equal access to the ballot through automatic voter registration, national early voting standards, restored preclearance, and enforceable protections against suppression and subversion.
3. **Electoral College Reform** - Complete the National Popular Vote Interstate Compact, enforce elector fidelity, prohibit substitution schemes, and shift toward proportional allocation to reflect the actual will of voters.
4. **Redistricting Reform** - Mandate independent commissions with measurable fairness metrics to draw congressional and state legislative maps. End the partisan ratchet effect by 2030 or risk permanent minority rule.
5. **Election Certification Integrity** - Protect election officials from coercion, criminalize false certification attempts, and establish nonpartisan federal safeguards to uphold accurate, lawful results.

II. Constraint – Restraining Abuses of Presidential Power

DEMOCRACY REQUIRES THAT NO PERSON—NOT even a president—stands above the law.

6. **Presidential Accountability** - End functional immunity. Establish that presidents may be indicted, prosecuted, and subpoenaed while in office for personal, criminal, or unconstitutional conduct.
7. **Oversight Independence and Protection** - Protect Inspectors General by statute. Enforce compliance with subpoenas. Strengthen whistleblower laws. Penalize obstruction of Congressional oversight and lawful review.
8. **Emergency Powers Reform** - Limit unilateral declarations. Require automatic expiration, congressional reauthorization, and defined legal scope for all national emergencies beyond 30 days.
9. **Executive Order Oversight** - Impose legislative review on executive orders that impact spending, constitutional rights, or separation of powers. Allow for override through fast-track Congressional vote.
10. **Pardon Power Constraints** - Ban self-pardons, secret pardons, and pardon-for-silence agreements. Require public reporting and DOJ review for all clemency actions taken by the President.

III. Function – Making Institutions Work for the Public

A REPUBLIC MUST BE able to govern effectively, equitably, and without sabotage.

11. **Supreme Court Term Limits** - Establish staggered 18-year terms for justices with mandatory retirement. Reduce political manipulation of timing and restore generational balance.
12. **Lower Court Expansion and Access to Justice** - Add judges where population growth and case backlog demand. Prioritize diversity pipelines, geographic equity, and a judiciary that reflects the people it serves.
13. **Supreme Court Ethics Code** - Impose binding ethics rules, gift bans, and mandatory recusals for conflicts of interest. Apply the same integrity standards to justices as to all federal judges.
14. **Insurrection Clause Enforcement** - Operationalize Section 3 of the Fourteenth Amendment to disqualify officials who aided or incited insurrection. Create a judicial process to enforce constitutional accountability.
15. **Transparency and FOIA Modernization** - Shorten response times, limit exemptions, and extend public transparency standards to privatized public functions and contracting agencies.

IV. Trust – Rebuilding Public Confidence in Shared Reality

Democracy cannot survive without truth, education, and a media system worthy of consent.

16. **Disinformation and Platform Transparency** - Require disclosure of political ad funding, origin, and targeting. Mandate civic audits of algorithmic manipulation in the lead-up to elections. Rein in profit-driven propaganda.
17. **Fairness in Broadcast Media** - Establish a modern Fairness Doctrine for publicly licensed broadcasters to

require balanced civic coverage, protect local journalism, and reduce partisan distortion.
18. **Civic Education and Democratic Literacy** - Fund universal K–12 civics instruction, national service opportunities, and adult democratic literacy programs to foster long-term participation and civic resilience.

THIS IS NOT A MENU. It is a map. These eighteen reforms are not independent demands. They are interlocking defenses against authoritarian rule. Fail to enact one, and the others grow weaker. Fail to enact enough, and democracy collapses again—this time, not by surprise, but by choice. The window for repair is open. But it will not stay open long.

APPENDIX B - THE LEGAL WEB OF PRESIDENTIAL CONSTRAINT

———— ✦ ————

The Constitution outlines the limits of power, but it is the law that gives those limits force. The presidency was not built to be bound by principle alone. It was built to be bound by law—by the steady accumulation of statutes passed in response to abuse, excess, and failure. Where the Constitution establishes broad authority, Congress supplies the specificity. Where the Framers left silence, Congress responds to history. This has been the design since the beginning: that law would evolve as the country did, adapting to its technologies, its failures, and its unfinished work.

As the only branch with the power to legislate, Congress bears the constitutional duty not just to check the President, but to defend the conditions of co-equality itself. It does this by passing laws that impose limits on executive behavior—laws that constrain appointments, budgets, emergency declarations, political retaliation, secrecy, and self-dealing. But it also legislates to protect the mechanisms of oversight: inspectors general, whistleblower pathways, subpoena enforcement, and public access to information. These laws do not restrain a king. They constrain an office—when that office is held to them.

This appendix presents the structure of those legal restraints. It is organized into fourteen categories across four domains: oversight, access, participation, and public power. Some laws bind the President directly; others protect those tasked with exposing abuse. A few remain theoretical—never enforced, or long neglected. But together, they form the legal architecture of democratic restraint. Each law listed here once answered a real threat. They may now be called to answer again.

The entries below are grouped by function and indexed for reference. Each law or doctrine is labeled with a two-part identifier: the first digit refers to its thematic group, the second to its order within that group. This system allows for precise citation in the main chapters and preserves clarity if the list expands in the future. While some laws appear thematically relevant to more than one category, each is listed only once for ease of navigation.

Grouped Sections and Reference Index

1. Oversight, Investigations, and Transparency (Items 1.1–1.8)
2. Legal and Budgetary Constraint (Items 2.1–2.6)
3. Criminal and Civil Law Restrictions (Items 3.1–3.8)
4. Lawsuits Against the President or Executive Agencies (Items 4.1–4.7)
5. Judicial and Immunity Doctrines (Items 5.1–5.5)
6. Laws Protecting the Press and Public Access (Items 6.1–6.7)
7. Civil Service and Labor Protections (Items 7.1–7.4)
8. Anti-Discrimination and DEI Framework (Items 8.1–8.4)

9. Environmental and Land Protection Laws (Items 9.1–9.7)
10. National Parks, Weather, and Climate Laws (Items 10.1–10.3)
11. Academic and Research Funding Protections (Items 11.1–11.2)
12. Torture, Detention, and Rendition Prohibitions (Items 12.1–12.3)
13. International Legal Commitments (Items 13.1–13.3)
14. Digital Power and Technological Constraint (Items 14.1–14.6)

NOTABLE LEGAL MARKERS

SOME ENTRIES ARE MARKED to indicate their current status:
- **(A)** Actively violated during Trump's presidency
- **(B)** Weakened or nullified by judicial decisions
- **(C)** Dormant or structurally ignored in current practice

1. Oversight, Investigations, and Transparency (1.1–1.8)

These laws empower independent review of presidential conduct, ensure the public's right to know, and create formal channels for exposing abuse. Together, they represent the front line of democratic self-defense: the capacity to watch, to speak, and to act without retaliation.

1.1 Inspector General Act (1978) — Created independent watchdogs in executive agencies to audit spending, investigate misconduct, and report findings to both Congress and the public. Designed after Watergate to ensure no president could again operate behind closed doors without internal scrutiny.

1.2 Whistleblower Protection Acts (1989, 2012) — Shield federal employees who expose wrongdoing—from illegal orders to corruption and waste. They prohibit retaliation and establish protected channels for disclosure, recognizing that internal resistance is sometimes the only line between legality and lawlessness.

1.3 Freedom of Information Act (1966; amended 1974, 1996, 2007) — Grants the public a legal right to access most government records. It is the statutory expression of the belief that democracy cannot function in darkness. Though often delayed or redacted, FOIA remains a cornerstone of investigative journalism and legal oversight.

1.4 Ethics in Government Act (1978) — Requires public officials —including the President—to file detailed financial disclosures, exposing potential conflicts of interest. It also created the Office of Government Ethics to enforce compliance, though the President appoints its leadership, limiting independence.

1.5 Government Accountability Office (GAO) Authority — As Congress's investigative arm, the GAO has power to audit executive actions, issue legal opinions on spending, and track program performance. Though it cannot compel enforcement, its findings serve as the evidentiary base for legislation and legal action.

1.6 Privacy Protection Act (1980) — Limits government searches and seizures targeting journalists. Enacted after law enforcement raids on newsrooms, it ensures that newsgathering materials cannot be seized without court approval—protecting freedom of the press from indirect censorship.

1.7 Presidential Records Act (1978) — Establishes that presidential records belong to the public, not the officeholder. Requires preservation of documents and communications, and mandates their transfer to the National Archives. Violations erode historical accountability and legal traceability.

1.8 Government in the Sunshine Act (1976) — Requires that meetings of federal agencies be open to public observation, with limited exemptions. Reinforces transparency not only in documents, but in deliberation itself—making secrecy the exception, not the default.

SECTION 2. Legal and Budgetary Constraint (2.1–2.6)
2. Legal and Budgetary Constraint (2.1–2.6)
These laws limit the President's power over money, emergencies, and appointments. They protect the constitutional balance of power by ensuring that executive actions comply with congressional intent and legal process.

2.1 Congressional Budget and Impoundment Control Act (1974) — Prohibits the President from withholding or deferring funds that Congress has appropriated. Central to Congress's constitutional power of the purse, this law was violated during Trump's Ukraine aid freeze and again in 2025 budget cancellations. **(B)**

2.2 National Emergencies Act (1976) — Requires the President to formally declare and justify national emergencies and report to Congress. Allows termination by joint resolution. Trump repeatedly invoked this law to redirect funds unilaterally. Legal, but distortive of the original purpose. **(C)**

2.3 War Powers Resolution (1973) — Requires the President to notify Congress within 48 hours of deploying armed forces and limits unauthorized military engagement to 60 days. Designed to rein in unilateral war-making. Routinely ignored by presidents from both parties. **(C)**

2.4 Federal Vacancies Reform Act (1998) — Restricts the President's ability to install unconfirmed "acting" officials indefinitely. Violations during both Trump terms, including backdoor staffing of DOGE, directly undermined Senate confirmation power. **(B)**

2.5 Administrative Procedure Act (1946) — Requires federal agencies to follow public rulemaking procedures and justify policy decisions. Courts have repeatedly struck down Trump-era rules as "arbitrary and capricious." Essential for curbing executive fiat. **(B)**

2.6 Mandamus Statute (28 U.S.C. §1361) — Allows courts to compel federal officials to perform legally required duties. Though rarely used, it remains a tool of last resort to force executive compliance with statute. **(C)**

Section 3. Criminal and Civil Law Restrictions (3.1–3.8)

These statutes define the legal boundaries of presidential and executive behavior. They prohibit misuse of office, political coercion, and personal enrichment through federal authority.

3.1 Hatch Act (1939) — Prohibits federal employees from engaging in partisan political activity in their official capacity. While the President is exempt, widespread violations under both Trump terms were not punished, rendering it performative. **(C)**

3.2 18 U.S.C. §208 – Conflict of Interest — Bars federal officials from participating in matters where they have a financial interest. The President is technically exempt. Trump and his family leveraged this loophole repeatedly for personal gain. **(A)**

3.3 18 U.S.C. §1001 – False Statements — Criminalizes knowingly making false statements to federal officials or agencies. No executive branch actors have been charged for dozens of documented falsehoods. **(C)**

3.4 Obstruction of Justice Statutes (§1505, §1512) — Criminalize interference with investigations, destruction of evidence, and witness tampering. Cited repeatedly in Mueller and January 6 investigations. No enforcement against Trump. **(C)**

3.5 Federal Election Campaign Act (FECA) & Bipartisan Campaign Reform Act (BCRA) — Regulate political fundraising and spending. Loopholes exploited through dark money networks and super PAC coordination, especially under Project 2025. **(B)**

3.6 Foreign Corrupt Practices Act (1977) — Prohibits bribery of foreign officials and misuse of U.S. power abroad. Trump's solicitation of foreign investigations into political opponents pushed this statute's boundaries with no consequence. (C)

3.7 False Claims Act (1863; updated 1986) — Enables whistleblowers to expose fraud against the government. Use has declined due to fear of retaliation and narrowing of protections. (C)

3.8 Logan Act (1799) — Prohibits unauthorized negotiation with foreign governments. Though rarely enforced, public revelations about shadow diplomacy by Trump allies raise credible violations. (C)

Section 4. Lawsuits Against the President or Executive Agencies (4.1–4.7)

These legal mechanisms allow individuals, organizations, and states to challenge unlawful executive actions. They form the foundation of accountability when other branches fail.

4.1 Administrative Procedure Act (APA) — Authorizes lawsuits to challenge agency actions as unlawful, arbitrary, or procedurally flawed. Courts have relied heavily on it to overturn Trump-era executive orders. Increasingly undercut by standing barriers. (B)

4.2 Federal Tort Claims Act (FTCA, 1946) — Allows lawsuits against the government for certain wrongful acts by employees. Rarely applies to the presidency directly but increasingly used against federal agencies involved in family separation, protest suppression, and border abuse. (C)

4.3 Freedom of Information Act (FOIA) — Grants the public a right to sue for access to government records. Weaponized delay and redaction have made enforcement slow and incomplete. (C)

4.4 Habeas Corpus (28 U.S.C. §§2241–2255) — Enables individuals to challenge unlawful detention. Still operational in courts, but weakened by executive claims of national security in immigration and protest cases. (C)

4.5 Bivens Doctrine (1971) — Allows lawsuits against federal officials for constitutional violations. Gutted by recent Supreme Court rulings, now functionally unavailable in most contexts. **(A)**

4.6 42 U.S.C. §1983 — Permits civil rights suits against state officials, but not federal ones. The federal gap remains a structural failure of accountability. **(C)**

4.7 Standing Doctrine — Requires plaintiffs to show injury and redressability. Expanded by conservative courts to dismiss meritorious cases against Trump and executive agencies. **(A)**

Section 5. Judicial and Immunity Doctrines (5.1–5.5)

These court precedents shape the legal boundaries—sometimes the lack thereof—on presidential accountability. They are not statutes, but they govern how and whether presidents can be held to law.

5.1 *Nixon v. Fitzgerald* (1982) — Grants the President absolute civil immunity for official acts. Created the foundation for presidential unaccountability while in office. Continues to shield abuse of power. **(C)**

5.2 *Clinton v. Jones* (1997) — Affirms that Presidents are not immune from civil suits for private conduct. Applied during Trump's first term; likely to be narrowed by future rulings. **(C)**

5.3 *Trump v. Vance* (2020) — Reaffirmed that the President is not above the law, but placed procedural hurdles in front of state criminal subpoenas. Celebrated at the time, now largely gutted by 2024–2025 court reinterpretations. **(B)**

5.4 *Trump v. Mazars* (2020) — Imposed strict limits on Congress's ability to subpoena the President's personal records. Widely interpreted to weaken legislative oversight. **(B)**

5.5 *Trump v. United States* (2024) — Currently or recently decided case likely to create or affirm sweeping criminal immunity for presidential acts. If allowed to stand, it ends the principle of equal justice under law. (A)

Section 6. Laws Protecting the Press and Public Access (6.1–6.7)

These laws uphold visibility into government operations, shield journalists from state retaliation, and guarantee that public power remains open to public scrutiny. Their survival is essential for democratic accountability.

6.1 Privacy Protection Act (1980) — Prevents government from searching or seizing journalists' materials without court approval. Still technically intact but threatened by informal harassment and digital surveillance tactics. (C)

6.2 DOJ Subpoena Guidelines (2021 revision) — Internal policy restricting subpoenas of journalists or their sources. Rewritten or ignored by Trump's DOJ in the second term; enforcement now depends entirely on political will. (B)

6.3 Freedom of Information Act (FOIA) — Previously listed (see 1.3, 4.3). Statutory cornerstone of public access, now weakened by systematic delay, redaction, and narrowing of standing. (C)

6.4 Federal Advisory Committee Act (FACA, 1972) — Requires transparency in executive advisory bodies. Routinely bypassed by "informal" Trump task forces like the 2025 "Efficiency Council." (B)

6.5 Government in the Sunshine Act (1976) — Previously listed (see 1.8). Mandates open meetings in federal agencies. Increasingly circumvented by digital-only deliberation and reclassification. (C)

6.6 Wiretap Act (Title III, 1968) — Prohibits unauthorized interception of electronic communications. DOGE surveillance operations may risk violating these provisions but remain unverified. (C)

6.7 *New York Times v. Sullivan* (1964) — Establishes the "actual malice" standard protecting press from libel suits by officials. Targeted for reversal by Trump allies and SCOTUS signals in 2025. (B)

. . .

SECTION 7. Civil Service and Labor Protections (7.1–7.4)

These laws safeguard the integrity of the federal workforce by prohibiting politically motivated hiring, firing, or surveillance. They ensure continuity, competence, and neutrality in public service.

7.1 Civil Service Reform Act (1978) — Protects federal workers from arbitrary dismissal and affirms merit-based employment.

7.2 Pendleton Act (1883) — Establishes the principle of competitive, nonpartisan hiring. A foundation of modern civil service.

7.3 Federal Service Labor-Management Relations Statute (1978) — Guarantees union rights for most federal employees. Protects collective bargaining and grievance processes.

7.4 Hatch Act (1939) — Already listed (see 3.1); bars partisan political activity by most executive branch employees.

SECTION 8. Anti-Discrimination and DEI Framework (8.1–8.4)

These laws define the boundaries of equity in federal employment. While they do not mandate proactive inclusion, they prohibit discrimination and provide the legal foundation for modern DEI programs—many of which are now being reversed.

8.1 Title VII of the Civil Rights Act (1964) — Prohibits employment discrimination based on race, sex, religion, or national origin. Still on the books but now reinterpreted narrowly in enforcement and litigation by Trump-appointed leadership at DOJ and EEOC. (C)

8.2 Americans with Disabilities Act (1990) — Bans discriminatory treatment of individuals with disabilities in federal hiring and services. Enforcement mechanisms remain technically available but underused and deprioritized. (C)

8.3 Equal Employment Opportunity Commission (EEOC) Rules — Enforces civil rights laws against workplace discrimination.

Under Trump's second term, internal leadership changes have muted enforcement and shifted investigative priorities. **(B)**

8.4 Executive Orders on DEI — Presidents have issued directives supporting or restricting agency-level DEI programs. Trump revoked most existing DEI orders in 2025 and replaced them with anti-DEI mandates. **(A)**

SECTION 9. **Environmental and Land Protection Laws (9.1–9.7)**

These laws were enacted to defend the ecological and public value of federal lands. They require that environmental risks be disclosed, species protected, and natural resources managed in the public interest. Trump's second term has systematically defied these standards.

9.1 National Environmental Policy Act (NEPA, 1970) — Requires environmental impact reviews for major federal actions. Trump's 2025 waivers on NEPA review for energy and infrastructure projects across 12 states constitute direct statutory violation. **(A)**

9.2 Federal Land Policy and Management Act (FLPMA, 1976) — Preserves public land and prohibits its arbitrary disposal. Bypassed through fast-track leasing under DOGE in late 2025, with no clear legal review. **(A)**

9.3 Antiquities Act (1906) — Allows designation and reduction of national monuments by executive order. Trump has used this power aggressively, revoking protection for over 4 million acres without scientific consultation. **(B)**

9.4 Endangered Species Act (ESA, 1973) — Prohibits actions that threaten protected species or habitats. Waived or ignored in over two dozen mining and pipeline approvals since February 2025. **(A)**

9.5 Mineral Leasing Act (1920) — Regulates leasing for extraction on public lands. Trump's second-term expansions in the Arctic and coastal zones show probable conflict with both FLPMA and NEPA. **(A)**

9.6 Outer Continental Shelf Lands Act (OCSLA) — Governs offshore energy leases. Executive actions in 2025 authorized leases without full environmental review, raising statutory compliance questions. **(B)**

9.7 National Historic Preservation Act (1966) — Requires cultural and historical impact reviews on federal projects. Preservation protocols were suspended by DOGE in at least five project zones, triggering multiple lawsuits. **(A)**

SECTION 10. National Parks, Weather, and Climate Laws (10.1–10.3)

These statutes safeguard the environmental, scientific, and recreational assets of the United States. They were designed to ensure that conservation, forecasting, and climate adaptation are conducted free from political interference. In Trump's second term, these laws have been circumvented or directly undermined.

10.1 National Parks Organic Act (1916) — Requires that national parks be preserved "unimpaired" for future generations. Trump's 2025 cuts to staffing, maintenance, and public access services in at least 37 national parks violate the spirit and likely the letter of this law. **(A)**

10.2 Weather Research and Forecasting Innovation Act (2017) — Mandates scientific integrity and transparency in weather data and climate forecasting. Trump's political interference in NOAA hurricane reporting and staff gag orders in April 2025 breach statutory reporting independence. **(A)**

10.3 Land and Water Conservation Fund Act (1965) — Provides federal grants for public parks, conservation easements, and outdoor recreation. Trump's 2025 budget removed all discretionary grant funding, effectively gutting the program without repeal. **(B)**

SECTION 11. Academic and Research Funding Protections (11.1–11.2)

Congress holds the constitutional power of the purse—including over science, research, and higher education. These laws were enacted to insulate scientific funding from partisan retaliation. In 2025, Trump's defunding of critical research programs violated that principle and the statutes behind it.

11.1 **Impoundment Control Act (1974)** — Prohibits the President from unilaterally withholding or canceling funds appropriated by Congress. Trump's May 2025 revocation of NIH, NSF, and CDC research grants—particularly those related to climate, vaccine deployment, and demographic modeling—was enacted without congressional rescission. (A)

11.2 **Authorizing Statutes for NIH/NSF** — Federal science agencies operate under congressionally authorized multi-year mandates. Trump's politically targeted cancellation of peer-reviewed academic grants (especially to Harvard, MIT, and the University of California system) in June 2025 likely violates both the statutory purpose and the nonpartisan criteria required by law. (A)

SECTION 12. Torture, Detention, and Rendition Prohibitions (12.1–12.3)

These laws and treaties prohibit the executive branch from using torture, indefinite detention, or rendition to countries where abuse is likely. They reflect both constitutional guarantees and binding international commitments. Recent actions by the Trump administration's ICE and DHS teams have tested their limits.

12.1 **Due Process Clauses (5th and 14th Amendments)** — Guarantee that no person—citizen or noncitizen—may be deprived of liberty without due process of law. The indefinite detention of asylum seekers at unlicensed border facilities without formal charging procedures or access to legal counsel violates these clauses. (A)

12.2 **Foreign Affairs Reform and Restructuring Act (1998)** —

Implements U.S. obligations under the Convention Against Torture. Forbids deportation to countries where individuals are "more likely than not" to be tortured. Reports of expedited removals to Egypt, Venezuela, and Saudi Arabia in spring 2025, without formal review, likely breach this statute. **(A)**

12.3 Convention Against Torture (CAT) — Ratified treaty prohibiting torture and refoulement. Binding under both international and domestic law. The U.S. remains obligated to enforce CAT protections regardless of presidential policy. Current violations by DHS and ICE are under legal challenge by the ACLU and other watchdog organizations. **(A)**

SECTION 13. **International Legal Commitments (13.1–13.3)**

The United States has ratified core treaties that form the backbone of international law and democratic legitimacy. These agreements are binding under the Supremacy Clause of the Constitution and reflect global norms on rights, war, and diplomacy. Violations not only breach international law—they erode U.S. credibility and moral authority.

13.1 International Covenant on Civil and Political Rights (ICCPR) — Ratified in 1992, this treaty guarantees freedoms of expression, assembly, due process, and equal protection. Although the U.S. declared it non-self-executing, its provisions still bind federal conduct and shape jurisprudence. ICE detention practices, digital surveillance, and protest suppression since 2025 likely violate Articles 9, 14, and 21. **(A)**

13.2 Geneva Conventions — These four treaties govern the treatment of civilians, prisoners of war, and wartime conduct. Allegations of black-site detention and "enhanced interrogation" of foreign nationals captured outside declared conflict zones raise serious Geneva compliance concerns. Trump officials have cited Article II powers to bypass Convention III protections. **(B)**

13.3 United Nations Charter and Related Instruments — The UN Charter commits member states to non-aggression, peaceful resolution of disputes, and respect for sovereignty. Trump's 2025 drone strike on a suspected cartel convoy inside Mexico—without Mexican consent or congressional authorization—has drawn UN scrutiny for violating Articles 2(4) and 33. **(A)**

Section 14. Digital Power and Technological Constraint (14.1–14.6)

While no confirmed legal violations by DOGE (the Department of Government Efficiency) have yet been publicly adjudicated, its structure—operated by Elon Musk under President Trump's direction—presents an unprecedented risk profile. DOGE's opaque access to sensitive federal databases, including Social Security, IRS, Medicare, and VA systems, has triggered bipartisan concern and multiple pending lawsuits. The laws below represent statutory boundaries most likely to be crossed.

14.1 Health Insurance Portability and Accountability Act (HIPAA, 1996) — Protects the confidentiality of medical records. DOGE's administrative authority over VA and Medicare databases raises substantial concerns about unauthorized access, particularly given reports of AI-driven eligibility reviews lacking medical oversight. **(B)**

14.2 Fair Credit Reporting Act (FCRA, 1970) — Regulates access to credit histories. Whistleblowers allege DOGE used financial screening tools to deny security clearances and terminate civil servants. If true, such use constitutes illegal profiling under FCRA. **(B)**

14.3 Privacy Act of 1974 — Requires that personal records held by federal agencies be secured, transparent, and accessible for review. DOGE's refusal to publish system-of-record notices and its use of proprietary software to manage personnel evaluations likely violates this statute. **(A)**

14.4 Gramm-Leach-Bliley Act (GLBA, 1999) — Protects consumer financial data from unauthorized use. If DOGE accessed Treasury-linked banking records (e.g., for Social Security recipients or federal aid applicants), this would constitute a breach under GLBA safeguards. **(C)**

14.5 Federal Information Security Modernization Act (FISMA, 2014) — Mandates cybersecurity standards and breach reporting. DOGE's non-cooperation with agency CIOs and cybersecurity audits has triggered three IG investigations. Absence of documented compliance strongly suggests FISMA violations. **(A)**

14.6 Presidential Policy Directive 41 (PPD-41, 2016) — Requires interagency coordination for cyber incidents. DOGE's unilateral response protocols and Musk's refusal to share source code with the Cybersecurity and Infrastructure Security Agency (CISA) may violate both the directive and internal OMB cybersecurity guidance. **(C)**

THESE LAWS ARE NOT A GUARANTEE. They are the legal limits on the presidency—and nearly all have now been weakened, violated, or ignored. They work only when enforced, respected, and upheld by officials with the courage to act. What binds a president is not statute alone—it is consequence. A democracy cannot survive a president determined to defy the law unless the law is enforced as a condition of holding office. If these limits continue to be bypassed, the result will not be political overreach. It will be autocracy.

APPENDIX C: THE SUMMARY OF PRESIDENTIAL CONSTRAINT

———— ✦ ————

This appendix summarizes the structural, statutory, and procedural mechanisms necessary to restore enforceable legal limits on presidential power. Each item includes: (1) the area of concern, and (2) the proposed reform. Together, these reforms define the architecture of a presidency bound by law, oversight, and democratic accountability.

1. **Presidential Accountability**
   Concern: Presidents have exploited ambiguity around legal immunity to evade prosecution for criminal, personal, and unconstitutional acts.
   Reform: Codify that no sitting or former president is immune from criminal indictment or prosecution for non-official conduct, including violations of the Constitution, obstruction of justice, or incitement to insurrection. Clarify that the presidency is not a shield against the rule of law.

. . .

2. Oversight Independence and Protection

Concern: Inspectors General, FOIA, whistleblower protections, and agency review processes have been defanged or circumvented.

Reform: Enact statutory independence for Inspectors General, including protections from removal without cause. Strengthen whistleblower laws with enforceable penalties for retaliation. Require full compliance with lawful congressional oversight and subpoena authority.

3. Emergency Powers Reform

Concern: Emergency declarations are increasingly used to bypass Congress and consolidate executive power indefinitely.

Reform: Require that all emergency declarations expire after 30 days unless renewed by Congress. Restrict emergency powers to areas directly related to the declared emergency, with automatic judicial review mechanisms.

4. Executive Order Oversight

Concern: Executive Orders are used to circumvent Congress, especially on rights, budgets, and immigration.

Reform: Require congressional review of any Executive Order that alters constitutional rights, reassigns federal spending, or undermines statutory limits. Allow pre-enforcement judicial review for constitutionally questionable orders.

5. Pardon Power Constraints

Concern: Pardons have been abused to obstruct justice, reward loyalists, and conceal crimes.

Reform: Prohibit self-pardons and secret pardons. Mandate public disclosure within 24 hours and require DOJ conflict-of-interest review for all clemency actions.

6. Campaign Finance Reform

Concern: Unlimited and undisclosed money has corrupted elections, policymaking, and public trust.

Reform: Overturn *Citizens United*. Ban dark money and foreign-influenced spending. Enact real-time disclosure and provide public financing alternatives.

7. Voting Rights Protection

Concern: Voter suppression and election subversion have escalated since the rollback of the Voting Rights Act.

Reform: Restore preclearance. Make vote-by-mail, early voting, and drop boxes universally available. Federalize voting access standards to ensure equal participation.

8. Electoral College Reform

Concern: Minority rule is now structurally protected by the Electoral College.

Reform: Complete the National Popular Vote Compact. Create statutory protections against false electors. Establish independent certification enforcement.

9. Redistricting Reform

Concern: Gerrymandering undermines fair representation and fuels political extremism.

Reform: Require all states to adopt independent redistricting commissions with transparent processes and fairness metrics.

10. Election Certification Integrity

Concern: Partisan actors have attempted to delay, block, or falsify election results.

Reform: Federally safeguard certification timelines. Criminalize false elector slates. Protect election workers from threats and political interference.

11. Supreme Court Term Limits

Concern: Lifetime tenure has made the Court unbalanced and unaccountable.

Reform: Enact 18-year staggered term limits for justices. Retain judicial independence while restoring generational rotation.

12. Lower Court Expansion and Diversity

Concern: Federal courts remain overloaded, ideologically skewed, and demographically unrepresentative.

Reform: Add new judgeships to match population growth. Prioritize regional and professional diversity. Establish public legal education pipelines.

13. Judicial Ethics and Accountability

Concern: The Supreme Court lacks a binding code of ethics, enabling corruption and influence.

Reform: Enforce mandatory ethics codes. Require recusals, financial disclosures, and public reporting of gifts and conflicts of interest.

. . .

14. Insurrection Clause Enforcement

Concern: Section 3 of the 14th Amendment has been rendered inoperative through judicial delay and inaction.

Reform: Create automatic enforcement mechanisms for officials found to have engaged in insurrection or rebellion.

15. Transparency and FOIA Modernization

Concern: Public records laws are slow, inconsistent, and easily evaded.

Reform: Modernize FOIA. Limit exemptions, shorten response times, and expand access to digital communications and privatized public functions.

16. Disinformation and Platform Regulation

Concern: Algorithmic manipulation and disinformation have eroded public trust and electoral integrity.

Reform: Mandate disclosure of political ad sources. Implement civic audits for algorithmic bias during election cycles. Ban AI-generated false content in campaigns.

17. Fairness in Broadcast Media

Concern: Broadcast media once held to balance requirements are now profit-driven and polarized.

Reform: Restore a modernized Fairness Doctrine. Require balance, fact-checking, and civic service standards for public-spectrum licensees.

. . .

18. Civic Education and Democratic Literacy

Concern: The public is unequipped to detect manipulation, resist authoritarianism, or understand constitutional government.

Reform: Fund universal civic education. Integrate democratic literacy, media evaluation, and public service opportunities into K-12 and post-secondary education.

19. Rebuilding Public Trust in Government

Concern: Decades of corruption, secrecy, and non-responsiveness have collapsed trust in institutions.

Reform: Institute transparency-by-design in policy development. Require public advisory boards, published metrics, and regular audits of federal agencies.

20. Presidential Constraint as Constitutional Norm

Concern: The presidency has escaped its constitutional limits through decades of drift and judicial permissiveness.

Reform: Codify legal, procedural, and structural constraints—including those outlined above—as baseline requirements for any presidency. No leader should ever again be allowed to reinterpret impunity as power.

APPENDIX D: THE UNWRITTEN GUARDRAILS
FIFTY TRADITIONS THAT ONCE RESTRAINED THE PRESIDENCY

---✦---

For most of American history, the presidency was constrained not only by law but by expectation. These unwritten norms—once honored by every president until Trump—formed a quiet but powerful fabric of restraint, woven from humility, transparency, and civic trust. Though unenforceable, they held the office in check. Their collapse did not just expose vulnerabilities. It rewrote the presidency in practice, even as the Constitution remained unchanged in theory.

I. TRANSPARENCY as a Civic Duty

1. **Release of personal tax returns** — Since Nixon, every president until Trump disclosed their tax records. The public had a right to know the sources, debts, and interests shaping executive power.

2. **Disclosure of medical status and physicals** — Presidents routinely released health summaries or full medical reports to assure the public of their capacity to serve.

3. **Publication of daily schedules** — Most presidents provided regular calendars showing their meetings, events, and locations. Trump largely ended this practice, replacing it with secrecy or self-promotion.

4. **Visitor logs to the White House and executive offices** — Until 2017, these logs were voluntarily released. Trump discontinued them entirely. Biden later restored limited disclosure.

5. **Routine White House press briefings** — Press Secretaries once held near-daily briefings with questions from across the media spectrum. Trump suspended these for over a year.

6. **Direct engagement through press conferences** — Presidents traditionally held regular press conferences—unscripted and open to follow-up. Trump preferred rallies and social media.

7. **Disclosure of foreign gifts and financial entanglements** — Though mandated in part by the Emoluments Clause, the broader tradition was to avoid even the appearance of influence by foreign actors.

8. **Explanation of executive orders upon signing** — Presidents typically released statements or held events to explain major orders. Trump often signed sweeping orders late at night with no notice.

9. **Voluntary financial disclosures beyond legal minimums** — Prior presidents went beyond FEC and ethics office requirements—offering full accounting of holdings, trusts, and debts. Trump provided only vague statements.

10. **Transparency in the presidential pardon process** — Traditionally, presidents issued pardons with input from the DOJ and released rationales. Trump bypassed this entirely, granting pardons to loyalists without explanation.

II. Accountability Without Coercion

11. **Voluntary compliance with congressional subpoenas** —

Presidents and aides historically cooperated with legislative oversight—even under scrutiny. Trump instructed mass defiance.

12. **Respect for Inspectors General** — IGs were traditionally viewed as internal guardians. Trump fired, sidelined, or intimidated multiple IGs investigating wrongdoing.

13. **Response to GAO audits and inquiries** — Presidents accepted the Government Accountability Office as a legitimate watchdog. Trump treated its findings as partisan attacks.

14. **Testimony by Cabinet officials and senior staff** — Agencies routinely sent leaders to testify before Congress. Under Trump, many refused or appeared only under threat of contempt.

15. **Acceptance of Special Counsel and Independent Counsel investigations** — From Watergate to Mueller, most presidents cooperated, even when resentful. Trump called the process treason and sought its destruction.

16. **No contact with DOJ about specific prosecutions** — Past presidents avoided direct interference with ongoing cases. Trump demanded investigations of enemies and leniency for allies.

17. **Protection of whistleblowers from retaliation** — Whistleblower laws were honored as shields for truth-tellers. Trump outed, vilified, and endangered those who reported misconduct or were suspected of leaks.

18. **Avoidance of personal conflicts of interest** — Presidents traditionally placed assets in blind trusts. Trump retained ownership of hundreds of businesses and openly profited.

19. **Respect for OMB independence in budget analysis** — The Office of Management and Budget historically offered neutral cost assessments. Trump's OMB under Vought became a propaganda arm.

20. **Cooperation with agency ethics officials** — Presidents and staff worked with the Office of Government Ethics to avoid conflicts. Trump defied the office's recommendations and attacked its leadership.

. . .

III. Respecting the Republic

21. **Deference to career civil servants** — Presidents once viewed apolitical career staff as vital stewards of government continuity. Trump cast them as a "deep state" and worked to replace them with loyalists.

22. **Non-use of federal agencies for partisan gain** — Past administrations separated governance from politics. Trump weaponized the DOJ, DHS, IRS, and Census Bureau for electoral and personal advantage.

23. **Refraining from commentary on active investigations** — Previous presidents avoided prejudicing legal outcomes. Trump routinely opined on guilt, demanded charges, and threatened judges.

24. **Respect for military apolitical norms** — Commanders-in-chief avoided using troops as political props. Trump had generals tear-gassed protestors for a photo op with a Bible.

25. **Protection of classified information** — Presidents historically protected state secrets. Trump shared Israeli intelligence with Russia in the Oval Office and hoarded classified documents after leaving office.

26. **Judicial independence honored in speech and action** — Earlier presidents avoided personal attacks on judges. Trump mocked, threatened, and pressured them—by name.

27. **Avoidance of brand promotion through office** — No prior president used the office to advertise personal businesses. Trump held state functions at his properties and redirected federal money toward them.

28. **Divestiture or blind trust of personal holdings** — Presidents like Carter and Obama divested assets or used blind trusts. Trump refused, claiming falsely that "the president can't have a conflict of interest."

29. **Consultation with prior presidents on sensitive matters** — Though informal, every president since Truman sought advice across party lines—except Trump, who severed those ties and treated predecessors as enemies.

30. **Refraining from lawsuits against one's own government** — No other president sued the National Archives, DOJ, or states to obstruct oversight. Trump made litigation a tool of delay and defiance.

IV. The Presidency as Example

31. **Peaceful concession of electoral defeat** — Every losing president or candidate in modern history conceded promptly—until Trump, who incited insurrection to remain in power.

32. **Use of the bully pulpit to unify in crisis** — Presidents traditionally addressed the nation with solemnity in hardship. Trump used crises—pandemics, protests, disasters—as stages for division or denial.

33. **Avoidance of personal insult in official speech** — Prior presidents disagreed without derision. Trump mocked physical appearances, disabilities, accents, and grief itself.

34. **Participation in national rituals and remembrances** — Presidents honored bipartisan norms by attending inaugurations, funerals, and days of mourning. Trump boycotted or minimized many such events.

35. **Limiting participation in partisan fundraising** — While all presidents raised funds, most kept it discreet. Trump monetized rallies, merchandised his image, and redirected funds to family and allies.

36. **Refusal to endorse candidates while in office** — Many presidents refrained from weighing into primaries or local contests. Trump openly endorsed loyalists and uses the threat of endorsing opponents to demand fealty.

37. **Engagement with both parties during national emergencies** — Past presidents rallied coalitions in wartime, disaster, or crisis. Trump used emergencies to punish opposition states and reward loyal governors.

38. **Presidential communication guided by truth** — Presidents, while political, avoided deliberate falsehoods in formal statements. Trump's falsehood count exceeded 30,000 during his first term alone.

39. **Respect for presidential transition rituals** — The handoff between administrations was treated as sacred. Trump sabotaged the 2020 transition, refused briefings, and tried to overturn results.

40. **Writing farewell letters to successors** — A quiet tradition since Reagan—passing on counsel and goodwill. Trump left no such note in 2021 and is unlikely to do so again.

V. The Presidency Is Not Personal Property

41. **Avoidance of personal profit while in office** — Presidents did not treat public office as a revenue stream. Trump directed government spending to his hotels, clubs, and properties.

42. **No use of federal forces for personal image-making** — Commanders-in-chief avoided theatrical military displays for personal glorification. Trump deployed troops against protestors for a staged Bible photo.

43. **Post-presidency silence to preserve national unity** — Departing presidents traditionally offered successors space to govern. Trump continued rallies, lawsuits, and a re-election campaign.

44. **Resignation or recusal of scandal-plagued officials** — Cabinet members once resigned over impropriety. Under Trump, criminally charged officials stayed or were reappointed.

45. **Use of Senate-confirmed officials in leadership roles** —

Presidents used "acting" designations sparingly. Trump ran the government with unconfirmed loyalists to avoid scrutiny.

46. **Respect for press freedom and media independence** — No modern president threatened to revoke credentials or punish outlets. Trump labeled journalists "enemies of the people."

47. **No regulatory retaliation against critics** — Presidents refrained from using agencies to punish dissent. Trump targeted car companies, universities, hospitals, and media companies.

48. **Rejection of foreign influence in elections** — Presidents saw foreign interference as disqualifying. Trump welcomed, solicited, and accepted help from adversarial states.

49. **Support for post-Watergate ethics reforms** — Presidents upheld bipartisan safeguards—FEC integrity, OGE independence, FOIA access. Trump hollowed them out or left them vacant.

50. **Governance as deliberation, not performance** — The office was once guided by strategy, counsel, and precedent. Trump governed via social media polls, personal whim, and spectacle.

These traditions were never codified because, until recently, they did not need to be. But precedent, once shattered, invites imitation. The collapse of these guardrails has revealed the presidency's dangerous dependence on self-restraint—and the system's failure to demand it. If democracy is to last, what was once voluntary must now be made structural. Custom must become law. Expectation must become enforceable. And no office, however powerful, must ever again presume itself above the republic.

APPENDIX E: NOTES ON JUDICIAL CORRUPTION AND INFLUENCE

———— ✦ ————

This appendix catalogs the unprecedented ethical breakdown now facing the United States judiciary. While courts were once seen as the final line of constitutional defense, recent years have revealed how vulnerable they are to political capture, personal enrichment, and ideological distortion. From solo dissents that abandon precedent to justices accepting lavish gifts from billionaires with business before the Court, the erosion is both procedural and moral. What follows is a structured account of five interconnected patterns: extreme rulings, ethical misconduct, partisan favoritism, personal attacks on judges, and the rise of dark-money influence. Together, they expose a Court in crisis.

It is divided into five sections:

1. Solo Dissents and Fringe Legal Positions
2. Undisclosed Gifts, Conflicts, and Partisan Activity
3. Failure to Recuse in Cases of Personal or Familial Involvement

4. Patterns of Retaliation Against Judges Who Ruled Against Trump
5. Dark-Money Legal Infrastructure and Case Placement Strategy

SECTION 1: Solo Dissents and Fringe Legal Positions — Justice Clarence Thomas

A series of solo dissents and extreme legal interpretations by Justice Thomas reflect a jurisprudence increasingly out of step with constitutional consensus and democratic norms.

1. *United States v. Rahimi (2024)* — Dissent against barring gun ownership for domestic abusers.
2. *Nelson v. Colorado (2017)* — Dissent denying refund of criminal fees after exoneration.
3. *Mahanoy v. B.L. (2021)* — Dissent supporting broad school control over off-campus speech.
4. *Snyder v. Louisiana (2008)* — Dissent against recognizing racial bias in jury selection.
5. *Hamdan v. Rumsfeld (2006)* — Dissent supporting Bush's military commissions at Guantanamo.
6. *U.S. Term Limits v. Thornton (1995)* — Dissent supporting state-imposed limits on Congress.
7. *Gonzales v. Raich (2005)* — Dissent against federal authority over intrastate medical marijuana.
8. *Counterman v. Colorado (2023)* — Dissent favoring conviction without proof of intent in threats.
9. *Foster v. Chatman (2016)* — Dissent minimizing racially motivated jury exclusion.
10. *Safford v. Redding (2009)* — Dissent defending a strip search of a middle-school student.

These decisions often elevate absolutist interpretations of rights or executive power over legal precedent and common-sense restraint.

Justice Clarence Thomas

Justice Thomas has repeatedly failed to disclose luxury travel, financial gifts, and property transactions involving conservative billionaire Harlan Crow and other wealthy donors. These include:

- Private jet flights, yacht cruises, and resort stays.
- Undisclosed sale of three family-owned Savannah parcels to Harlan Crow in 2014.
- Rent-free home for Thomas's mother provided by Crow.
- Tuition payments for his grandnephew.
- Expensive gifts such as historical artifacts and artwork.
- Undisclosed consulting payments to his wife, Ginni Thomas, directed through opaque financial arrangements.
- Participation in political fundraising events hosted by donors with business before the Court.
- Attendance at Bohemian Grove and Koch Network gatherings, with no public record.
- Repeated amended disclosures filed only after investigative reporting forced the issue.

Justice Samuel Alito

Justice Alito's conduct raises similar concerns:

- Accepted an undisclosed luxury fishing trip with

billionaire Paul Singer, who later had cases before the Court.
- Flew on Singer's private jet and failed to recuse in at least 10 related cases.
- Displayed symbols tied to "Stop the Steal" and January 6 movements outside his homes.
- Attended Koch Network fundraisers and accepted tickets from right-wing European aristocrats.
- Made public comments expressing hostility to political compromise and skepticism of oversight.
- Defended his actions preemptively through opinion pieces in ideologically aligned media.

Together, these patterns suggest not only ethical lapses but a rejection of judicial neutrality.

Section 3: Failure to Recuse in Cases of Personal or Familial Involvement

- Justice Thomas did not recuse from Supreme Court cases involving Trump's efforts to overturn the 2020 election—despite Ginni Thomas's active participation in those efforts.
- Thomas also refused to step aside in *Trump v. Anderson*, a case testing Trump's eligibility under Section 3 of the 14th Amendment.
- Justice Alito refused to recuse from January 6–related cases despite flying the upside-down U.S. flag and the "Appeal to Heaven" flag—both embraced by insurrectionists.
- Alito also declined to recuse in cases involving major

donors or partisan groups he associated with, including the Koch Network.
- Lower-court Trump appointees, including Judges Aileen Cannon and Matthew Kacsmaryk, similarly refused to recuse from cases where they had clear conflicts of interest or demonstrated bias.

These failures erode public confidence in the judiciary and suggest the existence of a two-tiered system—where conflicts are disqualifying for lower officials but not for those at the top.

Section 4: Patterns of Retaliation Against Judges Who Ruled Against Trump

DONALD TRUMP HAS REPEATEDLY USED social media, rallies, and official channels to attack judges who ruled against him. These attacks include:

- *Judge Gonzalo Curiel*: Trump called him biased because of his Mexican heritage.
- *Judge James Robart*: After blocking the Muslim travel ban, Trump labeled him a "so-called judge."
- *Judge Tanya Chutkan* and *Judge Juan Merchan*: Targeted by Trump during his criminal proceedings, including direct violations of gag orders.
- *Judge Amy Berman Jackson* and *Judge Emmet Sullivan*: Attacked for their roles in cases involving Trump allies.
- *Chief Justice Roberts*: Called a "nightmare" for conservatives over health care and voting rights rulings.
- Trump also incited online mobs who posted death

threats and memes calling for violence against targeted judges.

This sustained pattern of retaliation aims to chill judicial independence and weaponize the judiciary for personal and political gain.

Section 5: Dark-Money Legal Infrastructure and Case Placement Strategy

- **Leonard Leo's $1.6 billion network**, including the Marble Freedom Trust and the Judicial Crisis Network, strategically finances campaigns to shape the judiciary and funnel cases to favorable courts.
- **Amicus brief campaigns** coordinated by dark-money groups have swamped the Court, shaping conservative doctrine behind the scenes.
- **Targeted case placement** ensures lawsuits are filed before sympathetic Trump-appointed judges like Cannon, Kacsmaryk, or Walker.
- **Influence in judicial selection**, especially at the state level, has grown dramatically, with anonymous donors funding judicial elections and lobbying campaigns.
- **Resistance to transparency reforms**, including disclosure of amicus funding, judicial ethics enforcement, and recusal rules, ensures donor anonymity and ideological capture.

This infrastructure is not illegal—but it is corrosive. It transforms courts from neutral arbiters into ideological battlegrounds manipulated by wealth and influence.

. . .

THESE ARE NOT ISOLATED LAPSES. They form a pattern: of corrupted judgment, eroded impartiality, and unchecked power. When justices accept undisclosed gifts, refuse to recuse in cases of personal entanglement, or adopt fringe legal theories that rewrite constitutional norms, the consequence is not merely reputational—it is institutional collapse. The judiciary cannot constrain autocracy if it becomes its instrument. And democracy cannot survive if those who interpret the law are no longer bound by it. Oversight must not be optional. Recusal must not be voluntary. Ethics must not depend on honor. Reform must now be the condition of legitimacy.

APPENDIX F: MANIPULATION OF SUPREME COURT PROCEDURE TO ADVANCE IDEOLOGY

◆

The U.S. Supreme Court's procedural mechanisms—case selection, opinion drafting, and the application of precedent—are increasingly employed not as neutral tools of justice but as instruments to advance a specific ideological agenda. This manipulation—subtle, systematic, and cloaked in legal formalism—undermines judicial neutrality and corrodes democratic legitimacy.

One notable example is the Court's decision in *Citizens United v. FEC*, where Chief Justice Roberts orchestrated a re-argument of the case to address broader constitutional questions not initially presented by the parties. This strategic move facilitated a sweeping decision that overturned established campaign finance laws, illustrating how procedural choices can be leveraged to achieve predetermined ideological outcomes.

Similarly, in *Rucho v. Common Cause*, the Court declared partisan gerrymandering claims nonjusticiable political questions, effectively removing federal courts from addressing such issues. The decision offered no constitutional standard for when gerrymandering becomes unconstitutional, demonstrating how procedural abstention can serve to entrench partisan advantage under the guise of judicial restraint.

The Court's posture in *Loper Bright Enterprises v. Raimondo* further exemplifies this trend. By choosing to hear the case, the Court signaled its willingness to reconsider and potentially dismantle longstanding administrative law doctrines—especially *Chevron* deference—thus shifting the balance of power from executive agencies to the judiciary itself.

These instances reflect a broader pattern. The Court's decisions about what cases to hear, how to frame legal questions, and how broadly to rule are now shaped not only by law but by ideology. The cumulative effect is a judiciary that appears more invested in driving outcomes than in defending process—a dangerous inversion of its constitutional purpose.

The concept of "constitutional hardball"—where legal procedures are exploited for partisan gain—is now increasingly applicable to the Court itself. This approach shreds norms, severs the appearance of impartiality, and erodes the public trust necessary for democratic legitimacy.

Another tactic now exploited to circumvent full judicial scrutiny is the so-called "shadow docket"—a term coined to describe the Court's growing use of emergency orders and summary decisions without full briefing, oral argument, or signed opinions. Traditionally reserved for scheduling or procedural housekeeping, the shadow docket now shapes national policy in the dark.

The danger lies not only in the outcomes of these rulings but in the opaque manner in which they are delivered.

By avoiding the regular docket, the Court sidesteps transparency, evades public scrutiny, and shields itself from accountability. These unsigned, unexplained orders—often issued in the dead of night—can have sweeping national consequences without precedent, without debate, and without warning. Justice, in these cases, is neither seen nor explained.

Notable examples include the Court's midnight refusal to block Texas's SB 8 abortion ban—effectively nullifying *Roe v. Wade* protections without hearing argument—as well as multiple rulings altering voting procedures on the eve of elections, typically to the benefit of Republican-aligned interests. Many of these emerge from cases engineered through single-judge districts and fast-tracked to the Court by partisan actors.

These practices betray the Framers' design of a judiciary constrained by law and bound to the public it serves. Article III granted lifetime tenure not to facilitate unaccountable power, but to insulate judges from political pressure while ensuring fidelity to the rule of law. That fidelity is now in question.

To preserve the Court's legitimacy—and the democratic order it is sworn to uphold—procedural reform is essential. This includes mandatory explanations for emergency rulings, enforceable standards for granting certiorari, transparency in case selection, and the adoption of fixed terms for Justices. These changes would not politicize the Court. They would rescue it—from secrecy, from impunity, and from a creeping drift toward ideological rule. The Constitution grants the Court legitimacy only so long as it serves the law—not an agenda.

APPENDIX G: RESTORATION SPINE
WHAT MUST BE REBUILT, AND WHY

———✦———

A functioning democracy is not a list of policies. It is a system of interdependent conditions that either hold—or collapse together. We do not restore democracy by fixing symptoms. We restore it by rebuilding structure. In this book, we name the structure clearly.

Across the 18 chapters of the *American Restoration*, we identify four democratic conditions without which no republic can survive: **Consent. Constraint. Function. Trust.** These are not abstract values. They are operational tests. Where they fail, democracy fails. Where they hold, democracy holds.

None of these reforms are optional. None are theoretical. Every one addresses a failure already exploited, a weakness already abused. Together, they form a new foundation. Not for a different America—but for an America that finally lives up to its promise.

Some reforms are foundational. Others are protective. Six must come first—not because they are easiest, but because they shield the rest from repeal, obstruction, and judicial sabotage. These are the

Six That Hold: Court expansion, campaign finance reform, voting rights and fair maps, presidential accountability, independent oversight, and platform transparency.

They do not replace the full agenda. They defend it. Without them, every other reform is at risk of reversal. With them, democracy has a fighting chance.

What follows is the full democratic spine: eighteen reforms, each reinforcing one of the core conditions of democratic survival. Together, they define the structure—not just of a functioning government, but of a republic that endures.

CONDITION 1. Consent: The Power to Choose Government

Without the equal right to vote, speak, organize, and decide, democracy does not exist.

1. Campaign Finance Reform

Restore legislative authority to regulate money in politics. Enact real-time transparency, advertising limits, public financing pilots, and truth-in-campaign rules.

2. Voting Rights Protection

Guarantee universal and equal access to the ballot through automatic registration, national early voting, restored preclearance, and robust federal enforcement.

3. Electoral College Reform

Complete the National Popular Vote Compact, enforce elector fidelity, prohibit substitution schemes, and explore proportional allocation to better reflect the will of voters.

4. Redistricting Reform

Require independent commissions with measurable fairness metrics to draw congressional and state maps. End the gerrymander ratchet by 2030 to preserve democratic choice.

5. Election Certification Integrity

Criminalize false certification attempts, protect election workers from intimidation, and establish nonpartisan federal safeguards to uphold lawful outcomes.

CONDITION 2. Constraint: The Limits on Presidential Power

No democracy can survive when the executive is above the law.

6. Presidential Accountability

Establish that sitting presidents are not immune from indictment or subpoena for personal, criminal, or unconstitutional acts. Restore equality before the law.

7. Oversight Independence and Protection

Protect Inspectors General, empower whistleblowers, enforce congressional subpoenas, and punish obstruction of oversight.

8. Emergency Powers Reform

Limit unilateral declarations through automatic expiration and mandatory congressional reauthorization. End indefinite emergencies by executive fiat.

9. Executive Order Oversight

Require congressional review of executive orders affecting federal spending, constitutional rights, or balance of powers. Fast-track override mechanism.

10. Pardon Power Constraints

Ban self-pardons, secret pardons, and pardon-for-silence agreements. Require DOJ review and full public disclosure of all clemency decisions.

CONDITION 3. Function: The Capacity to Govern

Democracy must be able to act—fairly, capably, and without capture.

11. Supreme Court Term Limits

Impose 18-year staggered terms to depoliticize judicial appointments and restore generational balance.

12. Lower Court Expansion and Access to Justice

Add judges where needed to resolve backlogs and reduce partisan entrenchment. Expand access through diversity pipelines and geographic equity.

13. Supreme Court Ethics Code

Apply binding ethics rules, gift bans, and recusal requirements to justices. Make the highest court accountable to the same standards as all federal judges.

14. Insurrection Clause Enforcement

Operationalize Section 3 of the 14th Amendment to disqualify officials who incite or support insurrection. Create judicial review processes to enforce it fairly.

15. Transparency and FOIA Modernization

Shorten response timelines, limit overused exemptions, and extend open-government rules to privatized public functions.

CONDITION 4. Trust: The Foundation for Consent

Without truth, education, and inclusion, democracy cannot sustain public faith.

16. Disinformation and Platform Transparency

Disclose who pays for political ads, who is targeted, and how content is algorithmically promoted. Conduct civic audits before elections to detect manipulation.

17. Fairness in Broadcast Media

Reestablish a modern Fairness Doctrine for publicly licensed media. Require balanced civic coverage and protect local journalism from partisan takeover.

18. Civic Education and Democratic Literacy

Fund universal K–12 civics instruction, adult democratic literacy programs, and national service opportunities that prepare citizens for self-government.

TOGETHER, these reforms do more than fix broken laws. They rebuild the conditions for democratic life. They do not favor one party—they favor the public. They do not entrench power—they distribute it. They do not promise ease—they demand effort. But through them, democracy becomes possible again.

This is the spine of a restored republic. If it breaks, the body politic cannot stand. If it holds, the nation can rise.

APPENDIX H: EPIGRAPHS OF THE RESTORATION

---✦---

The following epigraphs opened each chapter of *American Restoration*. Taken together, they offer a moral arc for the work—one that moves from collapse and resistance to renewal and permanence. These are the words that framed the fight.

Epigraph: American Restoration

"No nation remains a democracy by accident. The people must defend its laws, rebuild its frame, and renew its soul."
— JP Vincent

Chapter 1: American Restoration - The Stakes

"You do not become a tyranny overnight. You become a tyranny by design, by neglect, and by delay."
— JP Vincent

Part I: Elections That Count Every Voice

"The ballot is stronger than the bullet."
— Abraham Lincoln

Chapter 3: The Restoration Agenda

"A representative cannot serve both the people and their patrons."
— JP Vincent

Chapter 4: Voting Rights Protection

A system that filters participation through race, class, or ZIP code is not broken. It is rigged."
— JP Vincent

Chapter 5: Electoral College Reform

"A democracy worthy of its people must let every voice count equally."
— Stacey Abrams

. . .

Chapter 6: Redistricting Reform

"The lines that divide us do more than shape elections—they shape who matters."
— JP Vincent

Chapter 7: Election Certification and Peaceful Transition

"The law must finish what the people begin."
— JP Vincent

Chapter 8: Elections That Work - Five Reforms, One Democracy

"The price of freedom is eternal vigilance."
— Thomas Jefferson.

Part II - The Limits to Presidential Power

"The Constitution was never meant to survive a man without shame."
— JP Vincent

Chapter 10: Power Without Boundary

> "A constitution is not the end of a struggle. It is the record of it—and the path to keep fighting."
> — JP Vincent

Chapter 11: Law Without Consequence

> "The sea did what it liked, and what it liked was destruction."
> — Charles Dickens, *A Tale of Two Cities*

Chapter 12: Office Without Honor

> "The presidency is not merely an administrative office. That is the least of it. It is preeminently a place of moral leadership."
> — Franklin D. Roosevelt

Chapter 13: Constraint Without Exception

> "The price of apathy towards public affairs is to be ruled by evil men."
> — Plato

Part III. A Judiciary That Upholds Law, Not Loyalty

> "Judges were never meant to be kings in robes."
> — JP Vincent

. . .

Chapter 15: Judicial Assignment Reform and Case Integrity

"Justice is not served when outcome is a matter of address."
— Learned Hand

Chapter 16: Judicial Ethics Reform and Federal Accountability

"Trust is not what frees power from oversight. It is what makes oversight necessary."
— J.P. Vincent

Chapter 17: Court Transparency and Shadow Docket Oversight

"People in an open society do not demand infallibility from their institutions. But it is difficult for them to accept what they are prohibited from observing."
— Chief Justice Warren Burger, *Richmond Newspapers v. Virginia* (1980)

Chapter 18: Supreme Court Term Limits and Generational Balance

"Laws are not made to last forever, but to endure until they no longer serve justice."
— Montesquieu

. . .

Chapter 19: Lower Court Expansion and Access to Justice

"No institution serves the people by accident. It does so by design, or not at all."
— JP Vincent

Chapter 20: Transparency Reform and Public Access to Information

"Justice must not only be done, but must also be seen to be done."
— Lord Hewart, *R v Sussex Justices, Ex parte McCarthy* (1924)

Chapter 21: The Rule of Law Is What We Build It To Be

"A government of laws, and not of men."
—John Adams

Part IV. Rebuilding an Informed Public

"Freedom is the freedom to say that two plus two make four. If that is granted, all else follows."
— George Orwell, *1984*

Chapter 23: Disinformation and Platform Transparency

"If liberty means anything at all, it means the right to tell people what they do not want to hear."
— George Orwell

Chapter 24: Fairness in Broadcast Media

"It isn't what I don't know that gets me in trouble—it's what I know for sure that ain't so."
— Mark Twain

Chapter 25: Civic Education and Democratic Literacy

"Surely we can teach each other how to stay free."
— JP Vincent

Chapter 26: The Six That Hold

"The republic survives not on trust, but on design—on checks that withstand betrayal."
— Learned Hand

Chapter 27: If We Are to Last

"We were not given a future. We were given the tools to build one."
— JP Vincent

APPENDIX I: SELECTED SOURCES AND CITATIONS

———— ✦ ————

This appendix offers a representative selection of the legal decisions, government documents, investigative journalism, and scholarly works that inform the arguments of *American Restoration*. It does not attempt a line-by-line citation but reflects the core legal and factual sources behind each reform.

—

I. Constitutional and Legal Sources

- U.S. Constitution: Articles I–III; Amendments I, XIV, XV, XVII, XIX, XXIV, XXVI
- *The Federalist Papers* (esp. Nos. 10, 51, 68)
- *Trump v. Anderson*, 602 U.S. ___ (2024) – decision

disqualifying state-level removal of Trump from ballots based on 14th Amendment Section 3
- *Trump v. United States*, Docket No. 23-939 (2025) – U.S. Supreme Court case on presidential criminal immunity
- *Dobbs v. Jackson Women's Health Organization*, 597 U.S. 215 (2022)
- Executive Orders from 2017–2025, accessed via federalregister.gov
- Electoral Count Reform and Presidential Transition Improvement Act of 2022
- Final Report of the Select Committee to Investigate the January 6th Attack (2022)

II. Government and Oversight Reports

- Office of the Inspector General (DOJ): Reports on FBI, politicization, whistleblower retaliation (2019–2024)
- Government Accountability Office (GAO): Reports on misuse of funds, inspector general firings, and emergency powers
- Brennan Center for Justice: "Emergency Powers and the Erosion of Constitutional Government" (2020); "Voting Laws Roundup" (2024)
- Congressional Research Service (CRS): Reports on pardon power, executive orders, war powers, and intelligence oversight
- Project on Government Oversight (POGO): Reports on IG independence and Trump-era obstruction of oversight

III. Investigative Journalism and News Analysis

- *ProPublica*: Investigative series on Justices Clarence Thomas and Samuel Alito's undisclosed gifts and luxury travel
- *The New York Times*: Reporting on Trump's legal defense, financial interests, and judicial manipulation
- *The Washington Post*: Exposés on Project 2025, loyalty purges, and federal agency sabotage
- *The Atlantic* and *The New Yorker*: Essays on democratic decline, Trumpism, and institutional decay
- *Reuters* and *Associated Press*: Election law enforcement and misinformation coverage
- *PBS Frontline*: "Democracy on the Brink," "Trump's American Carnage"
- *CNN* and *NPR*: Continuous coverage of federal indictments and constitutional challenges

IV. Books and Scholarly Works

- Timothy Snyder, *On Tyranny* (2017) and *The Road to Unfreedom* (2018)
- Steven Levitsky & Daniel Ziblatt, *How Democracies Die* (2018)
- Nancy MacLean, *Democracy in Chains* (2017)
- Michael Waldman, *The Fight to Vote* (2016)
- Corey Brettschneider, *The Oath and the Office* (2018)
- Bruce Ackerman, *We the People* series
- Akhil Reed Amar, *America's Constitution: A Biography* (2005)

V. Legal Analysis and Reform Frameworks

- Just Security Litigation Tracker: "Trump-Related Criminal and Civil Cases"
- Brookings Institution: "Reform the Presidency," "The Abuse of Emergency Powers"
- Democracy Docket (Marc Elias): Real-time legal coverage of voter suppression and gerrymandering
- Leadership Conference on Civil and Human Rights: Reports on disenfranchisement and civil rights rollbacks
- Brennan Center's National Task Force on Rule of Law and Democracy: Reports on restoring norms and institutional integrity

READER'S GUIDES

———✦———

The chapters of *American Restoration* expose what was broken and how it can be repaired. But understanding alone is not enough. These Reader's Guides are designed to extend the argument into action. Each guide offers a structured companion to its chapter: beginning with stakes, tracing the pattern of collapse, and ending with a practical path forward. They are not recaps. They are tools—made for classrooms, community meetings, organizing circles, and private reflection.

In a moment where democracy has become fragile not just in practice but in memory, we need structures that restore moral clarity. These guides aim to equip those willing to act: not with slogans, but with substance. They offer ways to reframe civic questions, anchor strategy in principle, and carry forward the work of repair with focus and resolve. This is how democratic renewal becomes something more than rhetoric—how it becomes real.

———✦———

Reader's Guide: Part I - Elections That Count Every Vote

The Stakes

No other reform matters if elections are not legitimate. A government cannot be held accountable by a public that cannot meaningfully choose its representatives. When elections are rigged by money, distorted by maps, suppressed by law, and overturned by partisanship, democracy becomes spectacle. This chapter lays the foundation for the entire *American Restoration*: ensuring that every vote can be cast, counted, and trusted—without fear, fraud, or obstruction. Without these five repairs, the republic cannot function. With them, self-government becomes possible again.

THE STRUCTURE

This chapter identifies five structural points of failure that now undermine electoral legitimacy:

1. Campaign Finance — elections controlled by wealth, not will.
2. Voting Rights — access manipulated to preserve power.
3. The Electoral College — a relic that distorts public voice.
4. Gerrymandering — engineered districts that entrench minority rule.
5. Certification and Transfer of Power — the final step now weaponized.

Each reform section follows the pattern of collapse, consequence, and remedy. Together, they form the keystone for every other chapter to come.

THE COLLAPSE

Campaigns are bought. Voters are purged. Outcomes are predetermined. And once ballots are cast, partisan actors are positioned to override the result. The illusion of democracy remains—but the system itself has been compromised. Each distortion is strategic. Each loophole was carved. The collapse of election integrity was not inevitable—it was engineered, in plain sight, and often in slow motion.

THE REMEDY

Fixing the system requires five urgent, structural changes:

1. Reform campaign finance laws to eliminate dark money and restore transparency.
2. Guarantee universal voting access through national standards and protections.
3. Replace the Electoral College with a system of direct national voting.
4. End gerrymandering by mandating independent redistricting commissions.
5. Protect certification with criminal penalties for interference and insulation from political retaliation.

These are not partisan demands. They are the democratic minimum.

WHAT COMES NEXT

Election reform must come first. Every other law proposed in this book depends on a Congress and executive chosen by real voters in real contests. Without this foundation, the remainder of *American Restoration* rests on sand. Politically, these reforms will be fought with false cries of overreach and fraud. But they are not overreach—they are overdue. Their passage will determine not only the survival of the agenda, but the survival of the system itself.

. . .

Three Things to Remember

- A vote that cannot be cast or counted is not a vote.
- The enemies of democracy rigged elections through law —not violence.
- Fixing elections isn't symbolic. It is survival.

Action List

- Ban dark money and require real-time transparency in campaign finance.
- Enact automatic, universal voter registration with vote-by-mail access.
- Abolish the Electoral College through constitutional amendment or compact.
- Establish independent redistricting commissions in all 50 states.
- Criminalize partisan certification interference and protect election officials.

Strategic Rationale

These reforms are the gateway to legitimacy. Without fair elections, progress on healthcare, justice, climate, or education will be temporary or reversed. Structurally sound elections create the conditions under which political competition can occur—not between oligarchs and the public, but between competing visions of public good.

. . .

What You Can Do

Support candidates who are committed to enacting electoral reform—not just in principle, but through specific proposals to repair campaign finance, redistricting, and vote certification. Strengthen the local press and watchdog organizations that monitor gerrymandering, voter suppression, and election interference by donating, subscribing, or amplifying their work. Join efforts to register voters and staff polling places, particularly in regions where access is most at risk. Push for state-level action where federal momentum has stalled—many of the most urgent reforms can begin locally. And speak clearly about the stakes: this is not just politics. Election sabotage is not a partisan tactic. It is the pathway to authoritarian rule.

Discussion Questions

1. The chapter argues that elections in the United States still occur, but no longer reflect the people or their will. What signs or examples most strongly support that claim in your view?
2. If campaign finance is described as "market capture" rather than representation, what reforms would truly sever the link between elected officials and donor dependency?
3. Voting access remains unequal across race, class, and geography. What would it take to make the right to vote truly universal—and why has that not yet been achieved?
4. The Electoral College is criticized for enabling minority rule. Should it be reformed or abolished? What might replace it—and how could that change reshape democracy?

5. Gerrymandering allows politicians to choose their voters. How can independent redistricting commissions restore fairness, and what are the barriers to their implementation?
6. Certification, once procedural, is now a political weapon. What legal and structural changes are needed to insulate this final step from manipulation or refusal?
7. This section insists that electoral reform is not just policy —it is the foundation of legitimacy. How do we persuade those who still see elections as mostly functional?
8. The chapter ends with a warning: that design must be answered with design. What does intentional, structural resistance look like in a democracy under strain?
9. Of the five reforms—finance, access, fairness, redistricting, and certification—which do you see as the keystone? Why?
10. What role can you play, locally or nationally, in making these electoral reforms real? What's one action you could take this month?

Reader's Guide: Chapter 3. Campaign Finance Reform

THE STAKES

American democracy is no longer driven by debate—it is dominated by dollars. Candidates are not chosen by communities, but by capital. Elections are flooded by dark money, manipulated by Super PACs, and shaped by ads designed to mislead, not inform. The result is not representative government, but financial capture. Campaign finance reform is not a secondary concern. It is the precondition for every other democratic function. Without it, power is neither public nor accountable—it is owned.

THE STRUCTURE

This chapter exposes the full scale of financial distortion in U.S. elections—from donor dominance and secret expenditures to deceptive advertising and relentless saturation. It recounts the historical arc from post-Watergate reform to post-Citizens United collapse, details the corrosive effects on policymaking, and highlights working models of reform in the U.S. and abroad. It closes by outlining a multi-pronged structural remedy.

THE COLLAPSE

Two Supreme Court decisions—*Buckley v. Valeo* (1976) and *Citizens United v. FEC* (2010)—opened the floodgates to unlimited, often anonymous spending. Candidates now spend up to half their time fundraising, beholden not to the public but to powerful patrons. Lies go unpunished. Ads are unregulated. Truth is drowned in volume. The media profits. The public loses faith. The system is corrupted not by one scandal, but by design.

THE REMEDY

- Enact real-time transparency for all political donations and expenditures.
- Cap contributions and limit total campaign expenditures.
- Mandate truth-in-advertising laws for political messaging.

- Expand public financing and small-dollar donor matching.
- Prohibit political advertising saturation and falsehood-based content.
- Encourage free, equal airtime for all qualified candidates.

What Comes Next

Reform must be structural, not symbolic. Disclosure without consequence is not enough. Public finance without limits is not reform. We must restore electoral integrity by rebuilding a system where speech cannot be bought and policy cannot be purchased.

Three Things to Remember

- Unlimited money distorts representation before a vote is ever cast.
- Political lies are legal in advertising—and that is by design.
- No other reform survives without campaign finance reform first.

The Action List

- Demand donation transparency from all candidates—federal, state, and local.
- Support public financing initiatives in your city or state.
- Reject candidates who rely on Super PACs or dark money.

- Push for truth-in-political-advertising laws where you live.
- Expose misleading ads and submit corrections to local media outlets.
- Call for Congress to overturn *Citizens United* and restore legislative authority.

Strategic Rationale

The fight for campaign finance reform is the fight for all other reforms. Without it, health policy answers to insurers, tax policy to billionaires, and environmental policy to extractive industries. Fixing this system will not make politics clean—but it will make it possible for public interest to compete. Democracy begins with the ability to hear and be heard. It ends when that right is auctioned off.

What You Can Do

Find one local, state, or national reform effort advancing campaign finance reform—and get involved. Whether you donate, organize, or amplify, your voice is a counterweight. The system is rigged to make you believe change is impossible. But the truth is simple: they have the money. We have the numbers. Let's use them.

Discussion Questions

1. This chapter opens with the claim that campaign finance reform is not a secondary concern but a precondition for democracy. Why is it foundational—and what evidence supports that claim?

2. The chapter traces the corruption of campaign finance back over a century. What lessons from earlier reform efforts—like the Tillman Act or post-Watergate laws—should guide today's strategy?
3. *Buckley v. Valeo* and *Citizens United* are described as turning points. How did these rulings reshape elections, and what would it take to reverse their impact?
4. If candidates spend up to 40% of their time fundraising, how does that distort representation and governance? What tradeoffs are being made—and who pays the price?
5. Political advertising is portrayed as a system of saturation, not persuasion. What reforms could meaningfully reduce its dominance without violating speech rights?
6. The chapter connects campaign finance to media distortion and public cynicism. How does unchecked political spending shape what citizens believe—and whether they participate?
7. Several international models are mentioned. What could the U.S. learn from France, the UK, Germany, or Australia—and how might those systems be adapted here?
8. Truth-in-advertising laws apply to products but not campaigns. Should political ads be held to similar standards? Who should enforce those standards—and how?
9. Local reforms like democracy vouchers and small-donor matching are described as hopeful but insufficient. What would it take to bring those reforms to scale nationally?
10. The chapter ends with a call to structural—not heroic—solutions. What kind of system would reward public service over private obedience? And how do we start building it now?

Reader's Guide: Chapter 4. Voting Rights Protection

The Stakes

The right to vote is the foundation of every other right in a democracy—but in the United States, that right has never been fully secured. It is not guaranteed by the Constitution, and it has been eroded through legislation, manipulation, and deliberate exclusion. A system that filters participation through race, class, or ZIP code is not broken—it is rigged. If we fail to guarantee access, we concede power to those who win not by persuasion, but by denial.

The Structure

This chapter traces the historical roots of voter exclusion, from the Constitution's original silence to modern suppression tactics. It examines state-level manipulation, court decisions that stripped protections, and the engineered barriers targeting marginalized communities. It closes by calling for national legislation, enforcement, and design-level reform to guarantee access and rebuild trust.

The Collapse

Voting is treated as a privilege, not a right. Courts have invalidated key protections, while state legislatures have passed thousands of bills to restrict access. Long lines, ID laws, purges, and intimidation disproportionately affect voters of color, the young, and the poor. Meanwhile, false claims of fraud justify real acts of sabotage. The system excludes by design—and claims legitimacy in doing so.

The Remedy

- Guarantee a national right to vote through federal law.
- Require automatic, universal registration for all eligible citizens.
- Expand access through early, mail, online, and in-person voting options.
- Enforce uniform standards for ballot handling, counting, and certification.
- Prohibit voter roll purges based on flawed data or partisan motives.
- Protect voters from intimidation and penalize suppression tactics.
- Build national infrastructure to modernize, audit, and secure elections.

What Comes Next

The next round of redistricting will begin after the 2030 elections. If voting rights are not secured by then, another decade of exclusion will be locked in. The window for action is short—but the tools already exist. Federal reform must come early in the new Congress, with implementation swift enough to protect the next redistricting cycle.

Three Things to Remember

- The Constitution does not guarantee the right to vote—it permits its denial.
- Suppression is no longer blunt—it is strategic, legal, and data-driven.

- Voting rights are not being lost by accident. They are being taken—on purpose.

Action List

- Pass federal voting rights legislation that mandates national standards.
- Rebuild and empower the Department of Justice's Voting Rights Section.
- Fund secure, inclusive national voting infrastructure.
- Penalize partisan roll purges, certification refusals, and intimidation tactics.
- Mandate automatic registration linked to any government interaction.
- Require states to offer multiple access methods, including online and mail voting.

Strategic Rationale

Voting is the gateway to all other reforms. If the electorate is narrowed, the system becomes unrepresentative by design. Every suppression tactic is a defense against the will of the majority—and every delay in reform makes exclusion more permanent. A just democracy does not require trust in the people—it guarantees their power. Securing voting rights now ensures that reform is not only possible, but legitimate.

What You Can Do

Join efforts to pass federal voting rights laws by contacting your representatives, supporting legal defense funds, and backing pro-democracy candidates. Volunteer to register voters, become a poll worker, or assist in election protection hotlines. Support litigation against voter suppression laws in your state. Your participation fights silence—and every action taken to expand access is an act of democratic defense.

Discussion Questions

1. The chapter opens with the claim that the right to vote is not guaranteed by the Constitution. How does this legal gap shape the ongoing fight for voting rights in the United States?
2. Many forms of voter suppression are described as "strategic," not accidental. What evidence supports this framing—and how can it be effectively countered?
3. The text contrasts exclusionary practices in the U.S. with inclusive models abroad. What lessons could the United States learn from other democracies—and what obstacles stand in the way?
4. This chapter asserts that a just democracy makes registration automatic and access universal. What would it take to implement such a system nationally—and what might it transform?
5. Laws restricting access are often defended as promoting "election integrity." How can we reframe the conversation to expose this as a strategy of exclusion rather than protection?
6. The chapter warns that Republicans have chosen restriction over persuasion. What does that imply about the future of bipartisanship on voting rights—and how should reformers respond?

7. Several modern reforms are proposed: early voting, online voting, and automatic registration. Which of these do you believe is most urgent, and why?
8. This chapter argues for a single federal voting standard. What are the risks and benefits of overriding state control in the name of universal access?
9. Time is presented as a political factor—especially the 2030 redistricting window. How does that deadline shape the urgency and strategy of current reform efforts?
10. The conclusion asserts that democracy must be self-made, not inherited. What role can you play in helping complete that unfinished work—and what is one action you can take now?

Reader's Guide: Chapter 5. Electoral College Reform

The Stakes

The presidency of the United States is the only office elected by the entire nation—yet it is not awarded by national vote. The Electoral College distorts representation, empowers minority rule, and renders millions of votes meaningless. In two of the last six elections, the presidency went to the candidate who lost the popular vote. This is not a safeguard. It is a threat. And each cycle it endures, the risk to legitimacy—and democracy itself—deepens.

THE STRUCTURE

This chapter traces the origins of the Electoral College as a logistical workaround, not a principled design. It explains how modern communication and voter education have nullified its original purpose, details its distortion of campaign strategy and governance, and explores both the risks of winner-take-all allocation and the legal avenues for reform, including the National Popular Vote Interstate Compact and proportional elector allocation.

The Collapse

The Electoral College no longer serves any functional democratic purpose. It silences voters in safe states, concentrates attention on a few battlegrounds, and enables presidents to claim mandates they did not earn. It incentivizes division over persuasion, geography over consensus, and minority rule over majoritarian legitimacy. If allowed to persist, it invites future elections where the outcome does not reflect the will of the people—and justifies power that does not belong.

The Remedy

- Complete ratification of the National Popular Vote Interstate Compact (NPVIC).
- Promote proportional elector allocation in all states.
- Enact national legislation binding electors to certified results.
- Offer federal incentives for states adopting fair vote-weighting systems.
- Restrict legislative overrides of popular will in presidential certification.
- Clarify that national vote equality is a constitutional interest subject to defense.

What Comes Next

Reform is legally and logistically achievable without a constitutional amendment. But it will be opposed by those who benefit from distortion. The task is not to wait for permission—it is to act where the law allows. That means mobilizing state legislatures, deploying federal tools, and preparing for judicial challenge with legislative precision and constitutional clarity.

Three Things to Remember

- The Electoral College was not sacred—it was a workaround for the 18th century.
- It consistently suppresses majority rule and inflates strategic geography.
- Legal, state-based reforms can neutralize its distortions without an amendment.

Action List

- Encourage remaining states to adopt the National Popular Vote Interstate Compact.
- Pass federal legislation mandating elector fidelity and penalizing faithless votes.
- Tie federal election funding to democratic metrics, including vote weight equity.
- Incentivize proportional elector allocation through grants and competitive awards.
- Direct DOJ and FEC to monitor and challenge systems that violate vote equality.

Strategic Rationale

Every other reform in this book depends on fair representation at the highest level. If a president can be elected while losing the majority, then all subsequent authority is tainted. Electoral College reform equalizes voice, restores legitimacy, and forces candidates to campaign—and govern—for the entire country, not a strategic fraction of it. That shift is foundational to any working democracy.

What You Can Do

Support state-level efforts to pass NPVIC legislation and encourage lawmakers in non-participating states to join. Write to state representatives, attend hearings, and push for proportional allocation where full national reform is politically blocked. Donate to organizations tracking and supporting Electoral College reform. And speak plainly: no democracy can endure if the people choose one president and the system installs another.

Discussion Questions

1. What original justifications did the Framers have for creating the Electoral College—and why do those justifications no longer apply?
2. How does the winner-take-all system in 48 states distort representation and voter influence in presidential elections?
3. What are the dangers of a system that allows a candidate to win the presidency while losing the national popular vote?

4. How does the Electoral College concentrate power in battleground states, and what are the consequences for national policy and public investment?
5. Why is the Electoral College described as a workaround rather than a foundational principle—and how has that ambiguity been exploited?
6. How does the U.S. compare with other democracies in terms of electing national leaders—and what could we learn from their systems?
7. What are the two viable reform strategies—NPVIC and proportional allocation—and what are the strengths and limitations of each?
8. Why is it critical to legally bind electors, and what risks do unbound electors pose in a close election?
9. How can Congress use its legislative power to encourage or enforce Electoral College reform without requiring a constitutional amendment?
10. The chapter argues that the Electoral College is part of a broader architecture of minority rule. How do these systems reinforce each other—and what happens if we reform one but not the others?
11. How might Electoral College reform change the tone, geography, and inclusiveness of presidential campaigns?
12. What steps can be taken now to build momentum for these reforms ahead of the 2029 legislative window—and what role can individuals play?

Reader's Guide: Chapter 6. Redistricting Reform

The Stakes

Redistricting shapes political power for a decade at a time—but in much of the United States, it has become a weapon to entrench minority rule. Gerrymandering enables legislators to pick their voters instead of the other way around. With safe seats, public accountability erodes, extremist candidates thrive, and the consent of the governed is replaced by cartographic manipulation. The distortion is legal, strategic, and ongoing—and if not corrected by 2030, will lock in a generation of structural injustice.

The Structure

The chapter begins by framing gerrymandering as a form of democratic sabotage, not just unfairness. It traces the constitutional basis for representation, shows how redistricting has evolved into a data-driven weapon, and documents how courts, legislatures, and party machines have reinforced its power. It ends with a dual solution: national standards and a targeted strategy to flip at least seven key legislatures before the next redistricting cycle.

The Collapse

The Supreme Court's 2019 ruling in *Rucho v. Common Cause* declared partisan gerrymandering a political question beyond judicial remedy. In its wake, Republican legislatures redoubled their efforts—ignoring state rulings, bypassing reforms, and consolidating control. This legal vacuum has allowed rigged maps to override voter intent, entrench supermajorities, and produce representatives insulated from electoral accountability. The collapse is not hypothetical. It is visible—and accelerating.

The Remedy

Congress must pass a Fair Maps Act setting enforceable national standards: banning partisan gerrymanders, requiring representational symmetry, mandating population parity, and ensuring transparency. States should be incentivized or compelled to adopt independent commissions or neutral processes. The goal is not aesthetic perfection, but outcome equity: districts that reflect real voting patterns, not partisan engineering.

What Comes Next

Time is short. The next redistricting cycle begins in 2030. Federal reform must pass by 2029. And Democrats must flip seven key legislatures—Arizona, Georgia, Pennsylvania, North Carolina, Wisconsin, Michigan, and New Hampshire—before maps are redrawn. These states are winnable, but only with national coordination and local investment. Miss the window, and another decade of minority rule is all but assured.

Three Things to Remember

- The Supreme Court has legalized partisan gerrymandering.
- Only Congress can impose a national fairness standard.
- The 2030 redistricting cycle will shape power until 2042.

Action List

- Pass a national Fair Maps Act setting legal standards for representational equity.

- Ban partisan gerrymandering through statutory definition and federal enforcement.
- Require population parity, public transparency, and judicial oversight for all maps.
- Incentivize states to adopt independent commissions for congressional redistricting.
- Condition federal election funding on compliance with anti-gerrymandering standards.

Strategic Rationale

The next redistricting cycle is not just a procedural event—it is the last opportunity to reset the structural conditions for democratic representation in the 2030s and 2040s. Gerrymandered legislatures have passed voting restrictions, shielded corruption, and insulated extremists. Reforming the map unlocks accountability, redistributes political power, and restores the link between vote and voice. Without redistricting reform, other reforms will die in rigged legislatures. With it, the door to functional democracy reopens.

What You Can Do

Support candidates in Arizona, Georgia, Pennsylvania, North Carolina, Wisconsin, Michigan, and New Hampshire who can flip legislative control before 2030. Volunteer with grassroots groups pushing for state redistricting reform. Donate to legal challenges against partisan maps. Spread awareness about how gerrymandering silences votes and skews policy. Every flipped legislature is a map redrawn—and a future reclaimed.

Discussion Questions

1. The chapter argues that redistricting has evolved from civic maintenance into "cartographic warfare." What are the most damaging consequences of this shift—for representation, legitimacy, and governance?
2. Gerrymandering is framed as both a political and moral failure. What does it mean to say that voters are "not governed by consent, but ruled"? Do you agree?
3. The distinction between racial and partisan gerrymandering is legally significant—but the outcomes often look similar. Should the law treat them equally? Why or why not?
4. What impact does gerrymandering have on the behavior and character of candidates who win in "safe" districts? How does this shape the tone of national politics?
5. The Supreme Court's decision in *Rucho v. Common Cause* declared partisan gerrymandering a "political question." What are the implications of this ruling for federal democracy—and for the role of courts in protecting it?
6. How do distorted maps concentrate not only power but also campaign money—and what does that mean for accountability?
7. The chapter compares U.S. redistricting with practices in Australia, Canada, and the U.K. What do these international models teach us about legitimacy and trust?
8. The text argues that no single method guarantees fairness, but a single standard is essential. What might that standard be—and how can it be enforced?
9. The chapter highlights 2030 as the critical deadline for reform. What are the most effective steps national and local organizers can take between now and then?
10. What strategies—legal, political, or grassroots—might be

most effective in flipping the seven key state legislatures before the next redistricting cycle?
11. How does redistricting reform connect to broader questions of democratic legitimacy, public trust, and national stability?
12. The final lines assert that we can "draw new ones—lines of fairness, of truth, of equal voice." What would it take—strategically and culturally—to make that vision real?

———— ✦ ————

Reader's Guide: Chapter 7. Election Certification and Peaceful Transition

The Stakes

Certification and transition are democracy's final defenses—and its most fragile. They convert counted votes into lawful power and ensure leadership changes hands peacefully. But recent years have exposed these processes as dangerously underprotected. The law does not compel good faith. And when sabotage is possible, sabotage becomes likely. Without binding legal guarantees, the next transfer of power may not occur at all.

The Structure

This chapter traces the breakdown of two once-assumed norms: the certification of lawful election results, and the peaceful transfer of executive power. It begins with the historical informality of both processes, examines their exploitation under Trump, and argues for federal reforms to make each step legally binding. The chapter ends with legislative proposals to secure both processes by 2030.

. . .

The Collapse

For centuries, certification and transition relied on integrity—not statute. That illusion collapsed in 2020, when Trump tried to overturn certified results through coordinated pressure, false electors, and incitement. It broke again in 2024, when his refusal to transition delayed briefings and planning. No laws were broken—because no laws existed to prevent it. Hope was never enough. Now we know.

The Remedy

The reforms are concrete. First, require states to criminalize false electors and certify results by a federal deadline. Second, protect election officials from harassment and coercion. Third, impose civil and criminal penalties for obstructing transition. Fourth, establish a nonpartisan transition authority to guarantee peaceful transfer. Democracy cannot rely on grace. It must rely on law.

What Comes Next

Certification and transfer reforms are foundational. Without them, every election remains vulnerable at its endpoint. Democrats must act swiftly if they achieve a trifecta in 2029. These changes are not just insurance—they are survival. The next crisis may not be averted by character. Only law can finish what the people begin.

Three Things to Remember

- The Electoral Count Act was never designed to withstand a lawless president—it assumed good faith.
- Trump's coordinated sabotage exploited gaps in certification, electors, and transition protocols.

- Without legal enforcement, the peaceful transfer of power is not guaranteed—it is optional.

Action List

- Criminalize false elector slates at both state and federal levels.
- Mandate timely certification of election results with uniform national deadlines.
- Establish civil and criminal penalties for obstructing presidential transition.
- Guarantee legal protection for election workers facing threats or coercion.
- Create a permanent nonpartisan authority to oversee transitions of power.

Strategic Rationale

Reform must target the system's most visible vulnerabilities. Certification and transition occur in full view of the nation—and the world—making them ripe for interference, delay, and sabotage. These moments test not only process but legitimacy. If the public cannot trust the transfer of power, democracy collapses into permanent brinkmanship. By securing these endpoints in law, we remove the temptation to defy the people—and restore confidence in the peaceful continuity of governance.

What You Can Do

Support candidates who back election security and transition law reform. Advocate for your state to criminalize false electors and to guarantee election official protections. Share accurate information about how certification and transition work—and where they remain vulnerable. Push media outlets to prioritize coverage of these legal gaps. And never accept obstruction or delay as normal—it isn't.

DISCUSSION QUESTIONS

1. The chapter states that certification is democracy's "final gate." Why is this step so critical—and what happens when it is left to tradition rather than law?
2. In 2020, the peaceful transition of power survived not because of legal safeguards, but because of individual choices. What are the dangers of relying on personal integrity rather than structural protection?
3. The chapter outlines Trump's multi-pronged effort to overturn the election. Which aspects of the system did he most effectively exploit—and which remain vulnerable today?
4. Transition failures in both 2020 and 2024 are presented as deliberate, not accidental. What specific harms resulted—and how might similar delays threaten future national security or public welfare?
5. The chapter identifies several legal voids: no penalties for false electors, no requirements for cooperation in transition, and no protections for election officials. Which of these is most urgent to address, and why?
6. Reforms like the 2022 Electoral Count Reform Act made partial progress. What further steps are needed to make certification and transition truly secure and enforceable?

7. Authoritarian regimes often delay, discredit, or disrupt power transfers. What parallels do you see between their tactics and recent U.S. behavior—and how do we ensure the U.S. doesn't follow the same path?
8. The chapter warns that the visibility of certification and transition makes them prime targets for interference. How can we defend these moments without undermining public confidence?
9. The idea that "losing is betrayal" has taken hold in some political circles. How can we restore the principle that accepting loss is a civic duty, not a personal failure?
10. The final lines argue that we do not need new ideals—only laws that reflect the ones we already claim to hold. What specific reforms do you support, and what can you do to help bring them about before 2028?

———— ✦ ————

Reader's Guide: Chapter 8. Elections That Work: Five Reforms, One Democracy

The Stakes

America does not have one election problem. It has five—each masking as separate when in fact they form a single failing system. Without simultaneous reform, each flaw reinforces the others. A rigged map silences turnout. A suppressed vote amplifies the value of money. Dark money bends outcomes before ballots are cast. Certification delays undo consent. And the Electoral College severs the people from the presidency. Reforming any one is progress. Reforming all five is democracy.

. . .

The Structure

This chapter outlines five foundational reforms—redistricting, voting rights, campaign finance, the Electoral College, and certification—not as a menu of options, but as an interdependent design. It reframes them not as policy debates but as structural imperatives, rooted in a single outcome: representative government that cannot be lawfully overturned.

The Collapse

Each reform area has been compromised by delay, sabotage, or systemic abuse. Districts are engineered to suppress dissent. Voters are purged. Billionaires flood elections with dark money. Presidents win despite losing the vote. And peaceful transitions depend on personality, not law. These are not abstract concerns. They are lived failures that cumulatively threaten the legitimacy of every election.

The Remedy

Fix all five—together. Mandate independent redistricting or proportional outcomes. Codify federal voting rights and equal access. Outlaw dark money and require full transparency. Eliminate or neutralize the Electoral College through national or proportional vote compacts. Require lawful certification and binding transfer of power. These are not discrete issues. They are five locks on one democratic door.

What Comes Next

No single reform will be enough. But taken together, they form a constitutional firewall against minority rule. These reforms must be passed no later than 2029 and implemented before redistricting and presidential election deadlines in 2030 and 2032. Delay risks another collapse. Completion marks the beginning of restored legitimacy.

Three Things to **Remember**

- No democratic reform holds unless all hold—rigged maps, blocked votes, dark money, and false certification are a system, not separate acts.
- Every past abuse—stolen districts, suppressed voters, bought elections—has already been mapped and is being repeated with precision.
- The only solution is full reform: five connected locks, one unbreakable chain securing electoral democracy.

Action List

- Enact a federal Fair Maps Act requiring proportional outcomes or independent commissions.
- Restore and expand the Voting Rights Act with federal oversight in high-risk states.
- Pass sweeping campaign finance reform with full donor transparency and public financing.
- Implement the National Popular Vote Compact or mandate proportional elector allocation.
- Mandate legal certification standards, criminalize false elector slates, and bind peaceful transfer by statute.

STRATEGIC RATIONALE

Partial reforms are now a liability. Each unaddressed weakness becomes an access point for authoritarian subversion. By treating these issues separately, the United States allowed a fragmented minority to dominate a fractured system. But the crisis has clarified the path: treat elections as a whole system—and rebuild it entirely. The architecture of democracy cannot rely on separate fixes. It requires a single foundation.

WHAT YOU CAN DO

Support and campaign for reform-minded candidates at every level. Volunteer for redistricting, voter registration, and election protection organizations. Donate to nonpartisan watchdog groups. Advocate for your state to join the National Popular Vote Compact. Speak clearly against voter suppression and electoral manipulation —especially in trusted personal and professional circles. Every action, every conversation, is a defense of the vote.

DISCUSSION QUESTIONS

1. The chapter argues that election reforms have historically been reactive—introduced only after major failures. What does this suggest about America's approach to democratic design, and why is a proactive, unified reform strategy necessary now?
2. How do the five reforms—redistricting, voting rights, campaign finance, the Electoral College, and certification —interact to form one functioning system? What happens when one is neglected?
3. Gerrymandering is framed not just as a political tool, but as a method of entrenching minority rule. In what ways

does this tactic threaten the principle of majority governance?

4. Voter suppression and voting access are described as strategic weapons. What are the long-term dangers of treating voting as a privilege rather than a right?

5. The chapter links dark money and campaign finance corruption to every other form of electoral manipulation. How does financial influence upstream undermine reforms downstream?

6. Why is the Electoral College considered incompatible with the principle of democratic equality—and how does its structure distort both campaigning and governance?

7. Certification was once assumed secure—but has now been shown to be a critical vulnerability. Why is it so essential that this step be protected by law rather than tradition?

8. The chapter warns that reform gaps, once exposed, will be widened and exploited. What examples from recent history support this—and how can unified reform cut off these avenues?

9. If only some reforms are implemented—say, finance reform without certification laws—how might that backfire? Can partial reform sometimes worsen systemic instability?

10. The author rejects idealism in favor of realism. In your view, what is the most realistic path forward to achieving all five reforms—and what role can citizens play in making that vision real?

───── ✦ ─────

Reader's Guide: Part II - The Limits to Presidential Power

The Stakes

The American presidency has become unconstrained—not by new laws, but by the erosion of those meant to contain it. Trump's second term confirms the collapse of constitutional, legal, and traditional limits. The danger is no longer hypothetical. It is operational. The tools of democratic restraint—executive boundaries, legal enforcement, institutional norms—have all failed simultaneously. What remains is a structure of impunity masquerading as democracy.

THE STRUCTURE

This chapter introduces the failure of presidential constraint by tracing how the three guardrails—constitutional design, statutory law, and democratic tradition—have been bypassed. It sets the stage for the next four chapters, each of which will examine one collapsed layer of restraint and the reforms required to rebuild it.

THE COLLAPSE

Trump has redefined the modern presidency by violating laws, defying subpoenas, erasing traditions, and weaponizing every tool of executive power. Courts are overwhelmed. Congress is complicit. Norms are ignored. The presidency is now functionally sovereign—unbound by checks and immune to consequence. The result is not failed oversight. It is no oversight.

THE REMEDY

The next four chapters detail the remedy:

- *Chapter 10* restores constitutional constraint.
- *Chapter 11* restores legal accountability.
- *Chapter 12* restores civic and institutional honor.
- *Chapter 13* designs a comprehensive structure to ensure permanent restraint.

This chapter names the collapse. The next four chapters rebuild.

What Comes Next

A republic cannot endure when its executive becomes monarchic. With Trump again in office, every day without reform strengthens impunity. The restoration of democratic constraint begins by diagnosing the full failure—and then rebuilding what collapsed, not in tradition alone, but in enforceable law.

Three Things to Remember

- The Constitution does not enforce itself. It relies on good faith—and Trump governs without it.
- No single breach caused this collapse. All three foundations—law, structure, and tradition—failed together.
- Other democracies prosecute criminal leaders. The U.S. protects them. That must change.

Action List

- Codify executive limits on emergency declarations, pardons, and agency funding powers.

- Enforce legal accountability for defiance of subpoenas, recordkeeping laws, and statutory obligations.
- Reform judicial and congressional oversight to prevent stall tactics and ensure enforceable checks.
- Establish binding transparency standards for presidential health, finances, access logs, and public statements.

Strategic Rationale

Unchecked executive power does not just erode democracy—it replaces it. The American presidency was designed to be powerful but contained. When all constraints fail, the system shifts from balance to rule. This chapter lays bare that shift. What follows must be more than opposition. It must be structural redesign. Every democracy that survives authoritarian drift does so by rebuilding the walls—stronger, clearer, and with no door left open.

What You Can Do

Support candidates and coalitions that pledge to reform presidential powers. Write and call your representatives to demand legal restraints on pardons, emergency declarations, and DOJ independence. Share this chapter with those still unsure of the urgency. And stay vigilant—because power never constrains itself. Only people can.

Discussion Questions

1. The chapter frames presidential restraint as a triangle of constitutional law, statutory enforcement, and

democratic tradition. What makes this structure so vulnerable to a single lawless actor?
2. Executive tools like the pardon power and emergency declarations were intended for rare use. What does it mean when they become the routine instruments of rule?
3. The Constitution assumes voluntary compliance. Should democratic systems be built to rely on character—or must we now design for bad faith?
4. This chapter argues that law is no longer enforced at scale or pace. What reforms would be necessary to make legal constraint functional again?
5. Tradition once carried the force of civic expectation. What does its collapse tell us about the cultural foundations of democracy?
6. The courts are still active—but overwhelmed. Can the judiciary alone sustain the rule of law when other branches have surrendered oversight?
7. The Office of Management and Budget is described as repurposed for political defunding. What are the risks when administrative tools are weaponized?
8. The chapter asserts that in the U.S., oversight fails not from legal complexity but political refusal. Do you agree—and if so, what does it imply for reform?
9. How does the American tolerance for impunity compare to the accountability shown in other democracies?
10. If one presidency can break the guardrails, what will it take—not just to repair them—but to ensure they hold next time?

——— ✦ ———

Reader's Guide: Chapter 10. Power Without Boundary

The Stakes

This chapter confronts the collapse of constitutional restraint on the presidency. It charts how Trump has violated nearly every foundational limit—converting the office from conditional trustee to unchecked sovereign. The danger is not that the Constitution failed, but that it was never built to survive a leader who rejects its constraints—and a party and Court that protect him.

THE STRUCTURE

We begin with the Framers' design: a presidency bound by law, limited by structure, and accountable to the people. We trace how each safeguard—Congressional limits, judicial enforcement, public constraint—functioned for 250 years. Then we document Trump's systematic destruction of that model through violation, defiance, and manipulation, culminating in a presidency no longer subject to law or consequence.

THE COLLAPSE

Trump has treated constitutional limits as optional. He has ignored the Emoluments Clause, violated the Bill of Rights, and declared himself immune from prosecution. His abuses are not theoretical. They are daily, active, and celebrated by his party. With the Court enabling him and Congress shielding him, the core assumption of the Constitution—that no man is above the law—has been shattered.

THE REMEDY

This chapter is diagnostic. The remedy comes in Chapter 13. But the argument here is clear: no reform is possible without first acknowledging collapse. The Constitution must be rebuilt—not through blind faith in old norms, but through law, accountability, and structural redesign that makes obedience non-negotiable. The oath must be reclaimed—and made enforceable.

What Comes Next

The next two chapters detail the failure of legal enforcement and the collapse of democratic norms. Chapter 13 then outlines the structural reforms required to rebuild constraint. Together, they form a recovery plan: not to weaken the presidency, but to restore the republic it was meant to serve.

Three Things to Remember

- The Constitution assumed honorable leaders. It offers no remedy for dishonor.
- Trump has violated constitutional limits not in secret, but in public—and remains unpunished.
- If we do not enforce the oath, we invite the next lawless president to finish what Trump began.

Action List

- Pass legislation to clarify Section 3 of the 14th Amendment and enforce disqualification for insurrectionists.

- Pass legislation to prohibit presidential self-dealing, with independent enforcement mechanisms.
- Require mandatory judicial review for executive actions that undermine constitutional rights and overstep Congressional limits.
- Restore congressional checks on war powers, emergency declarations, and treaty abrogations.
- Codify public accountability standards for the presidency—tax returns, financial disclosures, health transparency.

Strategic Rationale

The presidency must not remain the one office in American government exempt from enforcement. A republic cannot coexist with sovereign immunity. Structural accountability is not a partisan demand—it is the condition of continued self-government. If we cannot constrain executive power by law, we will be ruled by personality—and the law will serve only those who break it.

What You Can Do

Support candidates who vow to restore constitutional accountability. Call for judicial reform to end impunity at the highest levels. Share this chapter and its message widely. Teach the truth: the Constitution is a living defense only if we enforce it. Join movements that push for presidential constraint—not to weaken the office, but to make it honorable again.

Discussion Questions

1. The chapter argues that the Constitution was built on assumptions of honor and good faith. Can a system that relies on such assumptions ever be truly resilient against lawless leadership?
2. What is the significance of the Emoluments Clause, and why has its violation under Trump drawn so little consequence?
3. The Founders designed a presidency of limited, contingent power. Which constitutional mechanisms have failed most visibly—and why?
4. Trump's actions are presented not as aberrations, but as proof that constraint depends on enforcement. What happens when enforcement becomes selective or disappears?
5. The chapter lists multiple Amendments violated by Trump's conduct. Which of these violations do you find most dangerous to the republic—and why?
6. Judicial restraint has historically checked the presidency. What has changed in the court system that allows executive overreach to go unpunished?
7. The Constitution's Framers saw public protest, press freedom, and elections as ultimate checks on power. Are these tools still sufficient—or have they been eroded beyond function?
8. The Constitution, as written, contains tools for defense: impeachment, judicial review, public accountability. Why have these tools failed to deter or punish Trump?
9. If other democracies can convict former presidents, what does the United States' failure to do so say about its commitment to constitutional equality?
10. The chapter ends with a call to take the oath ourselves. What would it mean in practice for citizens to preserve,

protect, and defend the Constitution when others in power will not?

Reader's Guide: Chapter 11. Law Without Consequence

The Stakes

The American presidency was never meant to be above the law. Yet under Trump's second term, the structures of legal constraint—statutory oversight, agency compliance, judicial enforcement—have been bypassed, defied, or abandoned. This chapter examines how the web of laws once designed to restrain presidential power has been shredded, not through repeal, but through deliberate noncompliance, systemic exhaustion, and institutional complicity. The risk is not abstract. It is active. Unless the machinery of legal accountability is restored, America will no longer be a government of laws—but a theater of unchecked authority.

THE STRUCTURE

This chapter traces five escalating failures:

1. Congressional Inaction – Enabling illegality by declining to investigate or legislate.
2. Judicial Complicity – Especially from the Supreme Court, which has refused to uphold limits.
3. Statutory Defiance – Direct violations of binding laws like FOIA, NEPA, and the Impoundment Control Act.
4. New Instruments of Power – The emergence of extralegal entities like DOGE.
5. Civic Erosion – The normalization of illegality as the public grows fatigued or confused.

. . .

The Collapse

What once worked through deterrence now fails through scale. Trump has issued more executive orders than any modern president, many in direct violation of statute. The Department of Justice defends him. The courts are overwhelmed. Inspectors general are fired or ignored. Congress refuses to act. And the press is targeted, surveilled, and sued. The legal web still exists—but it hangs limp, bypassed by speed, shamelessness, and sheer volume. What law forbids, Trump declares. What law demands, he denies. Without consequence, even the clearest statutes cease to matter.

The Remedy

Legal repair must happen on these levels:

- Reinforce Statutory Constraints: Reauthorize and modernize oversight laws (see Appendix B).
- Protect Inspectors General: Make removal subject to bipartisan review or court approval.
- Reform the DOJ: Insulate prosecutorial decisions from executive influence.
- Limit Emergency Powers: Require judicial or congressional review after fixed intervals.
- Restore FOIA and Records Laws: Enforce mandatory compliance with strict penalties for evasion.

What Comes Next

This chapter is not the end of the legal story—it is a warning. The legal web that once constrained the presidency was real, but it was never self-sustaining. If the public no longer expects accountability, and if institutions no longer pursue it, law becomes pageantry. The chapters that follow explore further collapse—and what must be done to reverse it before no remedies remain.

Three Things to Remember

- Law requires enforcement—without it, legality becomes theater.
- Impunity invites escalation—unchecked power always grows bolder.
- The legal web is recoverable—but only if citizens act to restore it.

Action List

- Repeal or invalidate unconstitutional provisions of budgetary legislation.
- Codify statutory independence for inspectors general and oversight agencies.
- Impose limits and judicial review on emergency powers and executive waivers.
- Restore the enforceability of FOIA, PRA, and the Impoundment Control Act.
- Reform judicial appointments to require ethical compliance and recusal standards.

Strategic Rationale

Lawful government depends not just on laws, but on fidelity to them. Trump has exposed the vulnerability of a system that assumes compliance and underfunds enforcement. Structural repair must come before crisis, not after. Strengthening legal scaffolding now will reduce the need for protest, litigation, and collapse later. Law must once again mean something—not just for the governed, but for those who govern.

What You Can Do

Support legal defense funds and watchdog organizations fighting in court. Share verified reporting on Trump's unlawful actions. Push your representatives to demand accountability, reject unconstitutional proposals, and fund real oversight. Support judicial reform candidates and donate to outlets defending press freedom. Hold the line in conversations, letters, forums. The law can be restored—but only if the people demand it, loudly and without apology.

Discussion Questions

1. This chapter distinguishes between the existence of law and the enforcement of law. Can a democracy survive when its laws are intact on paper but ignored in practice?
2. Congress has historically passed laws in response to executive abuse. Why has the current Congress abandoned that role, and what are the consequences of that failure?
3. The legal web created after Watergate, Vietnam, and Iraq is compared to an institutional immune system. What does that metaphor reveal about the nature of democratic defense?

4. The Supreme Court's embrace of "presidential immunity" is presented as judicial complicity. How do you interpret the Court's role in legitimizing or resisting executive overreach?
5. Schedule F and the "Big Beautiful Budget Bill" are used to show how Trump defies statutory law. Why have these actions not triggered a legal or political backlash?
6. Agencies like DOGE operate outside public oversight and legal charter. What dangers arise when new executive structures are created without democratic legitimacy?
7. The press and judiciary are described as the last functioning tools of legal resistance. What actions—legal, financial, or civic—are needed to defend these institutions?
8. Trump's second term is characterized by deliberate lawbreaking without consequence. How has this normalized illegality, and what are the risks of public resignation?
9. If enforcement continues to fail at the federal level, what role can state governments, civil society, or individual citizens play in reasserting legal accountability?
10. The chapter ends with a call to action: "The law is not a wall. It is a warning." What does that mean to you—and what are you prepared to do if institutions continue to fail?

Reader's Guide: Chapter 12. Office Without Honor

The Stakes

The collapse of civic restraint in the presidency is not simply a cultural decline—it is a constitutional emergency. While the law can check power, it cannot compel decency. The presidency was long governed by norms: humility, transparency, engagement, and honor. Trump revealed these norms as optional. In doing so, he transformed the office from a public trust into a personal instrument of power. This chapter argues that the erosion of honor is not cosmetic—it is foundational. Without internal restraint, no legal boundary holds. And without public expectation, no democratic safeguard survives.

The Structure

This chapter begins with the constitutional design of the presidency and the nonlegal restraints—humility, transparency, engagement, and honor—that evolved to shape its moral authority. It then traces the erosion of those norms, from Washington's example to Trump's systematic demolition. Each era of expectation is unpacked in turn, culminating in the assertion that Trump's presidency was not an aberration, but a blueprint. The chapter moves from individual violations to institutional mutation, cultural absorption, and the normalization of shamelessness. It closes with a sober blueprint for restoration—not nostalgic, but legal and civic—anchored in the idea that if honor is no longer voluntary, it must be enforced by law, vigilance, and memory.

The Collapse

Trump's presidency has modeled lawless advantage: corruption without consequence, power without duty. His disdain for ethical norms encouraged not just individual violations but systemic erosion. Agencies obey loyalty, not law. Oversight is ignored. Shame has vanished. The result is a presidency detached from principle—one that does not reflect the republic it serves, but the ambition of the man who holds it. Worse still, that model is now being copied. A generation is watching—and learning—that dishonor is rewarded.

THE REMEDY

We cannot legislate character, but we can legislate constraint. Reforms must include:

- Mandatory financial, medical, and ethical disclosures
- Required publication of visitor logs and executive actions
- Enforceable prohibitions on self-dealing and retaliatory appointments
- Codification of transition protocols and oversight compliance
- Strengthened authority and independence for ethics offices
- Public education about the role and limits of the presidency

WHAT COMES **Next**

Restoring honor is not about nostalgia. It is about survival. If honor cannot be assumed, it must be enforced. If shame will not constrain, law must. And if neither suffice, the public must reassert its right to demand that those in power serve rather than rule. This is not merely about one man, one term, or one party. It is about the future of the presidency—and whether it will remain a role of civic responsibility or become a throne of personal entitlement.

THREE THINGS TO **Remember**

- The presidency was long governed by invisible norms—until Trump made them optional.
- Without shame, the office becomes a vessel for corruption, spectacle, and personal rule.
- Restoration will require both legal reform and public reawakening of ethical expectation.

Action List

- Legislate mandatory disclosure requirements for all presidential candidates and officeholders.
- Expand legal protections for ethics offices and whistleblowers.
- Codify public access to visitor logs, agency directives, and transition processes.
- Prohibit the use of public office for private enrichment, including business promotion and campaign activity. on federal property.
- Require independent certification of all presidential financial holdings and conflicts of interest.

Strategic Rationale

Honor cannot be enforced by statute alone, but law can create the conditions under which dishonor is exposed, constrained, and punished. This chapter exposes how cultural erosion enabled structural decay. The remedy is not to demand virtue but to expect transparency, traceability, and consequence. By embedding these expectations in enforceable code, we not only preserve the office—we protect the republic it is meant to serve.

. . .

WHAT YOU CAN DO

Call for mandatory presidential disclosure laws at the state and federal levels. Support watchdog groups that track conflicts of interest and violations of ethical norms. Refuse to normalize dishonor—speak, write, and organize in defense of dignity in public office. Demand that news outlets report breaches of civic expectation, not just legal transgressions. And vote for leaders who understand that restraint is not weakness—it is the foundation of democracy.

DISCUSSION QUESTIONS

1. The chapter opens by stating that the presidency was built on fear, not trust, and later held together by norms, not law. What does this suggest about the strengths—and vulnerabilities—of the office?
2. Tradition, transparency, engagement, and honor are described as successive layers of restraint. Which of these do you believe was most critical in preserving democratic legitimacy?
3. Many of Trump's most damaging actions were not illegal, but shameless. Should shame and honor play a role in democratic governance—or is that unrealistic in modern politics?
4. How did the erosion of small traditions—like tax returns or press briefings—pave the way for larger violations? Can you identify a moment when you noticed this shift?
5. The chapter warns that Trump didn't just abandon norms—he showed that violating them brought reward,

not punishment. What role did the public, press, or Congress play in enabling that dynamic?

6. If tradition can no longer be trusted to restrain a President, what kinds of legal reforms might realistically restore transparency, accountability, and dignity to the office?

7. The chapter describes a cultural shift: younger generations growing up without seeing honor in leadership. How might this influence their expectations of democracy—or their cynicism toward it?

8. The text notes that "a presidency without shame is not a strong presidency—it is a hollow one." Do you agree? How does moral authority differ from institutional power?

9. How should we respond when elected officials mock accountability, exploit tradition, and reward disobedience to law and truth? What practical steps can be taken—by citizens or institutions?

10. The final paragraphs argue that restoration must be active, deliberate, and demanded—not nostalgic. What does that restoration look like in your community, your vote, or your voice?

Reader's Guide: Chapter 13. Constraint Without Exception

The Stakes

The American presidency was never designed to rely on goodwill. It was intended to be restrained—by law, by institution, and by civic expectation. Trump's second term reveals how quickly those restraints can collapse when shame disappears, enforcement fails, and the public grows exhausted. This chapter argues that constitutional democracy cannot survive if constraint is optional. Every power must have a limit. Every office must have accountability. Without that, there is no republic—only rule.

The Structure

This chapter traces the failure of each form of presidential restraint—structural, legal, and cultural—and outlines the reforms and responsibilities necessary to restore constraint. It ends by showing that the restoration of civic constraint does not begin in Washington. It begins with daily acts of defiance, accountability, and solidarity by citizens who refuse to disappear.

The Collapse

The Constitution divided powers but could not ensure conscience. Laws established checks, but courts failed to enforce them. Traditions shaped expectations, but Trump erased them. What remained was impunity. The final breach came not through destruction, but through a systematic bypassing of every safeguard —executed shamelessly and defended politically. The result is not strong leadership. It is unbounded rule.

The Remedy

Restraint must be made real. That means codifying norms into law, denying power to the shameless, and guaranteeing enforcement —without exception. Presidents who defy lawful orders must face arrest. Justices who invent immunity must be removed. The right to recall, remove, and refuse must belong to the people. Tradition is not enough. Consequence must return.

. . .

WHAT COMES Next

Constraint begins in culture: with truth spoken, laws followed, and power explained. Restoration will not come from courts or Congress alone. It will come from civic habit—practiced daily, relentlessly, by millions. Silence must end. Action must begin. It will be slow. It will be hard. It will be scattered. But it will work—if we insist on it, together.

THREE THINGS TO Remember

- No restraint survives without enforcement.
- Shamelessness is more dangerous than ambition.
- Constraint is not tradition—it must be law, expectation, and habit.

ACTION LIST

- Pass binding laws to replace broken norms.
- Impeach officials—including justices—who violate their oaths.
- Support recall mechanisms at every level of government.
- Demand enforcement of ethics, transparency, and disclosure laws.
- Organize to block shameless candidates from winning office.

STRATEGIC RATIONALE

When norms collapse, bad actors multiply. Trump proved that one man can expose the fragility of the entire system if power is unbounded and shame is irrelevant. This chapter argues that future survival demands structural, legal, and cultural enforcement of limits. Without that, authoritarianism becomes not a threat—but an inevitability.

What You Can Do

Start where you are. Identify power without oversight—locally, statewide, nationally—and challenge it. Support investigative journalism. Demand FOIA access. Push for ethics reform. Refuse silence where enforcement is missing. Join watchdog groups. Volunteer for candidates who pledge to restore accountability. Help others understand that laws without teeth are invitations to impunity. What you do may not feel decisive—but it adds weight. Every act counts. Every voice matters. And civic constraint begins with the expectation that someone—anyone—must answer to us.

Discussion Questions

1. The chapter describes the Constitution as a structure built on restraint, not efficiency. What did that tradeoff protect—and how has it been exploited?
2. "The law did its job defining restraint. Tradition did its job modeling it. But the courts failed to enforce." Do you agree with this assessment? Which branch failed most clearly, and why?
3. Trump is said to have "found a blueprint" for impunity by violating every boundary at once. Why was this strategy so effective—and what does that suggest about current enforcement mechanisms?

4. Can you recall a moment when you realized the system was failing—not theoretically, but visibly? What institutions, if any, still seemed to hold?
5. The chapter draws a sharp line between honor and constraint. If we cannot legislate character, what can be done to keep those without it from holding power?
6. One proposal is to enshrine previously unwritten norms —like financial disclosure or recusal—into law. Which unwritten norms do you believe should now become enforceable standards?
7. The text argues that when judges, senators, or presidents ignore the law without consequence, legitimacy collapses. What practical steps might restore public faith in that legitimacy?
8. "The most effective constraint on power is to deny it to those who will not be bound." What systems—legal, electoral, or civic—would need to change to make that possible?
9. The chapter ends by reframing civic action as a personal, unglamorous habit: "You don't need permission. You need only to start." What does this suggest about how democracies are restored?
10. Of all the ideas in this chapter—restraint, consequence, expectation, culture, refusal—which one do you think is most important for preserving freedom? Which do you personally find hardest?

——— ✦ ———

Reader's Guide: Part III - A Judiciary That Upholds Law, Not Loyalty

The Stakes

The legitimacy of a democratic republic depends on the courts. Without integrity, transparency, and impartiality, judicial power becomes not a shield against tyranny, but a tool of it. This chapter argues that Trump and the modern Republican Party have transformed the courts—from institutions meant to uphold the rule of law into instruments that protect executive lawlessness and partisan power. If the courts fall, law becomes theater. And democracy becomes myth.

The Structure

The chapter begins by revisiting the original purpose of Article III and the vulnerabilities left by the Framers. It then traces the politicization of the judiciary under the Republican Party and Trump. Finally, it introduces six institutional reforms—each targeting a specific failure—and argues that these reforms do not politicize the courts, but preserve their role as arbiters of law, not power.

The Collapse

Judicial independence has become judicial impunity. Venue shopping allows litigants to choose their judge. Ethics are unenforced. Critical rulings are issued anonymously or without explanation. FOIA exemptions and court understaffing block scrutiny. Life tenure without limits ensures capture across generations. And Supreme Court Justices now invent legal doctrines to shield Trump and suppress accountability. The courts, meant to check power, now serve it.

The Remedy

Six reforms can restore integrity:

1. Judicial Assignment Reform to eliminate venue abuse and ensure impartiality.
2. Judicial Ethics Reform to apply a binding code of conduct to all federal judges.
3. Court Transparency and Shadow Docket Oversight to ensure public access and accountability.
4. Supreme Court Term Limits to rebalance generational capture.
5. Lower Court Expansion to reduce delay, manipulation, and ideological bottlenecks.
6. FOIA and Administrative Transparency to expose concealed public actions and restore visibility.

What Comes Next

None of these reforms is radical. All are necessary. Courts cannot demand public trust—they must earn it. That means ruling transparently, behaving ethically, and applying law without fear or favor. The goal is not to punish the judiciary but to restore its purpose. Because when courts kneel to the throne, the republic falls with them. But when they stand, so does the Constitution.

Three Things to Remember

- Judicial independence is not judicial impunity.
- Secrecy is not neutrality—it is manipulation.

- Courts that serve power destroy law. Courts that serve law constrain power.

Action List

- Pass legislation to randomize federal case assignments and prevent judge-shopping.
- Apply a single enforceable code of ethics to all Article III judges.
- Mandate real-time public access to federal trials of national consequence.
- Impose 18-year term limits on Supreme Court Justices.
- Expand lower courts to match population and caseload growth.
- Reform FOIA to shorten delays, close loopholes, and apply standards to public contractors.

Strategic Rationale

Trump's capture of the judiciary was not accidental—it was systematic. Courts once designed to check power have become accelerants of its abuse. The reforms proposed here are not partisan demands. They are democratic necessities. Without visible, ethical, and accessible courts, law becomes a mask for power. Rebuilding the courts is not a side project—it is the front line of democratic defense.

What You Can Do

You can demand judicial accountability by amplifying the need for reform—speak plainly about the ethical violations, secrecy, and bias now visible in the courts. Support organizations that monitor judicial misconduct and track shadow docket abuse. Call your senators to support court expansion, ethics legislation, and FOIA reform. Vote in state judicial elections and educate others on how court power works. Share legal journalism and expose procedural manipulation. Refuse to accept the myth of untouchable judges—every democracy needs judges who serve the people, not the powerful.

Discussion Questions

1. The chapter states that judicial independence was never meant to become judicial impunity. How can we restore this balance without undermining the legitimacy of the judiciary?
2. How did the Framers' incomplete judicial framework—particularly the absence of mandatory ethics rules—leave the courts vulnerable to partisan capture?
3. What role did Trump's strategic use of judicial appointments and venue manipulation play in accelerating existing structural weaknesses?
4. How does the "shadow docket" challenge traditional understandings of transparency and public accountability in the judiciary?
5. In what ways can term limits for Supreme Court Justices rebalance power without violating constitutional principles?
6. Why is the expansion of lower courts essential—not just to reduce delays—but to defend against ideological manipulation?
7. How do privatized government functions, particularly in

the legal system, threaten transparency and democratic oversight?

8. The chapter insists that these reforms do not attack judicial independence but complete the original constitutional design. Do you agree? Why or why not?
9. What would it take for the public to once again believe that courts serve the law—not the party or the president?
10. Which of the six reforms described feels most urgent to you, and what might be required to enact it at the federal level?

Reader's Guide: Chapter 15. Judicial Assignment Reform and Case Integrity

The Stakes

Justice in a democracy depends not only on law, but on the belief that law is applied fairly, without regard to geography, politics, or personality. Today, that belief is collapsing. Courts have become tools of political strategy—where the selection of venue can determine the outcome, and one judge can overrule national policy. This chapter argues that venue manipulation is not a procedural glitch—it is an existential threat to judicial legitimacy. If assignment can be rigged, then so can justice.

THE STRUCTURE

This chapter begins by tracing the historical origins of judicial case assignment, explains how single-judge divisions evolved into partisan weapons, and details how venue manipulation undermines the rule of law. It then outlines three essential reforms: nationwide randomization of case assignment, the use of multi-judge panels for nationwide injunctions, and the creation of a Federal Office of Judicial Integrity. It concludes with a call to restore trust—not through rhetoric, but through structural reform.

The Collapse

Venue shopping has become doctrine. Partisan actors now file cases not where harm occurred, but where the judge is predictable. In districts like Amarillo, Texas, one ideologue has become a one-man veto on national policy. Supreme Court justices operate without binding ethics rules. Recusal is optional. Transparency is minimal. What began as judicial independence has decayed into ideological orchestration. This is not accidental. It is deliberate sabotage—of process, precedent, and public trust.

The Remedy

Congress must mandate national random assignment for any case with potential national impact. Three-judge panels should be required for nationwide injunctions. A Federal Office of Judicial Integrity must track anomalies and review recusal patterns. Ethics must be codified and enforced. Judicial discretion cannot remain a vehicle for political power. These reforms are not radical. They are the minimum required for public trust in law to survive.

What Comes Next

Without change, belief in the neutrality of the courts will vanish. That collapse won't come all at once—it will fade through cynicism, inconsistency, and silence. Judicial authority rests on public consent. Rebuilding that consent requires visible fairness, structural reform, and a renewed insistence that process—not politics—determines outcomes. This is not punishment. It is preservation.

. . .

THREE THINGS TO **Remember**

- Venue shopping is not strategy. It is sabotage.
- Judicial legitimacy begins with random, fair assignment.
- Reform is not partisan—it is patriotic.

ACTION LIST

- Mandate national random assignment for federal cases with national impact.
- Require three-judge panels for nationwide injunctions.
- Establish a Federal Office of Judicial Integrity to monitor case assignment and recusal.
- Codify and enforce ethics rules for all federal judges, including Supreme Court Justices.
- Eliminate loopholes that allow administrative framing to avoid reform triggers.

STRATEGIC RATIONALE

Judicial capture does not always look like corruption. Sometimes it looks like procedure—quiet, technical, and devastating. This chapter shows how the manipulation of assignment rules has eroded the court's neutrality and created ideological strongholds in key jurisdictions. The most dangerous threat to justice is not lawbreaking, but law-bending. If reform is delayed again, we may preserve the appearance of courts—while losing their purpose entirely.

. . .

What You Can Do

Learn how venue shopping works—and teach others. Support legislation that requires fair assignment and ethics oversight. Challenge local courts and legal institutions to publish their assignment procedures and recusal data. Write letters. Attend hearings. Ask your representatives where they stand on judicial reform. And when you vote, prioritize candidates who understand that without neutral courts, democracy cannot function. You don't have to know everything about the judiciary to defend it. You only have to refuse to let it be rigged in silence.

Discussion Questions

1. Why does the chapter argue that judicial manipulation is not merely a procedural flaw but a systemic threat to democratic legitimacy?
2. In what ways has the creation of single-judge divisions, originally for logistical purposes, become a tool for political influence?
3. How has venue shopping—especially in places like Amarillo—distorted the public's perception of judicial neutrality?
4. The chapter critiques the rise of nationwide injunctions. Should such rulings be allowed at all, and if so, under what conditions?
5. What are the risks of limiting judicial reforms to only explicitly constitutional cases, rather than broader administrative and regulatory ones?
6. Do you agree that random assignment and three-judge

panels are necessary for restoring public trust? Why or why not?

7. How might a Federal Office of Judicial Integrity change the current landscape of oversight? Would it be enough?
8. The chapter warns that judges without enforceable ethics codes function more like sovereigns than public servants. What minimum ethical standards should apply?
9. Opponents argue that these reforms would politicize the judiciary. How can reformers respond to that claim effectively?
10. If legitimacy rests on public trust, what actions—legal, political, or civic—are most essential to prevent the erosion of judicial authority?

Reader's Guide: Judicial Ethics Reform and Federal Accountability

The Stakes

The judiciary was designed to be impartial, trusted, and bound by law—not elevated beyond it. But today, the courts face a crisis of legitimacy. The absence of a binding ethics code for the Supreme Court, the failure of recusal in the face of obvious conflicts, and a culture of voluntary compliance have led to an erosion of public trust. When citizens see judges accept undisclosed gifts and rule on cases involving political allies, the presumption of fairness disappears. This chapter contends that judicial ethics are not ornamental —they are constitutional—and that without real accountability, the courts will become instruments of power, not arbiters of law.

. . .

The Structure

The chapter opens by clarifying the original purpose of judicial independence as a protection from political coercion—not a license for impunity. It revisits the post-Watergate reforms and the origins of the judiciary's partial ethics framework, then examines the current failures in disclosure, recusal, and oversight. Mid-chapter, it focuses on recent examples of misconduct by Justices Thomas and Alito, followed by Congress's refusal to enforce reform. The chapter closes with a detailed prescription: one enforceable code of ethics, real-time transparency, independent review, and uniform application to all Article III judges—including the Supreme Court.

The Collapse

Judicial independence has been twisted into exceptionalism. Justices are exempt from the very rules they demand of others. Recusal is treated as voluntary. Financial entanglements are hidden. Ethics oversight is fragmented and toothless. Thomas and Alito have accepted undisclosed benefits from partisan actors while ruling in their favor. Project 2025 has further dismantled institutional checks. And congressional Republicans have blocked every serious reform effort. Trust in the Court has plunged, with fewer than half of Americans believing it rules based on law rather than politics. What began as a safeguard of neutrality has decayed into a system that shields power instead of checking it.

The Remedy

Congress must pass one binding code of judicial ethics covering all Article III judges, without exception. It must require public, real-time disclosures of gifts, travel, finances, and outside income. Recusal must be mandatory when conflicts exist. An independent oversight body must have the power to investigate violations and recommend discipline—including public reprimand and impeachment referral. Justices must no longer be permitted to decide for themselves whether they are compromised. Ethics must be enforced, not assumed. And every American must be able to trust that justice is delivered by those bound to fairness—not shielded from scrutiny.

What Comes Next

If judicial legitimacy collapses, law itself will lose meaning. People will stop believing in fair rulings. Courts will become partisan arenas. Violence and chaos will rise as citizens abandon the hope of lawful redress. We are already seeing it—on January 6, in threats to judges, in political violence across the country. Courts were built to withstand partisanship. But they cannot survive without constraint. We must rebuild that constraint—not as punishment, but as preservation. Ethics is not a partisan issue. It is the foundation of public trust. And that trust is what separates a constitutional democracy from a constitutional facade.

Three Things to Remember

- Judicial independence was never meant to shield judges from accountability.
- Voluntary ethics compliance has failed—visible, enforceable rules are now essential.
- Without trust in courts, the rule of law collapses into the rule of power.

Action List

- Pass legislation creating one binding judicial ethics code for all Article III judges.
- Mandate real-time public disclosure of all gifts, financial interests, and outside income.
- Require automatic recusal for conflicts of interest—no exceptions.
- Establish an independent ethics oversight body empowered to investigate and recommend discipline.
- Restore DOJ cooperation with ethics enforcement and reverse Project 2025 sabotage of judicial transparency.

Strategic Rationale

The judiciary's power depends entirely on the belief that its rulings are fair. That belief is now vanishing. This chapter demonstrates how systemic ethical failure—left unaddressed—will transform the courts into tools of partisan control. The collapse of recusal, the refusal of the Supreme Court to bind itself to any code, and the overt alliance with ideological actors expose a fundamental breach. This is not about decorum. It is about constitutional survival. To protect the republic, we must reassert that no judge is above the law.

What You Can Do

Start by learning how judicial ethics systems work—and where they fail. Share that knowledge with others. Support legislation that applies ethical standards equally across the judiciary. Attend candidate forums and ask local, state, and federal candidates where they stand on Supreme Court ethics reform. Write to your representatives. Demand an end to judicial exceptionalism. Volunteer with civic education groups that explain how courts shape democracy.

Speak up when misconduct is revealed. When a branch of government cannot police itself, the people must insist that it be policed. You don't need to be a lawyer to defend the courts. You need only to expect—and demand—integrity.

DISCUSSION QUESTIONS

1. What is the constitutional rationale for lifetime tenure and salary protection for judges, and how has that rationale been misinterpreted or abused in recent decades?
2. How did the Framers' experience with monarchy influence their expectations for judicial accountability in the U.S. system?
3. Why has the Supreme Court historically exempted itself from the Code of Conduct that applies to lower federal courts, and what are the consequences of that exemption?
4. What structural differences exist between the ethical oversight of lower courts and that of the Supreme Court, and how do these differences affect public trust?
5. Why is voluntary self-regulation by Supreme Court Justices inadequate in the current political and legal climate?
6. How have specific examples—such as those involving Justices Thomas and Alito—revealed systemic failures in judicial recusal and disclosure?
7. What role has Congress played in either advancing or obstructing judicial ethics reform, and what political motivations appear to drive that role?
8. How does the current state of judicial ethics influence

the broader legitimacy of the legal system, especially in high-stakes cases like civil rights or election disputes?
9. In what ways does the lack of enforceable judicial ethics contribute to democratic fragility and rising political violence?
10. What reforms are necessary to ensure that all federal judges, including Supreme Court Justices, are held to enforceable standards of transparency and accountability?

––––– ✦ –––––

Reader's Guide: Court Transparency and Shadow Docket Oversight

The Stakes

The judiciary was never meant to operate in darkness. In a democracy, law gains its authority not by force, but by legitimacy—and legitimacy requires visibility. This chapter exposes how courts, especially the Supreme Court, have increasingly withdrawn from public scrutiny. Shadow docket rulings, paywalled court records, and camera bans are not procedural quirks. They are forms of concealment that erode trust. The danger is not just what the public doesn't see—it's what can now be done in the dark.

The Structure

This chapter opens with the constitutional basis for courtroom openness, drawing on the Sixth Amendment and historical practice. It then traces the shift from civic visibility to institutional obscurity: banning cameras, paywalling court records, and relying on unsigned emergency rulings. It details how Trump and his allies have weaponized this opacity for legal delay and political advantage.

It concludes with three structural reforms: live access to federal proceedings, a rebuilt public record system, and mandatory transparency for emergency rulings.

THE COLLAPSE

Justice has grown increasingly hidden. From camera bans to the monetization of PACER, the federal judiciary now functions largely out of sight. The shadow docket—a system of unsigned, unexplained emergency rulings—has become a routine tool of executive power. Under Trump, it enabled not only policy imposition but prosecutorial evasion. Republican efforts to modernize judicial transparency have been blocked or buried, creating a judiciary that is procedurally powerful but publicly invisible. That invisibility is not caution—it is concealment.

THE REMEDY

Congress must restore visibility by enacting three key reforms: (1) require real-time audiovisual access to all federal hearings of national consequence; (2) eliminate the PACER paywall and establish a free, unified public access system for court records; and (3) require that all emergency judicial actions altering rights or policy be signed, explained, and reviewed. These are not radical steps. They are constitutional necessities. Justice must not only be done—it must be seen.

WHAT COMES NEXT

If shadow docket governance becomes standard, the law will cease to function as a constraint on power. Every unsigned stay, every unexplained order, chips away at public faith. When courts operate invisibly, they cannot command legitimacy. And when legitimacy collapses, the rule of law collapses with it. We are not yet governed by silence—but we are growing accustomed to it. That silence must be broken.

Three Things to Remember

- The judiciary cannot remain legitimate if it cannot be seen.
- The shadow docket is not judicial restraint—it is procedural evasion.
- Visibility is not ornament. It is a constitutional shield.

Action List

- Mandate audiovisual access to federal hearings with national impact.
- Rebuild PACER as a free, open, searchable public infrastructure.
- Require all emergency rulings to include authorship, reasoning, and review timelines.
- Prohibit the use of unsigned, unexplained orders to change national policy.
- Introduce and pass legislation enforcing judicial transparency standards.

Strategic Rationale

Opacity is not a neutral condition—it is a choice. When courts retreat from view, they invite manipulation. The shadow docket is not a glitch. It is a method of unaccountable governance that weakens the judiciary's moral standing and facilitates executive overreach. This chapter shows how concealment has become a tactic—and why public visibility is the only way to defend judicial legitimacy in an era of political assault.

What You Can Do

Help lift the curtain. Educate others about the shadow docket and its impact. Support journalism that challenges judicial secrecy and explains the courts. Advocate for transparency legislation—and ask your elected officials where they stand. Attend public hearings, demand digital access, and push for reform of court-record systems. When justice is hidden, democracy is weakened. But if we make the system visible again, we make it answerable. And that is how we defend it.

Discussion Questions

1. What does it mean for justice to be "seen," and why is public visibility a constitutional safeguard rather than a symbolic gesture?
2. How has the physical and digital inaccessibility of the courts (e.g., closed courtrooms, PACER fees) shaped public understanding and trust in the judiciary?
3. Why did the emergence of the shadow docket represent more than just a procedural shift? What are the implications for democratic accountability?
4. In what ways has the Republican legal movement leveraged judicial opacity to achieve policy outcomes without full public scrutiny?

5. How did Trump's first and second terms differ in their use of emergency court filings, and what does this reveal about the evolving nature of executive overreach?
6. How does delay function as a tool of impunity within the legal system, especially under the current Supreme Court's use of the shadow docket?
7. What philosophical and civic consequences arise when justice is inaccessible or invisible to the public?
8. What reforms are proposed to restore judicial transparency, and how might they rebalance the relationship between the courts and the public?
9. How does the current state of court access violate the spirit, if not the letter, of the Sixth Amendment and the broader constitutional commitment to public oversight?
10. Why is visibility described in the final paragraph as more than a virtue—as a shield? What does that suggest about the future of democracy if judicial secrecy becomes normalized?

———— ✦ ————

Reader's Guide: Supreme Court Term Limits and Generational Balance

The Stakes

The Supreme Court is no longer a guardian of democratic rhythm. With appointments stretching into half-centuries, the Court reflects past ideologies long after the public has moved on. This chapter argues that life tenure without term limits distorts justice, entrenches minority rule, and renders the Court a relic. Without rotation, renewal becomes impossible—and the law loses its legitimacy.

. . .

The Structure

This chapter opens with a historical framing of judicial tenure, contrasting past expectations with today's ideological entrenchment. It documents how term limits were neither envisioned nor barred by the Framers and how lifetime appointments have become a tool of minority rule. The chapter outlines the constitutional pathway to 18-year staggered terms and closes with a call to restore legitimacy through rotation and generational balance.

The Collapse

What began as judicial independence has metastasized into judicial permanence. The Court is no longer responsive to the people but locked in the strategies of presidents long gone. Youthful appointees are chosen not for wisdom but for longevity. Public trust erodes with every ideologically driven ruling. The result is a body unmoored from time—one that rules not with fresh judgment, but with calcified power.

The Remedy

Congress should enact legislation imposing 18-year term limits for active Supreme Court service. Justices would transition to senior status thereafter, retaining salary and title but stepping back from full participation. Every two years, a new Justice would be appointed, restoring predictable turnover, generational relevance, and public trust. The reform requires no constitutional amendment —only political will.

What Comes Next

Without reform, the Court will grow even more removed from the public it governs. Legal legitimacy will fracture along partisan lines. Every decision will be seen as legacy power, not democratic deliberation. Reforming the rhythm of judicial service is essential—not just to protect the Court, but to preserve faith in the rule of law itself.

Three Things to **Remember**

- The Constitution allows life tenure—but not permanent dominance.
- Rotation renews legitimacy; stagnation breeds distrust.
- Term limits restore balance, not by force, but by design.

Action List

- Enact 18-year term limits for active Supreme Court service via statute.
- Transition Justices to senior status with lifetime title and salary after active terms.
- Appoint one new Justice every two years to establish regular turnover.
- Support the Supreme Court Term Limits and Regular Appointments Act.
- Normalize the dignity of retirement and end strategic manipulation of vacancies.

Strategic Rationale

Lifetime service once protected judicial courage; now it protects ideological conquest. This chapter shows how generational entrenchment corrodes democratic legitimacy. Term limits do not weaken the Court—they renew it. Regular, predictable turnover ensures that no political movement can hijack the judiciary for decades. The law must live in time, not in stasis.

What You Can Do

Talk to others about how term limits strengthen democracy. Write to your representatives to support term-limit legislation. Challenge the myth that reform means politicizing the Court—remind them it's already been politicized by design. Celebrate judicial retirement as civic dignity, not loss. Defend the idea that public trust is earned not by robes alone, but by rhythm, rotation, and renewal.

Discussion Questions

1. What assumptions did the Framers make about judicial tenure, and how have changes in life expectancy and political strategy upended those assumptions?
2. How does life tenure, once seen as a safeguard of independence, now function as a tool of ideological entrenchment?
3. In what ways has the politicization of Supreme Court appointments changed the Court's public legitimacy and internal functioning?
4. What are the consequences of Justices remaining in power for decades, particularly when their decisions affect generations they may no longer understand?
5. How has the confirmation process evolved, and what does it reveal about the increasing view of the Court as a partisan instrument?

6. Why is judicial visibility not enough to ensure legitimacy—why must there also be generational turnover?
7. What does it mean for democracy when Supreme Court rulings reflect partisan manipulation rather than public consensus?
8. How does the proposed 18-year term limit structure preserve judicial independence while restoring democratic rhythm?
9. Why do other democracies impose term limits or retirement ages on their high courts, and what lessons should the U.S. draw from them?
10. The chapter closes by contrasting possession and service. How might this distinction change how Americans view the role of the judiciary?

―――― ✦ ――――

Reader's Guide: Lower Court Expansion and Access to Justice

The Stakes

The Constitution grants Congress the power to build and shape the federal courts—but for nearly half a century, it has failed to do so. The result is a judiciary that is overburdened, under-resourced, demographically skewed, and structurally manipulated. Justice delayed is no longer rare. It is systemic. And for millions of Americans, access to justice depends on geography, wealth, or political strategy. This chapter argues that judicial expansion is not radical—it is routine, long overdue, and essential to rebuilding a fair, functioning democracy.

THE STRUCTURE

This chapter begins with the constitutional foundation for lower courts, then traces the historical precedent for judicial expansion as democratic maintenance. It explains how Republicans weaponized delay to create a judiciary of ideological loyalty and geographic imbalance, culminating in Trump's strategic manipulation of venues and vacancies. The chapter then outlines an agenda: expanding judgeships, modernizing access, diversifying the judicial pipeline, repairing timelines, correcting geographic distortions, and embedding periodic review. It concludes by calling on Congress to reclaim its constitutional duty—to build a judiciary worthy of the republic it serves.

THE COLLAPSE

Judicial imbalance is no accident—it is design. Republicans froze court expansion while flooding the bench with ideologues. Trump then turned that captured structure into a weapon of delay, obstruction, and personal protection. Dockets are overloaded. Courts in liberal regions are starved. Immigration districts lack judges with relevant expertise. Legal aid is inaccessible. Rural communities are court deserts. Delay is now a governing tool. Access has become a privilege. And justice, for many, is not denied outright—it simply never arrives.

THE REMEDY

Congress must authorize scaled judicial expansion across a decade, guided by caseloads and systemic delays. It must fund not only new judges, but the full infrastructure of modern justice—staff, technology, e-filing, multilingual services, and remote access. The pipeline must open to defenders, civil rights advocates, and legal aid lawyers. Judicial geography must be rebalanced to reflect real need. Confirmation procedures must be fixed, and a permanent, nonpartisan Judicial Capacity Review Commission established to make expansion a democratic norm. This is not court-packing. It is court restoration.

What Comes Next

Without reform, the judiciary will remain a bottleneck, a shield for the powerful, and a symbol of civic exclusion. Delay will become erasure. Venue shopping will deepen inequality. And public trust in law will decay into cynicism. But with reform, the courts can become what they were always meant to be: engines of justice, guardians of equal protection, and pillars of democratic life. The tools exist. The precedent is clear. What remains is the will to act.

Three Things to Remember

- Judicial delay is not neutral—it is strategic sabotage.
- A judiciary built only for the powerful cannot deliver equal justice.
- Court expansion is constitutional maintenance, not political rupture.

Action List

- Authorize new judgeships through a decade-long, data-driven expansion plan.
- Fund the full infrastructure of access: staffing, technology, legal aid, and multilingual support.
- Rebalance judicial geography to serve diverse, high-caseload regions equitably.

- Diversify the nomination pipeline to include defenders, civil rights advocates, and legal aid attorneys.
- Create a nonpartisan Judicial Capacity Review Commission with ten-year review cycles.
- Reform Senate confirmation procedures to prevent obstruction and abuse.
- Modernize public legal education to teach procedural access and civic empowerment.

STRATEGIC RATIONALE

A broken judiciary weakens every other reform. Courts are where laws are interpreted, challenged, and enforced. Without timely, fair, and universal access, every promise of democracy is delayed or denied. This chapter makes clear: judicial scarcity is not efficiency—it is exclusion. Restoration begins with expansion, transparency, and the rebalancing of power. Courts that are overwhelmed cannot serve. Courts that are captured cannot protect. To defend the republic, we must build courts that reflect it.

WHAT YOU CAN DO

Learn how your local federal courts are structured—and where vacancies, delays, or access issues exist. Support candidates who commit to expanding judicial capacity and diversifying appointments. Advocate for remote access, language support, and universal e-filing in your district. Challenge myths about court-packing by explaining the constitutional role of Congress in shaping the judiciary. Volunteer with legal aid organizations or civic education efforts that make the law more accessible. And above all, vote for leaders who believe the courts should serve everyone—not just the powerful few.

DISCUSSION QUESTIONS

1. How does the Constitution empower Congress to expand the lower courts, and why is this responsibility foundational to justice?
2. What historical precedents demonstrate that judicial expansion is a routine act of constitutional maintenance?
3. In what ways did Republican strategy since the 1980s deliberately block judicial expansion for ideological gain?
4. How did Trump's use of judicial appointments reflect broader trends in politicizing the judiciary?
5. Why is the failure to expand the judiciary considered a structural collapse rather than simple oversight?
6. How can increasing court capacity help ensure timely justice and equal access under the law?
7. What barriers exist in diversifying the judiciary, and how might reform open the bench to underrepresented legal professionals?
8. How does geographic imbalance in judicial appointments affect access to justice across different regions?
9. Why is public legal education critical to restoring trust and functionality in the judiciary?
10. What institutional safeguards are proposed to ensure judicial expansion remains a nonpartisan and enduring reform?

Reader's Guide: Transparency Reform and Public Access to Information

The Stakes

Justice is not merely a function—it is a performance of accountability. When that performance is hidden, trust evaporates. This chapter shows how American justice, once conducted in full view of the people, has been pushed behind paywalls, outsourced into secrecy, and cloaked in procedural darkness. The danger is not only corruption but replacement: public institutions hollowed out and sold off to the highest bidder. Without transparency, democracy cannot be defended—because the public cannot see what is being taken.

The Structure

The chapter begins with the historical foundations of judicial transparency—from early public trials to the First Amendment and the codification of access. It traces the evolution of legal openness through FOIA and shows how Republican administrations gradually dismantled its reach. It then details the privatization of court functions and the emergence of opacity as strategy under Trump, culminating in the creation of DOGE. The final section outlines legislative and structural reforms needed to restore democratic visibility.

The Collapse

Transparency was never inevitable—it was maintained by law and expectation. When those falter, concealment thrives. From sealed surveillance dockets and outsourced case management to press restrictions and obstructed FOIA requests, access to the courts has been functionally denied. DOGE, under Trump's second term, operated as an unaccountable agency beyond public view. What began as administrative secrecy became systemic suppression. Courts cannot enforce justice when their workings are invisible—and power cannot be constrained when no one can see how it moves.

The Remedy

Congress must extend FOIA to all entities executing public functions, including contractors. Deadlines must be enforceable. All judicial contracts, surveillance protocols, and administrative decisions must be published. Paywalls on court records must be eliminated. Courts must disclose how they use technology to manage cases. A presumption of visibility must guide every reform. Transparency must be rebuilt as democratic infrastructure: visible dockets, accessible systems, public oversight. This is not exposure for spectacle—it is visibility for accountability.

What Comes Next

Without reform, privatization will continue to hollow out democratic governance. Services once accountable to Congress will serve investors instead. Silence will become strategy. Secrecy will become structure. And the public—unaware of what's gone—will be unable to reclaim it. This is not an abstract loss. It is the auctioning of the Republic. Unless we see what is being done in our name, we cannot stop it. Transparency is not the goal. It is the condition that makes every other reform possible.

Three Things to Remember

- Transparency is not data—it is civic sight.

- Public services without public oversight are not democratic.
- The dismantling of visibility is the first step toward authoritarian rule.

Action List

- Expand FOIA to include contractors, subcontractors, and public-function intermediaries.
- Require real-time public access to court dockets, recusal notices, and administrative decisions.
- Abolish PACER fees and build a public, searchable legal record system.
- Mandate transparency in surveillance orders and outsourced judicial functions.
- Enact fixed deadlines and penalties for FOIA violations and delays.
- Create review mechanisms for national security and proprietary exemptions.

Strategic Rationale

Opacity is not neutral. It favors those with power, connections, and the means to manipulate unseen. The retreat from transparency has enabled authoritarian maneuvering—placing public functions behind corporate walls and political shields. This chapter exposes how secrecy became a governing strategy and argues that visibility is the only democratic antidote. Without public access, law becomes theater. With it, the people regain the tools to judge, resist, and restore. Justice cannot serve unless it can be seen.

What You Can Do

Learn how to file FOIA requests—and teach others. Demand transparency from your courts, local agencies, and public contractors. Support reforms that eliminate paywalls and increase public access to government data. Attend hearings. Ask elected officials where they stand on judicial openness and transparency legislation. Advocate for accessible systems, visible processes, and enforceable disclosure laws. The power to see is the power to protect. And in a democracy, that power belongs to the people—not the few who benefit from silence.

Discussion Questions

1. How did early American legal traditions distinguish the new republic from monarchic secrecy?
2. Why was the First Amendment critical not only for speech but also for public access to government action?
3. How does courtroom transparency contribute to both justice and democratic legitimacy?
4. What is the relationship between stare decisis and the public's ability to trace judicial reasoning?
5. How did the Freedom of Information Act (FOIA) attempt to codify transparency, and what have been its key weaknesses?
6. In what ways did Trump's first and second terms dismantle traditional transparency norms, particularly in the courts?
7. How does privatization of legal and governmental functions erode public accountability?

8. What distinctions should be maintained between justifiable secrecy and dangerous concealment?
9. Why is the public's ability to "see" justice essential to maintaining civic trust and the rule of law?
10. What reforms to transparency law and judicial procedure are most urgent to restore democratic oversight?

Reader's Guide: The Rule of Law is What We Build It to Be

The Stakes

Judicial authority depends not on force, but on trust. When rulings arrive unsigned, ethics violations go unpunished, and case assignments are manipulated for outcome, that trust fractures. Today, the courts are not merely in crisis—they are being actively repurposed. Not to check power, but to prolong it. If Americans no longer believe the law governs equally, they will not obey it. And if no one demands better, what breaks next is not procedure—it is democracy itself.

THE STRUCTURE

This chapter traces the decline of judicial legitimacy and the weaponization of structural gaps. It shows how Republican strategists and Trump allies transformed the judiciary from constraint into shield. It then presents six integrated reforms to restore transparency, enforce ethics, end partisan control, and revive generational balance—each grounded in Article III's congressional mandate to structure the courts.

THE COLLAPSE

The courts were designed for independence but assumed integrity. That assumption collapsed. Lifetime appointments became partisan strongholds. Shadow dockets erased accountability. Judicial impunity spread from the Supreme Court downward. Trump's second term intensified the decay: courts were flooded with delay motions, assignments rigged by geography, and rulings delivered without reason. The system now favors the powerful, rewards secrecy, and abandons its constitutional role. This is not dysfunction. It is design, weaponized.

The Remedy

To restore the courts, we must enact six critical reforms:

1. Judicial Assignment Reform to end venue shopping and restore impartiality.
2. Judicial Ethics Reform to enforce a binding code across all Article III judges.
3. Court Transparency Expansion to eliminate shadow rulings and abolish paywalls.
4. Lower Court Expansion to meet the scale of modern litigation and delay.
5. Supreme Court Term Limits to prevent ideological entrenchment and restore generational legitimacy.
6. Confirmation Reform to ensure transparent, time-bound, and merit-based judicial appointments.

These reforms do not diminish the courts. They rescue them—by ending impunity, restoring accountability, and renewing public faith in equal justice under law.

What Comes Next

Congress must act. These reforms are not constitutionally prohibited—they are constitutionally required. Article III gives Congress the power to structure the federal judiciary. It has used that power before. It must do so again. Ethics, assignments, transparency, term limits, and court capacity must be legislated—not left to judicial preference. The courts will not reform themselves. But they will respond to law.

Three Things to Remember

- A captured court does not limit power. It legalizes its abuse.
- Congress was given the authority to fix this. It must now find the will.
- If law no longer binds the powerful, it no longer protects the rest.

Action List

- Enact enforceable judicial ethics laws, binding on all Article III judges.
- Pass legislation mandating random assignment of federal trial judges.
- Ban unsigned rulings that alter rights, block enforcement, or suspend policy.
- Legislate an 18-year active term limit for Supreme Court Justices via rotation to senior status.
- Authorize phased expansion of lower courts, tied to caseload and delay metrics.

- Codify transparent confirmation procedures with public disclosures and deadlines.

Strategic Rationale

These reforms are not incremental—they are foundational. They target the six ways power currently bypasses accountability: secrecy, impunity, delay, manipulation, imbalance, and ideological permanence. Together, they restore the rule of law as a democratic guardrail, not a ceremonial relic. Reform makes the courts neither partisan nor passive—but functional, legitimate, and defensible against authoritarian capture.

What You Can Do

Call your senators and representatives to support term limits, ethics enforcement, and judicial expansion. Join organizations tracking court corruption and mobilizing reform. File FOIA requests. Attend court hearings. Demand transparency. Vote for candidates who treat the courts as engines of equality, not tools of power. The Constitution gave us this authority. The moment demands that we use it.

Discussion Questions

1. What factors have contributed to the growing public distrust in the judiciary, and how do these threaten democratic legitimacy?
2. How did the Framers' assumptions about judicial virtue shape the original design of the courts, and where did those assumptions fall short?

3. In what ways has the modern Republican Party reshaped judicial appointment and confirmation to entrench long-term control?
4. How does Trump's second-term use of the judiciary differ from his first, and what are the broader consequences of that shift?
5. What is the difference between judicial independence and judicial impunity, and how can reform preserve the former while eliminating the latter?
6. Why are unsigned opinions, hidden dockets, and delayed rulings dangerous to the rule of law?
7. What are the six proposed reforms, and how do they work together to restore integrity and accessibility to the courts?
8. Why is it essential for Congress—not the judiciary itself—to enact structural court reform?
9. How does legislative inaction enable judicial decay, and what are the constitutional responsibilities of Congress in this regard?
10. What does the chapter mean by saying "we are the authors now," and how can citizens reclaim their power in shaping the judiciary?

Reader's Guide: Part IV: Rebuilding an Informed Public

The Stakes

Democracy cannot function without shared understanding. The collapse of public trust in media, education, and information systems has fragmented American civic life. Without visibility into algorithms, fairness in media, and universal civic education, citizens cannot discern fact from fiction, or power from performance. Misinformation is no longer an error—it is a strategy, used to destabilize consent and paralyze opposition. If the public cannot agree on what is real, it cannot resist what is wrong. Truth is not optional. It is what democracy breathes.

The Structure

This chapter identifies three core failures that have eroded public understanding: unregulated algorithmic influence, the collapse of media accountability, and the disappearance of meaningful civic education. It then outlines structural reforms that would restore public oversight of digital platforms, reestablish media standards, and embed civic knowledge as a national priority—not only in schools, but throughout adult public life. These reforms are not cosmetic. They are foundational. Because consent must be informed —or it is not consent at all.

The Collapse

Platform algorithms now shape belief with no accountability. The repeal of the Fairness Doctrine removed any public duty from powerful broadcasters. Schools, stripped of honest civics, have left generations without the tools to understand or defend democracy. Lies move faster than facts. The press, once adversarial, often abdicates its role. Adults, ashamed of what they do not know, disengage. Disinformation is no longer isolated—it is systemic. The public is not only uninformed. It is being unformed.

The Remedy

We propose three structural reforms:

- Platform Transparency: Require auditability of algorithms, public disclosure of political advertising, and real-time exposure of disinformation campaigns.
- Media Fairness: Reinstate public interest obligations for broadcasters, require corrections and disclosures, and ensure platforms distinguish journalism from propaganda.
- Civic Education: Fully fund modern civics that teaches democratic function, disinformation detection, and the practice of public service—at every age.

These reforms give citizens the tools to think, decide, and govern together.

What Comes Next

This is only the beginning. Public understanding must be rebuilt not once, but constantly, across platforms, professions, and generations. The reforms outlined here create conditions for truth to survive—but their success depends on cultural will, institutional leadership, and public engagement. We must choose a country in which knowing matters, in which service is honorable, and in which truth is something more than a casualty of strategy.

Three Things to Remember

- Truth is not censorship's victim. It is democracy's precondition.
- Misinformation thrives where regulation, education, and civic culture fail.
- No public can govern itself if it cannot trust what it sees.

. . .

Action List

- Enact federal legislation requiring public algorithm audits and content transparency from digital platforms.
- Reinstate public interest broadcasting standards and create enforceable fairness rules for cable and streaming platforms.
- Mandate robust, modern civic education in every state, with federal funding tied to clear curriculum standards.
- Fund and empower lifelong civic learning through libraries, universities, unions, and local institutions.
- Create a National Civic Service Program encouraging young people to serve in elected office, public institutions, and the military with training in ethics and governance.

Strategic Rationale

These reforms rebuild the scaffolding of democracy. When citizens understand how power works, they are harder to mislead. When platforms are visible, disinformation loses its shield. When public discourse has structure, truth can stand longer than spin. We do not demand uniformity of thought—we demand the conditions that make thinking possible. These reforms are not cultural grievances. They are constitutional restorations.

What You Can Do

Support and demand civic education in your community. Ask school boards, libraries, and local media how they are preparing citizens to resist disinformation. Organize public forums that teach media literacy and civic participation. Volunteer for programs that bridge generational divides in knowledge. Write to your representatives to support platform regulation and media standards. Democracy is not sustained by knowledge alone—but without it, nothing else can hold.

Discussion Questions

1. What does it mean to say that democracy begins in the mind rather than the ballot box?
2. How have modern information systems—platforms, media, and education—failed in their role to support democracy?
3. In what ways has disinformation been structurally enabled rather than merely tolerated?
4. How does Trump's use of lies as spectacle reflect a deeper collapse in institutional safeguards?
5. What are the dangers of epistemic collapse, and how does it differ from political polarization?
6. How do engagement-based algorithms contribute to the spread and profitability of falsehoods?
7. Why is civic education described as "infrastructure" rather than enrichment, and what reforms are proposed?
8. What role can public institutions—libraries, unions, faith groups—play in rebuilding democratic literacy?
9. How does the chapter reframe public service and military service as tools for democratic renewal?
10. Why is truth described as the infrastructure of consent, and what must be done to preserve it?

Reader's Guide: Disinformation and Platform Transparency

The Stakes

Truth is not self-sustaining. Without it, democracy cannot function—only react. In today's media ecosystem, lies are not accidents. They are infrastructure. Platforms profit from distortion, politicians exploit it, and the public suffers its consequences. When private amplification replaces public understanding, the result is not liberty but control.

THE STRUCTURE

The Constitution protects speech from government censorship but is silent on platform manipulation. Section 230 granted platforms immunity for user content to encourage moderation. Instead, it fostered impunity. Over time, moderation was dismantled, truth was punished, and disinformation became central to political power —especially under Trump's second term.

THE COLLAPSE

Trump's allies systematically undermined moderation, reframed platform accountability as censorship, and turned public speech into a weapon of authoritarian governance. Platforms, under pressure or willingly complicit, abandoned responsibility. What began as neglect became strategy: silence dissent, elevate cruelty, erase dissenters—and reward flattery over fact. Truth became the casualty. Children became the collateral.

THE REMEDY

We must rewrite Section 230 to require real transparency and active moderation. Satire and criticism must remain protected, but

AI abuse and digital harassment must not. A new federal oversight body must audit algorithms, enforce standards, and ensure no speech platform is beyond the reach of law, accountability, or democratic principle.

What Comes Next

Without truth, no vote is informed, no law holds, no institution survives. Reforms in transparency, moderation, and platform accountability must come first—or nothing else endures. The goal is not control. It is the restoration of civic space where facts can breathe, disagreement can flourish, and democracy can survive.

Three Things to Remember

- Disinformation is not noise—it is architecture. Lies now form the scaffolding of political power.
- Amplification is not a right. It is a system of private control used to punish truth and profit from fear.
- You cannot govern a people disconnected from reality. Truth is not a luxury. It is the condition for consent.

Action List

- Rewrite Section 230 to revoke immunity for platforms that amplify disinformation for profit.
- Create a federal authority to audit, report on, and enforce algorithmic transparency and moderation standards.
- Define and protect satire, criticism, and dissent—while distinguishing them from impersonation and harm.

- Criminalize cyberstalking, synthetic harassment, and AI-driven abuse—especially targeting minors and vulnerable users.
- Require age verification, independent appeal processes, and public algorithmic audits for major platforms.

Strategic Rationale

If citizens cannot distinguish fact from fiction, democracy cannot survive. Every other reform—from climate to courts—relies on an informed public capable of judgment. Rebuilding shared truth is not optional. It is the precondition for resistance, repair, and renewal.

What You Can Do

Support platform accountability legislation and demand transparency from digital services you use. Share this chapter with others to clarify what is at stake. Back independent journalism that still upholds truth. Refuse to amplify propaganda—no matter how tempting the outrage. And teach others, especially young people, to ask: who benefits from the lie?

Discussion Questions

1. How does the distinction between the right to speak and the power to amplify shape our understanding of free speech in the digital age?
2. In what ways has Section 230 enabled or obstructed accountability for online disinformation and abuse?

3. How did platform decisions to appease Trump's administration alter public access to truthful information?
4. What role did Republican messaging play in delegitimizing content moderation and fact-checking?
5. How has Trump used social media platforms as instruments of governance and control rather than communication?
6. What are the dangers of laws targeting deepfakes that may protect the powerful while exposing the vulnerable?
7. How has Elon Musk's transformation of Twitter into X reshaped the landscape of digital speech and platform responsibility?
8. What is the impact of disinformation becoming an infrastructure of governance rather than an incidental byproduct?
9. Why is independent enforcement essential in regulating platform conduct and safeguarding democratic discourse?
10. What reforms are necessary to balance free expression with the protection of truth, dignity, and vulnerable populations online?

Reader's Guide: Fairness in Broadcast Media

The Stakes

Without shared facts, there is no shared future. The airwaves that once informed the nation now echo with partisan distortion, coordinated disinformation, and spectacle disguised as news. Deregulation turned truth into opinion, journalism into performance, and the press into a battleground of loyalty tests. If we cannot trust what we hear, we cannot consent to be governed.

The Structure

The Constitution protects speech—but not the right to deceive at scale. Congress is empowered to regulate broadcasting in the public interest. The Fairness Doctrine, repealed in 1987, once enforced balance and accountability in public broadcasting. Since its demise, consolidation and deregulation have turned a shared civic resource into a private megaphone for power.

The Collapse

The repeal of the Fairness Doctrine marked the collapse of public standards in media. Fox News, talk radio, and partisan networks transformed journalism into identity-based entertainment. Local news withered. Regulatory oversight vanished. Trump weaponized this landscape—elevating propaganda, punishing dissent, and redefining media as loyalty theater. Truth became optional. Fiction became governance.

The Remedy

We do not need to resurrect the Fairness Doctrine. But we must restore its principle: if you use the public airwaves, you owe the public fairness. A modern framework must enforce transparency, balance, and accountability across all major broadcasting platforms. This includes revising FCC standards, banning media monopolies, requiring public ad disclosures, and funding nonpartisan journalism. The goal is not censorship—but the conditions for informed democracy.

. . .

What Comes Next

Regulatory reform will face fierce resistance. But the First Amendment is not a shield for deception. The public must reclaim its airwaves. Networks that claim journalistic authority must meet basic standards of accuracy and disclosure. Truth must be visible. Lies must be named. And the media must serve the people—not the powerful.

Three Things to Remember

- Broadcasting is not a right. It is a licensed use of public infrastructure, and must serve the public interest—not political propaganda.
- The repeal of the Fairness Doctrine was not technological. It was ideological—and its consequences have been catastrophic for civic trust.
- Truth is not fragile. But without standards, access, or accountability, it can be drowned out—leaving democracy exposed to spectacle, distortion, and control.

Action List

- Rebuild the FCC with independent commissioners, public interest mandates, and enforcement authority over fairness, ownership, and access.
- Ban cross-ownership and media monopolies that collapse local journalism and manufacture consent.
- Enforce political ad transparency across broadcast, cable, and digital media—with public archives and real-time disclosure.

- Establish a civic labeling standard to distinguish journalism from opinion and entertainment from propaganda.
- Create a national public media fund to support investigative journalism, local news, and community-driven reporting.

Strategic Rationale

No democracy can survive without trusted channels of information. When propaganda outpaces journalism, civic unity dissolves. Restoring standards is not nostalgia—it is necessity. The media landscape has changed, but the public interest remains. These reforms are how we reclaim the ability to think clearly, argue fairly, and govern together.

What You Can Do

Call for FCC reform. Support independent journalism and local news. Demand full disclosure in political advertising. Share this guide. And challenge networks, candidates, and corporations that profit from distortion. The airwaves belong to the people. It's time we take them back.

Discussion Questions

1. How did the repeal of the Fairness Doctrine alter the structure and tone of American broadcast media?
2. What legal and constitutional foundations support public oversight of the airwaves?

3. In what ways has media deregulation contributed to the erosion of shared reality in the U.S.?
4. How do historical examples of authoritarian media manipulation echo in today's U.S. media landscape?
5. What is the difference between censorship and accountability in the context of broadcast regulation?
6. How do partisan media ecosystems influence identity, belief, and civic behavior?
7. What reforms are proposed to restore standards without infringing on First Amendment rights?
8. How has corporate consolidation of media affected local journalism and democratic accountability?
9. Should platforms that carry political content be subject to the same rules as broadcasters? Why or why not?
10. What principles should guide the restoration of public interest standards in a fragmented media environment?

---- ✦ ----

Reader's Guide: Civic Education and Democratic Literacy

The Stakes

Without civic understanding, democracy cannot survive. The Constitution assumes a literate public—not in letters, but in liberty. It rests its promise of self-government on the belief that people can be taught to govern themselves. But today, that foundation is eroding. A public that no longer knows what government is, what it does, or how to influence it cannot meaningfully consent to its authority. When civic knowledge collapses, so does democratic legitimacy—and in its place rises confusion, manipulation, and authoritarian rule.

. . .

The Structure

This chapter traces the constitutional logic that assumes civic literacy, the historical investments that once supported it, and the political sabotage that has undermined it. It contrasts U.S. retreat from civic education with international efforts to preserve democratic understanding, exposes the weaponization of ignorance under Trump, and concludes with a plan to rebuild civic knowledge as infrastructure—not just in schools, but across a lifelong public sphere.

The Collapse

The deliberate dismantling of civic education has been central to Republican strategy for decades. From censorship laws like Florida's Stop WOKE Act to defunded school systems and whitewashed curricula, the goal is not neutrality—it is engineered ignorance. When voters cannot distinguish law from performance, power from spectacle, or rights from rhetoric, democracy is no longer deliberative. It is hollow—and easily hijacked.

The Remedy

We must rebuild civic education as public infrastructure. Every student in every state must be taught the principles, institutions, and responsibilities of democratic life. Curriculum must be factual, inclusive, and protected from political distortion. Adult civic education must become mainstream—delivered through trusted institutions like libraries, unions, and public broadcasting. Participation must be restored as honor, and public service made a viable path for all. Without civic literacy, liberty decays. With it, democracy can renew.

. . .

What Comes Next

The next chapter continues this thread by examining how public broadcasting, independent media, and local journalism must be protected and rebuilt to sustain a truly informed public. Together with civic education and platform transparency, these reforms form the foundation of a functioning, participatory democracy.

Three Things to Remember

- Civic education is not nostalgia—it is constitutional infrastructure.
- Ignorance is not apolitical—it is the strategy of authoritarianism.
- A people who do not understand power cannot control it.

Action List

- Require universal, fact-based civic education in all 50 states, aligned with constitutional principles and democratic history.
- Fund adult civic education programs through public libraries, community centers, and trusted local institutions.
- Restore and protect the teaching of protest, dissent, and social justice movements as essential parts of American history.
- Ban state censorship of educational content related to race, power, and civic responsibility.
- Create public service and civic leadership pipelines to

encourage young people to participate in democracy—not just as voters, but as leaders.

Strategic Rationale

Authoritarians do not fear protest. They fear understanding. When people grasp how power works, they ask questions, demand accountability, and resist manipulation. Civic education teaches the skills of democracy: reason, dissent, debate, and judgment. Rebuilding it is not merely reform. It is a declaration that self-government still matters, and that the next generation must be equipped to defend it.

What You Can Do

Speak up for honest, inclusive civics instruction in your local schools and communities. Organize or support public workshops that explain government processes and voting rights. Join or fund organizations that defend educational freedom, including iCivics and Generation Citizen. Demand that school boards reject censorship and prioritize constitutional literacy. Encourage young people to run for office, serve in public roles, or become civic educators themselves. And wherever possible, treat the teaching of democracy not as a partisan act—but as a moral one, vital to freedom and our shared future.

Discussion Questions

1. Why did the Framers of the Constitution assume civic education without explicitly mandating it?

2. How did the teaching of civics in the U.S. evolve from the founding through the Cold War?
3. What role did the Cold War play in elevating civic education as a national priority?
4. How does the U.S. approach to civic education today compare with that of Germany, Finland, or Australia?
5. In what ways have recent Republican-led efforts sabotaged civic understanding?
6. Why is the collapse of civic education a threat not just to knowledge, but to constitutional legitimacy?
7. How did Trump's ignorance and misinformation strategy exploit civic illiteracy?
8. What are the key differences between civic education and patriotic indoctrination?
9. Why must civic education extend beyond K–12 classrooms to adult institutions and public spaces?
10. How can civic participation—including public service and military service—be reframed as democratic labor?

Reader's Guide: The Six That Hold

The Stakes

Without structural protection, every reform passed can be overturned. What we restore today can be dismantled tomorrow—unless we secure the foundation first.

THE STRUCTURE

This chapter identifies six reforms that serve as democratic fortifications: Supreme Court reform, campaign finance reform, voting rights, presidential constraint, independent oversight, and disinformation regulation. Each is explained in terms of how it protects the others—and who will try to undo it.

The Collapse

Trump's second term exploited the very gaps these six reforms are meant to close. The courts shielded lawbreaking. Donors bought immunity. Platforms fueled distortion. The system failed not by accident, but because these defenses were never built—or were deliberately removed.

The Remedy

Pass the six that hold. Expand the Supreme Court. Ban dark money. Secure the vote. Rein in emergency powers. Enforce oversight. Defend truth. These reforms must be enacted not as ideals, but as sequencing—within the first four years of renewed power.

What Comes Next

Reform must be made permanent before it is challenged. That means electing leaders with courage, not caution. It means treating these six reforms as foundational, not optional. Without them, American Restoration will remain vulnerable to reversal.

Three Things to Remember

- A reform not protected is a reform waiting to be repealed.
- The Court will strike down what we do—unless we fix it first.
- These six must be law before the next wave of sabotage begins.

Action List

- Demand immediate Court expansion and ethical constraints.
- Pressure legislators to pass campaign finance reform before 2026.
- Support national and state efforts to secure voting rights and fair maps.
- Advocate for legislation limiting presidential emergency powers.
- Back whistleblower protection and enforceable oversight statutes.
- Push for transparency and accountability in digital platforms and political ads.

Strategic Rationale

REFORM WITHOUT PROTECTION IS FRAGILE. The far right has shown how quickly a single election can erase years of progress. These six reforms form a defensive wall around democracy itself. Without them, even the best policies will fall.

What You Can Do

- Write to your representatives demanding prioritization of these six reforms.

- Join or support groups targeting Supreme Court expansion and ethics reform.
- Volunteer for candidates who commit to defending voting access and campaign finance limits.
- Donate to journalism outlets covering court capture, dark money, and disinformation.
- Share this chapter and explain why these six are not just policies—they are the plan.

Discussion Questions

1. What kinds of leaders are most likely to pursue these six reforms—and what will it take to elect them?
2. Which reform do you think would provoke the fiercest backlash, and why?
3. What happens if only some of the six are passed—can the others hold without them?
4. What systems or institutions benefit most from the status quo, and how will they try to fight back?
5. What will it take to defend these reforms after they're passed—against courts, campaigns, and public fatigue?
6. What would it look like if these six reforms were successfully implemented—how would daily democracy feel different?
7. Why is campaign finance reform so often supported in principle but delayed in practice?
8. Do you believe expanding the Supreme Court is justifiable—and if so, how would you explain it to a skeptical audience?
9. In your view, what is the difference between censorship and disinformation regulation?

10. If you had to convince someone that these six reforms are the foundation for all the others, what argument would you make?

Reader's Guide: If We Are to Last

The Stakes

What happens now will determine whether American democracy endures—or becomes another fallen republic, remembered more for its myth than its function. The United States is not immune to collapse. It is, in fact, following a familiar path: erosion of truth, concentration of power, abandonment of principle, and public disengagement. Around the world, billions still long for what we take for granted. This is our last clear moment to choose whether democracy survives us—or dies in our hands.

THE STRUCTURE

This chapter opens by dismantling the myth that Trump alone broke the system, tracing the collapse back through decades of drift and decay. It recounts the parallel rise of resistance and restoration. It then turns inward: confronting the moral failure of leadership, the urgency of institutional reform, and the need for principled, courageous public servants. The chapter closes with a generational hand-off: a call to act, to participate, and to preserve what others only dream of having.

THE COLLAPSE

The system was not destroyed overnight. It was hollowed out from within—by dark money, court manipulation, voter suppression, media capture, and elite cowardice. Trump simply accelerated a long decline. Institutions that should have constrained him did not. Leadership that should have acted waited. The public was distracted while power consolidated. This is not a singular crisis. It is the end stage of decades of erosion.

The Remedy

We must not only resist authoritarianism—we must reconstruct democracy. That means:

- Codifying democratic rights and access.
- Building resilient public institutions that serve all, not just some.
- Electing leaders with courage, not calculation.
- Practicing democracy daily, not just episodically.
- Designing a system that functions visibly, fairly, and inclusively.

American Restoration offers a full blueprint. But without securing the six foundational reforms identified in the previous chapter, even the best policies remain vulnerable. Their success depends on bold and tireless leadership—and public participation.

What Comes Next

This chapter closes Volume II of *American Restoration* by setting the stage for Volume III *American Redemption*. While this volume exposed what was lost and how to restore it, the next turns to protection and permanence: how to rebuild constraint, defend rights from rollback, and ensure this collapse never happens again. The handoff is made. The next work begins.

. . .

Three Things to **Remember**

- Trump did not break democracy. He proved it was already broken.
- What others around the world still dream of, we are letting collapse.
- This is not the end. It is the handoff. What happens next is up to us.

Action List

- Find, support, and elect courageous leaders who act before it's popular or safe.
- Refuse delay dressed as propriety—demand action from those in power now.
- Make democracy a daily practice: show up, speak out, hold the line.
- Tell the full truth about what broke, who profits, and how we rebuild it.
- Design visible, fair, inclusive systems that cannot be silently dismantled.
- Honor global democratic hopes by refusing to surrender our own.

Strategic Rationale

A democracy cannot survive without participants, defenders, and truth-tellers. This chapter exposes how our systems were hollowed from within—and insists that rebuilding must be deliberate, structural, and moral. It underscores that reform is not enough:

we must create institutions worthy of the name "republic," and leaders worthy of the public's trust. Anything less invites collapse again.

What You Can Do

Don't wait for perfect leaders. Support the ones who speak clearly, act early, and risk consequence. Run for office. Organize your workplace, your neighborhood, your school board. Protect those who speak out. Refuse silence when lies are told. The next phase of democracy will not be written by institutions. It will be written by citizens who showed up. Start now. Start where you are. And do not stop.

Discussion Questions

1. What structural weaknesses in U.S. democracy did Trump exploit rather than create, and why did previous leaders hesitate to act on them?
2. How did moral failure—not just institutional failure—contribute to the erosion of democratic norms?
3. In what ways did local action and public resolve provide a counterbalance to federal collapse?
4. What does it mean to say "law alone is not enough" in the context of restoring democratic governance?
5. Why is it essential to reject the idea of returning to a "better past" and instead build what never fully existed?
6. How do dignity, care, and education function as democratic infrastructure—not just policy goals?
7. What kind of leadership does this chapter suggest is necessary for renewal, and where might it be found?

8. How does participation, rather than trust, form the true foundation of democratic practice?
9. Why is it important to acknowledge how the world views American backsliding—and what responsibility comes with that?
10. How can this generation turn a legacy of collapse into a foundation for construction and long-term democratic renewal?

These guides were written not only to inform, but to endure. Their purpose is not to win arguments, but to cultivate readiness—for truth, for responsibility, and for the long labor of democratic restoration. They mark a shift in tone from outrage to stewardship: a recognition that the republic will not be rebuilt by spectacle, but by disciplined, collaborative work.

What you do with these guides is up to you. Share them. Teach them. Use them to train others. The fight for democracy is not episodic—it is daily, deliberate, and shared. Let these be part of that rhythm: tools not just for understanding the republic we lost, but for building the one that must come next.

AFTERWORD

American Restoration is not the end of the fight. It is the beginning of the construction. The chapters here do not claim perfection or permanence. They do not promise success. But they offer the clearest map we could draw, in the clearest language we could write, at a moment when clarity itself is under assault. These reforms are not the only way forward. But they are a way. They are a foundation —deliberately laid to recover what the Constitution promised and to prevent again what nearly destroyed it.

If these reforms are debated, revised, improved—good. That is the point. No one will gather us all together in Philadelphia this time. No parchment will carry us forward. We must do it ourselves —scattered, diverse, angry, determined—and yet, together. This book is not a blueprint handed down. It is a torch handed on. Not a cathedral built, but stones set out, ready for the work ahead.

What comes next depends not on the plan, but on the people. What remains now is not inspiration. It is execution. Each reform demands effort—not someday, but starting now. The work cannot depend on a single leader or faction, but on citizens who are done being told to wait, to settle, to accept the erosion of their own power. Many are angry. Many are afraid. Some don't yet know where to begin. So begin here. Open the Reader's Guides. Read "What You Can Do." Pick one act—or three, or ten. Speak. Share. Organize. Fail. Begin again. This is not a test of perfection. It is a test of participation. You are not alone. And no action is too small when joined with thousands more.

The reforms undertaken may evolve. Some may falter. But the will to rebuild must endure. Democracy is not disqualified by sabotage. It is proven by what we do next. This republic can still be restored—and handed down with more care than we gave it. And with more permanence than we were given.

This task is generational. It must be shared. The work begins now—with we the people, with as many as we can bring alongside us, and with the clarity forged in everything we've endured and everything we refuse to let happen again. There is no perfect fix. But there is principled construction. There is a path.

Let's begin again. Now. Until the work is done.

The world is watching. So are our children.

Jim Vincent
— June, 2025

COLOPHON

American Restoration is the second volume in an ongoing body of work focused on democratic renewal, resistance to authoritarianism, and the policies and principles that must define a just republic. This volume expands upon the constitutional framework established in *American Renewal* and begins the deeper work of applying its vision through structural reform, public accountability, and institutional repair.

ALSO BY JIM VINCENT

American Renewal

Volume I of The American Renewal Trilogy

A manifesto for resistance, a blueprint for survival, and a plan to outlast authoritarian rule. Written to confront the second Trump presidency with truth, clarity, and strategic resolve.

American Restoration

Volume II of The American Renewal Trilogy

A comprehensive plan to rebuild the foundations of American democracy. Eighteen reforms necessary for rebuilding the foundations of democracy.

American Redemption *(forthcoming)*

Volume III of The American Renewal Trilogy

Eighteen legislative reforms to fulfill the constitutional promises—justice, peace, defense, prosperity, liberty, and unity—and build a republic that serves all its people.

Essays on Tyranny

A collection of essays on the collapse of American political norms between 2000 and 2024, and the cultural, moral, and institutional choices that made authoritarianism possible.

The Quiet Habit of Giving

A book about love, loss, and repair. Based on the six emotional needs that sustain long relationships—Admiration, Belonging, Control, Freedom, Security, and Validation—and what happens when they are missing.

For more, visit jimvincentus.substack.com.

ABOUT THE AUTHOR

Jim Vincent is a U.S. citizen, born and raised in the United States, where he lived for fifty years. He now resides in Australia, with children and grandchildren still living in the country he calls home. His writing reflects both an unbreakable connection to the American experiment—and a deep concern for its survival.

As an American living overseas, Vincent brings a perspective shaped by two advantages: distance from the tribal divisions that dominate U.S. politics, and the lived experience of another functioning democracy. From that vantage point, he sees with greater clarity what has been lost in the United States—and what remains possible.

He is the founder of *Jim Vincent US*, an independent publication focused on resisting authoritarianism and rebuilding democratic power. His work is trusted for its clarity, strategy, and moral purpose. He writes not for applause, but for action—believing that the republic must be reclaimed, not remembered.

He can be reached at https://jimvincentus.substack.com/